D0223929

FANTASY

THE LIBERATION OF IMAGINATION

San Diego Christian College
2100 Greenfield Drive
El Cajon, CA 92019

Genres in Context

THE SHORT STORY
The Reality of Artifice
Charles E. May

FANTASY
The Liberation of Imagination
Richard Mathews

BIOGRAPHY
Writing Lives
Catherine N. Parke

THE SEA VOYAGE NARRATIVE
Robert Foulke

SCIENCE FICTION BEFORE 1900
Imagination Discovers Technology
Paul K. Alkon

SCIENCE FICTION AFTER 1900
From the Steam Man to the Stars
Brooks Landon

NATURE WRITING
The Pastoral Impulse in America
Don Scheese

THE FAIRY TALE
The Magic Mirror of Imagination
Steven Swann Jones

TRAVEL WRITING
The Self and the World
Casey Blanton

809.915
M429f

25.16

FANTASY

THE LIBERATION OF IMAGINATION

Richard Mathews

Routledge
New York and London

Published in 2002 by
Routledge
29 West 35th Street
New York, NY 10001

Published in Great Britain by
Routledge
11 New Fetter Lane
London EC4P 4EE

Routledge is an imprint of the Taylor & Francis Group.

Originally published in hardcover by Twayne Publishers, an imprint of The Gale Group.
This paperback edition published by arrangement with Twayne Publishers.

Copyright © 1997 by Twayne Publishers

First Routledge paperback edition 2002

Printed in the United States of America on acid-free paper.

All rights reserved. No part of this book may be reprinted or reproduced or utilized in any
form or by any electronic, mechanical, or other means, now known or hereafter invented,
including photocopying and recording, or in any information storage or retrieval system, without permission in writing from the publisher.

10 9 8 7 6 5 4 3 2 1

Cataloging-in-Publication Data available from the Library of Congress.

ISBN 0–415–93890–2 (pbk)

For Emily and Joseph,
who opened my eyes to new readings

In every cry of every man,
In every Infant's cry of fear,
In every voice, in every ban,
The mind-forged manacles I hear.

—William Blake, "London," 1794

General Editor's Statement

Genre studies have been a central concern of Anglo-American and European literary theory for at least the past quarter century, and the academic interest has been reflected, for example, in new college courses in slave narratives, autobiography, biography, nature writing, and the literature of travel as well as in the rapid expansion of genre theory itself. Genre has also become an indispensable term for trade publishers and the vast readership they serve. Indeed, few general bookstores do not have sections devoted to science fiction, romance, and mystery fiction. Still, genre is among the slipperiest of literary terms, as any examination of genre theories and their histories will suggest.

In conceiving this series we have tried to avoid, on the one hand, the comically pedantic spirit that informs Polonius's recitation of kinds of drama, and on the other hand, the equally unhelpful insistence that every literary production is a unique expression that must not be forced into any system of classification. We have instead developed our list of genres, which range from ancient comedy to the Western, with the conviction that by common consent kinds of literature do exist—not as fixed categories but as fluid ones that change over time as the result of the complex interplay of authors, audiences, and literary and cultural institutions. As individual titles in the series demonstrate, the idea of genre offers us provocative ways to study both the continuities and adaptability of literature as a familiar and inexhaustible source of human imagination.

Recognition of the fluid boundaries both within and among genres will provide, we believe, a useful array of perspectives from which to study literature's complex development. Genres, as traditional but open ways of understanding the world, contribute to our capacity to respond to narrative and expressive forms and offer means with which to discern moral significances embodied in these forms. Genres, in short, serve ethical as well as aesthetic purposes, and the volumes in this series attempt to demonstrate how this double benefit has been achieved as these genres have been transformed over the years. Each title in the series should be measured against this large ambition.

Ron Gottesman

Contents

Chapter 6
Darkening Antiquity: Sword and Sorcery
(Robert E. Howard's Conan Series)   118

Chapter 7
Completing the Circle: Language, Power, and Vision
(Ursula K. Le Guin's Earthsea Cycle)   135

Preface

Fantasy unlocks imagination. By the time William Blake decried the "mind-forged manacles" at the end of the eighteenth century, he had begun his own mythic process to release imagination from its chains of reason. But Blake was a poet, a visionary, and a madman, and the liberation he sought came more quickly in poetry than in prose. In fact, as the nineteenth century began, romantic poets started to reclaim the fantastic imagination in diverse works, from Coleridge's "Kubla Kahn" and "The Rime of the Ancient Mariner" to Keats's "Lamia," Byron's "Childe Harold," and Christina Rossetti's "Goblin Market."

Prose was a different genre and a different story. It was created in the language, form, and syntax that had systematically demythologized and scientized the world. Under its rational insistence, superstition had gradually been supplanted by recorded observation, hypothesis, experiment, and fact. At an earlier time, before the scientific method prescribed empirical tests for theories, human thought had been free to entertain nearly any imaginative truth. But by the eighteenth century, the chains of reason were in place.

This book is intended for students and general audiences as a guide to a fuller appreciation of the creative possibilities literary fantasy unleashes. Because of the oceanic scope of the subject and the nature of its revolutionary form, I have found my task to be like trying to grasp water. My hands sometimes come up wet or even dripping, but they are empty nonetheless. Beyond them I can see the oceans and unceasing waves, the rivers and white water, the transformations in the water cycle as dews evaporate and reform into mists. My hope is that the mists collected here may condense as reservoirs for readers, that they may then generate the energy for further study and illumination.

In keeping with the editorial guidelines of Twayne's Studies in Literary Themes and Genres, I have focused on only a few influential works that suggest some of the primary characteristics and patterns of fantasy: William Morris's *The Well at the World's End* (1896); Robert E. Howard's *The Hour of the Dragon* (1935); T. H. White's *The Once and Future King* (1938–1958); J. R. R. Tolkien's *The Lord of the Rings* (1954–1955); and Ursula K. Le Guin's Earthsea Cycle (1968–1990). Because fantasy is a truly international genre, much could and should be said of its milestone works in other languages and cultures, and I have included some along the way, but within the tight compass of this volume I have chosen to concentrate on English and American exemplars. In Great Britain and the United States the genre crystallized in ways that are striking even from an international perspective. Perhaps because both countries in their rush to be at the forefront of industrial and postindustrial technologies manacled their literary imaginations more firmly, their literary counterrevolution was all the more striking and self-conscious. In England and the U.S. in particular, modern fantasy has been a movement conscious of itself, alluding to and building on its own traditions and unafraid to explore new directions, to hybridize with mainstream, science fiction, horror, and experimental fiction of all kinds.

Fantasy is a literature of liberation and subversion. Its target may be politics, economics, religion, psychology, or sexuality. It seeks to liberate the feminine, the unconscious, the repressed, the past, the present, and the future.

Acknowledgments

Portions of chapters 2 and 3 previously appeared in somewhat different form as essays on *The Well at the World's End* and *The Lord of the Rings* in *Survey of Modern Fantasy Literature*, copyright 1983 by Salem Press, and are included here by permission of Salem Press.

This work could not have been completed without the encouragement, patience, and help of many friends and colleagues, including Brian Garman, Mary Jane Schenck, Suzanne Hiebert, Anita Scharf, and Ellen White; University of Tampa librarians Marlyn Cook Pethe, Mickey Wells, and Art Bagley; and University of South Florida librarians Phyllis McEwen and Paul Camp.

A special note of appreciation goes to Ron Gottesman, whose sage comments and insights helped me past many a sticking point. For substantial contributions of information, learning, and critical perspectives, I'm grateful to Christopher Tolkien, Verlyn Flieger, Brian Attebery, John D. Rateliff, Douglas A. Anderson, Robert Reginald, R. C. H. Briggs, Carol and Deena Johnson, and Neil Barron. Research for this project was funded in part by a summer faculty research grant from the Charles Dana Foundation. Finally, I thank my wife, Julie Empric, whose intelligence, scholarly example, and support have guided me throughout this work.

Chronology

ca. 2000 B.C.E.	*The Epic of Gilgamesh* (Assyria/Babylonia)
ca. 750 B.C.E.	Homer's *The Odyssey*
ca. 620–560 B.C.E.	*Aesop's Fables*
ca. 500 B.C.E.	Valmiki's *Ramayana* (India)
ca. 400 B.C.E.– C.E. 400	*Mahabharata* (India)
19 B.C.E.	Virgil's *Aeneid*
17 B.C.E.	Ovid's *Metamorphoses* (Italy)
ca. 120–180	Lucius Apuleius's *The Golden Ass* (North Africa)
ca. 725	*Beowulf*
ca. 1200	*Nibelungenlied* (Germany)
ca. 1200	Snorri Sturluson's *Prose Edda* (Iceland)
ca. 1210	Wolfram von Eschenbach's *Parzifal* (Germany)
ca. 1320	Dante Alighieri's *The Divine Comedy* (Italy)
ca. 1370	*Sir Gawain and the Green Knight*
ca. 1375	*Grettir's Saga* (Iceland)
ca. 1400	*The Mabinogion* (Wales), a compilation of medieval Welsh prose tales

FANTASY

1889   Mark Twain's *A Connecticut Yankee in King Arthur's Court*

1890   William Morris's *The House of the Wolfings; News from Nowhere* serialized in *Commonweal* (published in book form in 1891)

1896   H. Rider Haggard's *She*

1900   L. Frank Baum's *The Wonderful Wizard of Oz*

1900   Ernest Bramah's *The Wallet of Kai Lung* (the first of a series of Oriental fantasies featuring the wandering storyteller Kai Lung)

1904   James Barrie's *Peter Pan*

1904   W. H. Hudson's *Green Mansions*

1905   Lord Dunsany's *The Gods of Pegana*

1911   Algernon Blackwood's *The Centaur*

1911   H. G. Wells's *The Country of the Blind and Other Stories*

1912   Carl Gustav Jung's *Psychology of the Unconscious*

1912   James Stephens's *The Crock of Gold*

1914   Edgar Rice Burroughs's *Tarzan of the Apes*

1915   Charlotte Perkins Gilman's *Herland,* a lost-race story featuring a feminist utopia; appeared in Gilman's magazine *Forerunner*

1918   A. Merritt's *The Moon Pool* published in *All-Story* magazine

1920   David Lindsay's *A Voyage to Arcturus*

1921   James Branch Cabell's *Figures of Earth,* the first of a series of stories featuring Dom Manuel of Poictesme and his descendants

1922   E. R. Eddison's *The Worm Ouroboros*

1923   *Weird Tales,* a pulp magazine of fantasy and horror, begins publication

1926   Thorne Smith's *Topper*

1929–1940   Farnsworth Wright's tenure as editor of *Weird Tales*

FANTASY

1930–1931 Charles Williams's *War in Heaven, The Place of the Lion,* and *Many Dimensions*

1934 Pamela L. Travers's *Mary Poppins*

1935 Robert E. Howard's *Hour of the Dragon*

1936 Evangeline Walton's retelling of Celtic myths from *The Mabinogion,* which would eventually comprise several volumes, commences with *The Virgin and the Swine* (retitled *The Island of the Mighty* in the 1970 Ballantine edition)

1937 J. R. R. Tolkien's *The Hobbit*

1938 T. H. White's *The Sword in the Stone*

1939–1943 The pulp magazine *Unknown* (later called *Unknown Worlds*) publishes innovative fantasy fiction under the editorship of John W. Campbell Jr.

1941 L. Sprague de Camp's *The Incomplete Enchanter*

1945 George Orwell's *Animal Farm*

1946 Mervyn Peake's *Titus Groan,* the first book in the Gormenghast series

1948 Fletcher Pratt (under the pseudonym George U. Fletcher), *The Well of the Unicorn*

1949 *The Magazine of Fantasy and Science Fiction,* founded by Anthony Boucher and J. Francis McComas, begins monthly publication

1950 C. S. Lewis's *The Lion, the Witch and the Wardrobe,* the first work in the Chronicles of Narnia

1952–1980 *Fantastic,* a monthly or bimonthly magazine of fantastic literature (later merged with *Amazing Science Fiction Stories*)

1954–1955 J. R. R. Tolkien's *The Lord of the Rings*

1960 Peter Beagle's *A Fine and Private Place*

1962 Jorge Luis Borges's *Ficciones*

1962 Ray Bradbury's *Something Wicked This Way Comes*

1963 Michael Moorcock's Elric Saga begins with *The Stealer of Souls*

1963   Andre Norton's *Witch World,* a novel that begins a popular series of stories in a matriarchal parallel world

1964   Lloyd Alexander's *The Book of Three,* the first novel in the five-part Chronicles of Prydain, which also includes *The Black Cauldron* (1965)

1966   John Norman's Gor series begins with *Tarnsman of Gor*

1966   John Barth's *Giles Goat-Boy*

1967   The Mythopoeic Society is founded to study and discuss fantasy literature, especially the works of the Inklings

1967   Donald Barthelme's *Snow White*

1968   Peter Beagle's *The Last Unicorn*

1968   Ursula K. Le Guin's *A Wizard of Earthsea*

1968   Fritz Leiber's Fafhrd and the Gray Mouser series begins with *Swords in the Mist, Swords against Wizardry,* and *The Swords of Lankhmar*

1968   Anne McCaffrey's Dragon series begins with *Dragonflight*

1969   Roger Zelazny's *Creatures of Light and Darkness*

1970   Gabriel García Márquez's *One Hundred Years of Solitude*

1970   Roger Zelazny's Amber series begins with *Nine Princes in Amber*

1970   The Science Fiction Research Association is founded

1971   The British Fantasy Society is founded

1972   Richard Adams's *Watership Down*

1977   Piers Anthony's Xanth series begins with *A Spell for Chameleon*

1977   Stephen R. Donaldson's *Chronicles of Thomas Covenant the Unbeliever*

1979   *Thieve's World* is published, the first of the shared-world concept of anthologies of assorted stories in which various authors explore a common sustained story line and set of characters

FANTASY

1980   Piers Anthony's *Split Infinity*, the first work in the Apprentice Adept series, which combines science fiction and fantasy in two parallel worlds

1981   John Crowley's *Little, Big*

1982   The International Association for the Fantastic in the Arts (IAFA) is established

1982   The innovative British magazine *Interzone*, edited by David Pringle, begins publication

1983   Piers Anthony's Incarnations of Immortality series begins with *On a Pale Horse*

1984   Robert Holdstock's *Mythago Wood*

1984   William Gibson's *Neuromancer*

1988   Elizabeth Ann Scarborough's *The Healer's War*

1989   Salman Rushdie's *The Satanic Verses*

1990   Ursula K. Le Guin's *Tehanu: The Last Book of Earthsea*

1990   Tom DeHaven's *Walker of Worlds*, the first work in the King's Tramp trilogy

1991   John Barth's *The Last Voyage of Somebody the Sailor*

1991   John Grant's *Albion*

1994   John Barth's *Once Upon a Time: A Floating Opera*

1994   John Crowley's *Love and Sleep*

1994   Elizabeth Ann Scarborough's *The Godmother*

Chapter 1

FROM ANTIQUITY TO INFINITY: THE DEVELOPMENT OF MODERN FANTASY

antasy enables us to enter worlds of infinite possibility. The maps and contours of fantasy are circumscribed only by imagination itself. The breathtaking sweep of its scope can be awesome and even frightening, but this powerful, vivid mode of human consciousness has been part of artistic expression from the earliest known oral and written texts right up to the present day. In fact, the literary genre of modern fantasy is characterized by a narrative frame that unites timeless mythic patterns with contemporary individual experiences. Its stories at their hearts are *about* the relationship between the individual and the infinite.

Although it is difficult to define literary fantasy precisely, most critics agree it is a type of fiction that evokes wonder, mystery, or magic—a sense of possibility beyond the ordinary, material, rationally predictable world in which we live. As a literary genre, modern fantasy is clearly related to the magical stories of myth, legend, fairy tale, and folklore from all over the world. There are also elements of fantasy in even the most realistic literature, just as daydream and imagination hover at the edges of our waking minds. Fantasy as a distinct literary genre, however, may best be thought of as a fiction that elicits wonder through elements of the supernatural or impossible. It consciously breaks free from mundane reality.

Because fantasy is so pervasive in the early literature of every culture—from Egypt, Babylonia, China, India, and Persia to Greece, Rome, and the West—and is inseparable from the greatest tales and legends of antiquity, which are filled with transformations, marvels, and supernatural events, one critic has observed that "fantasy forms the mainstream of Western literature until the Renaissance."[1] But the literary paths of realism and fantasy began to diverge in the 1600s as new systems of learning from the Renaissance brought about a rejection of superstition in favor of science and reason. Until the scientific method began to tame and frame the world, the human imagination had had free rein to explain mundane reality by referring to supernatural forces. Trees might be transformed human spirits and the sun pulled by a chariot across the sky. The great resources of human reason gradually reduced the number of acceptable explanations, however, leaving less room for unrestrained belief and imagination.

By the nineteenth century, history began to be conceived as falling into three broad developmental periods: ancient, medieval, and modern. The medieval period was viewed as the "Dark Ages," and as scientific reasoning took root even the great ancient civilizations were increasingly regarded as primitive, superstitious, and unenlightened. Despite a few stunning celebrations of fantasy in the Renaissance, including Shakespeare's *A Midsummer Night's Dream*, the trend toward a literature purified by reason and reality was unmistakable.

In *The Rise of the Novel*, Ian Watt brilliantly describes the changes that helped shape realistic fiction and documents its full emergence as a genre in the eighteenth century. Fantasy as a modern literary category all its own took shape through a dialectic with this new literature of realism. The insightful and influential modern authors who crafted fantasy as an alternative literary form seem intuitively to have understood that they could create a complex and appealing counterpoint to popular fiction about ordinary life by imbuing their writing with ancient human impulses toward myth and romance. Thus fantasy as a genre emerged in the shape of novels and short stories, the two most significant modern structures for contemporary fiction.

These modes of realistic fiction first rose to popularity during the eighteenth century through books by Samuel Richardson, Henry Fielding, Tobias Smollett, Laurence Sterne, and Frances Burney, then flowered into the great age of literary realism in the nineteenth century in the writing of Jane Austen, Charles Dickens, William Makepeace Thackeray, Anthony Trollope, George Eliot, Thomas Hardy, and others. The widespread interest in and market for stories of real life with ordinary, believable characters grew and flourished concurrently with the increasing dominance of the scientific method, the expansion of the industrial revolution, and the unfolding of related historical developments, including changes in printing and publishing technologies, increasing literacy, and a rising middle class. The emergence of realism as the mainstream focus for the literary imagination created a clear dialectical pole against which the fantasy genre could counterthrust as a specialized mode of fiction. In fact, fantasy especially utilized the novel—the most ambitious and popular vehicle for realism—as its primary literary vehicle as well.

Unlike realistic fiction, fantasy does not require logic—technological, chemical, or alien—to explain the startling actions or twists of character and plot recorded on its pages; such events may be explained by magic or not explained at all. The presence of these magical or impossible elements in a fictional form (a novel or short story), in which realism and logical causality are expected, creates a tension between form and content in which the reader's "willing suspension of disbelief" can be exercised in surprising ways. Fantasy's fundamental departure from realism creates what influential literary theorist Tzvetan Todorov calls "hesitation" in the reader, whose instincts for credibility are stretched through narrative events beyond realistic explanation. Other critics, such as Harold Bloom, have argued convincingly that the best fantasy involves no hesitation but a sense of being caught up in and swept away by the "agonistic encounter of deep, strong reading."[2] In either case, the fantasy writer's freedom to depart from realism involves an obligation to coherence and to the establishment of a relationship with the reader's experience, perhaps best expressed in Robert Scholes's description of "fabulation" as "fiction that offers us a world clearly and radically discontinuous from the one we know, yet returns to confront that known world in some cognitive way."[3]

Fantasy is closely allied to other variations of the realistic novel, including gothic horror, science fiction, utopian fiction, and satire, and one way to clarify a generic identity for fantasy is to consider it in relationship to these. Significantly, each of these kindred genres more directly depends on and utilizes the conventions and contexts of realism, whereas fantasy consistently incorporates a radical departure from the real. The gothic tale of terror, the first significant generic rebellion against the realistic novel, developed a clear identity of its own, playing fear and dark terror against the light of reason. A series of startling books in exotic settings, from Horace Walpole's *Castle of Otranto* (1765) to the works of such writers as William Beckford, Ann Radcliffe, M. G. ("Monk") Lewis, and Charles Maturin, contained unexplained horrors, bleeding statues, and walking portraits. French and German authors also used supernatural elements to develop a wider range of expression than is possible in the realistic novel. Broadly speaking, these works were part of the romantic movement and include such milestones as Jacques Cazotte's *Le diable amoureux* (*The Devil in Love*, 1772), Ludwig Tieck's three-volume collection *Phantasus* (1812–1817), the early-nineteenth-century German tales of E. T. A. Hoffmann, and the works of Friedrich de la Motte Fouqué (most significantly *Undine*, 1811) and Wilhelm Meinhold (whose *Sidonia the Sorceress*, 1847–1848, was a great favorite of the Pre-Raphaelites and one of the books William Morris chose to publish at his Kelmscott Press). Yet despite frightening intrusions from the supernatural, these authors maintain their hold on familiar, material reality, evoking terror precisely because of this realistic grounding.

Science fiction is similarly anchored in the actual. It depicts events in a rational universe in which occurrences are subject to reasonable scientific explanation and causality, however futuristic, alien, or inventive the science. Orson Scott Card, a contemporary author who writes both fantasy and science fiction, explains the difference in simple, practical terms: "If the story is set in a universe that follows the same rules as ours, it's science fiction. If it's set in a universe that doesn't follow our rules, it's fantasy."[4] The presence of magic in fantasy is probably the most common departure from the "rules" of science fiction that help distinguish it from fantasy, but as Eric Rabkin rightly points out, fantasy and science fiction are most appropriately viewed as two ends of a spectrum, with blurred boundaries in the middle.[5] Within similar spectrum models we should also locate the shifts from fantasy to supernatural and horror fiction, fantasy to utopian or satirical writing, fantasy to realism. Utopian fiction may be distinguished from fantasy by the fact that it usually sticks closer to the realistic "rules," for the ideal society must be seen in relationship to the realistic present, and most utopias imply there is a way to change our present, real society into a more ideal society by means other than magic. Yet fantasy often includes utopian or dystopian elements, as might be expected given the philosophical and moral concerns also characteristic of the genre, so there are areas where these modes of writing overlap and coalesce, as in the numerous fantasy variations on the Arthurian utopia of Camelot or in such novels as Anatole France's *The White Stone*, Richard Brautigan's *In Watermelon Sugar*, and James Hilton's *Lost Horizon*.

Like science fiction and utopian writing, satire bears a similarly close relationship to fantasy, but it, too, is nearer to the real world than to pure fantasy. Satire aims to correct defects in the real world by holding them up for ridicule. Through laughter and logic satire seeks to amend or improve identifiable behaviors in real life lived by realistic rules. To the extent that the satirist fully creates an alternative impossible world, as Swift does in *Gulliver's Travels*, for example, satire may depart into fantasy, but usually the departure is tinged with the awareness of exaggeration and unbelievability, and the literary focus or thematic purpose turns us away from the fantastic toward the real. Despite these fundamental differences, the literary spectrum that includes gothic novels, science fiction, utopias, and satires forms a supportive continuum for fantasy. These allied modes, fed like fantasy from many ancient sources in myth and folklore, continue to contribute much to the evolution of the genre. There are no pure genres, and fantasy is no exception.

Foundations of Fantasy in the Ancient World

Nearly all of the surviving literature of the ancient world, from *The Epic of Gilgamesh* to *The Odyssey*, is rooted in fantasy, though at the time each work was composed much of it was believed by those who heard or read it to be true. In eras when matters of superstition and magic were popularly accepted as fact, much of what we see today as nonrealistic elements in literature did not necessarily seem impossible or imaginary. Nonetheless, it is clear that even the earliest fantastical prose fiction was constructed by its authors as *fiction* rather than as history. Although those who heard or read the texts may have believed them to be literally true, the artists who created them clearly placed significance on nonliteral metaphoric or mythic purposes. The aim of these early works seems to have been a desire equally to stimulate, educate, and entertain. In some cases there was also a desire to influence, impress, and control.

The oldest known examples of ancient fiction—texts we would now call fantasy—are magical tales from Egypt recorded on papyrus that has been dated about 2000 B.C.E. The earliest (ca. 2000–1900 B.C.E.), "The Tale of the Shipwrecked Sailor,"[6] is the story of a young man sailing on the Red Sea who is shipwrecked on a phantom island. There he meets the genie, or guarding spirit, of the place, a 50-foot snake with a 3-foot beard and a body overlaid with gold. Finally he escapes without harm, as the creature has assured him he will, and the island vanishes from sight. This oldest fantasy text contains archetypal narrative elements of the genre: an uninitiated hero on a sea journey is thrown off course by a storm, encounters an enchanted island, confronts a monster, and survives, wiser for the experience.[7]

One aspect of this and other ancient Egyptian fantasy texts that establishes them as fiction is that each tale is imaginatively presented within a larger narrative frame. The "Shipwrecked Sailor," told to entertain a superior officer during a tedious voyage, is a clear precursor, in both narrative frame and specific subject, of the cycle of Sinbad tales in *The Arabian Nights*. It is an episode also analogous to Odysseus's arrival at the Phaeacians' island in *The Odyssey*. And the marvelous monster is the clear prototype of the greatest fantasy monster of all time—the dragon, sometimes called the "wurm."

The narrative frame for three tales from the somewhat later transcribed Westcar Papyrus casts the storytelling back in time, as if the tales were being told about 2680 B.C.E., to Khufu (Cheops), builder of the Great Pyramid at Giza (Gizeh), across the Nile from Cairo.[8] Actually, the stories might well have been told at one time in his court. The first one is about a magician whose wife has been seduced. The magician reasserts his honor and power by making an enchanted wax crocodile that comes to life to kill his wife's lover. In "The Boating Party" a magician parts the waters of a lake in order to recover a malachite pendant in the shape of a fish that has been lost by a maiden of the court. In "The Magician Djedi," a magician exhibits his power to decapitate animals and later to restore them to life by cutting off and then rejoining the heads of a goose, a duck, and an ox. These stories, which were no doubt written down long after they were actually composed, seem to date from the third century B.C.E., a period from which no full texts have yet been recovered. But they make it clear that from the earliest literary history human beings have been involved in the creation and preservation of texts portraying archetypal patterns of deep mortal concern: the first tale draws connections between art and magic and links these with the most basic human problems in love relationships, including jealousy, honor, and justice. The second tale is an archetypal story about human control over nature. The third involves control of life and death. In each there appears a mixture of reality and magic, and each treats finite relationships with forces of the infinite.

Even more important in terms of influence and mythic scope is the great Babylonian text of about the same period (ca. 2000 B.C.E.) known as *The Epic of Gilgamesh*. The narrative establishes many motifs and archetypes, which recur in the Bible and in the Greek epics. The legendary King Gilgamesh is linked to an unlikely companion in the person of a wild man, Enkidu. Together they face a series of startling adventures, including one with Humbaba, a fire-breathing monster. A character named Utnapishtim is a prototype of Noah in the Bible, and the epic, perhaps best known for its account of a great flood similar to Noah's, predates the Old Testament.[9] After Enkidu dies, Gilgamesh quests for immortality, but a serpent robs him of the herb that promises eternal life, and Gilgamesh returns home to die. The wandering hero/king, the unlikely companion, the combination of king and savage, the elemental adventures (Gilgamesh faces challenges of earth, air, fire, and water), the conquest of a fire-breathing monster, and Gilgamesh's thwarted search for immortality—even his downfall through the agency of a serpent —are archetypes repeated so frequently in fantasy that they have become defining characteristics of the genre.

The ancient Egyptians attributed the gift of writing to the god Thoth, who was said to have bestowed it on humankind, so this link to the infinite or transcendent is mythically present in various accounts of the very act or gift of writing. In fact, *hieroglyph,* the term that combines the Greek words *heiros* (holy) and *gluphein* (to carve or engrave) to refer to the characters of Egyptian writing, means "writing of the gods." The Egyptian and Babylonian magical tales, although not primarily religious documents, exhibit awareness of the holiness inherent in the nature of language itself. An emphasis on the transcendent and creative power of words remains an integral characteristic of fantasy today. The self-reflexiveness so often claimed as modernist or postmodernist is in fact an ancient trope and theme.

Many of the influential fantasy texts of the ancient world make the sacred even more central and overt. The books of the Old Testament, written in Hebrew and Aramaic between 1000 and 100 B.C.E., preserve numerous tales of magic and power, from the creation of the world to the parting of the Red Sea, all of which are explicitly related to an infinite God. Though the Old Testament, like the more ancient Egyptian Book of the Dead,[10] is a religious rather than a purely literary text, both of these works, as well as other religious writings, exerted strong influences on the creation of the literary genre of fantasy. As in the "holy carving" of hieroglyphics, in these and other early texts the word was associated with the power to create and transform; it was part of a sacred story and frequently a sacred gift and trust. Litanies, prayers, hymns, and words of power were held as a matter of faith to touch eternity and bring the human spirit closer to it. Text was a means for clarifying, expressing, and celebrating the human relationship to the infinite.

Other pre-Christian tales from the third and fourth centuries B.C.E. are preserved in the *Mahabharata,* the greatest classical Sanskrit epic of ancient India, which was first recorded in its present form in about 400 to 500 B.C.E. It, too, is a repository of stories from much more ancient oral and folk traditions. This massive work, about eight times the length of *The Iliad* and *The Odyssey* combined, encompasses cosmic statements about politics, history, philosophy, and metaphysics. One of its oldest tales is an archetypal love story, the saga of Nala and Damayanti; it also includes the Bhagavad Gita, its best-known portion and widely published as an individual work. The cosmic struggles of this epic tale, complete with the transmigration of souls and elaborate supernatural interactions between gods and men, offers a nearly unequaled scale and scope for the fantastic imagination.

Another Sanskrit work, the *Pancatantra,* a collection of five books of beast fables composed about 200 B.C.E., is one of the earliest models for stories in which animals are endowed with human qualities and abilities, through their behavior revealing the moral strengths and weaknesses of human nature and offering insights into virtue and happiness. Fabulous talking animals are, of course, not unique to Indian literature. They have become a staple of the fantasy genre. The ancient fables best known today are probably the stories attributed to the semilegendary Greek writer Aesop; the details about his life history and when he lived are uncertain, but Aesop has exerted an enduring influence on the literary history of the fantastic. He is thought to have lived from about 620 to 560 B.C.E. and is said to have been a Phrygian slave who emerged from his period of servitude on the island of Samos to deliver tales full of folk wisdom. The manuscripts attributed to Aesop were first assembled in Latin in the second or third century C.E., but many of the tales have Middle Eastern, African, Mediterranean, or even ancient Indian and Sumerian origins. It is interesting to realize that there were international sources for Aesop's fables, for the fact that they are collected in Graeco-Roman texts demonstrates that early literature in oral and folk traditions was, in fact, global. Certain tales quite literally spread throughout the world even before they could be written or printed to become best-sellers by best tellers, and most of these tales were filled with fantasy. Aesop's fables and the *Pancatantra* exemplify the moral and ethical grounding, the global influence, and the tendency to cross boundaries typical of fantasy; in both collections the boundaries of communication are dispensed with so that we comprehend the language of animals.

The four greatest of the ancient works influencing the Western fantasy tradition—which are indeed watershed literary influences for the entire Western literary tradition—are the two Greek epics by Homer, *The Iliad* and *The Odyssey;* the Roman epic by Virgil, *The Aeneid;* and the Arabic of *Alf Laylah Wa-Laylah (The Thousand and One Nights),* commonly known as *The Arabian Nights,* a large collection of fantastic stories assembled by a Persian poet in the tenth century. However, many tales in *The Arabian Nights* existed much earlier, such as the story of Sinbad the sailor, which seems to predate even *The Odyssey*. Homer's two epics set lofty heroic and imaginative models as well as high literary standards in both form and language. *The Iliad,* probably composed in the eighth century B.C.E., tells of events that took place about 1180 B.C.E., when the hero Achilles joined other Greek warriors to lay siege to Troy. (Odysseus is also among those in the Greek forces assaulting Troy.) Achilles, full of pride, strength, and anger, is a hero doomed to prove himself through battle in a contest at once cruel and purifying. *The Odyssey,* the story of the return of Odysseus, king of Ithaca, to his home after the fall of Troy, presents a different sort of hero, one who survives by wit and wisdom rather than by the strength, bravery, and fury that characterize Achilles. Throughout both works, human history is shown to intersect with eternal forces; undying gods and goddesses display carelessness with life and death and show traits of fickleness, vanity, and whimsy that often make doomed mortals seem dignified by contrast.

The foremost epic of Roman culture is Virgil's *Aeneid,* composed in Latin in 30 to 19 B.C.E. It exemplifies a more self-conscious, sophisticated awareness of literary form and structure, including allusions to Greek history and myth and the portrayal of a more civilized ideal of heroism than that found in Homer. In the book, which recounts the founding of a glorious civilization, Aeneas displays a new and different attitude toward war. He seems to view suffering and death with profound sorrow and pity, as necessary consequences of a fight he is forced by destiny to participate in and win. The poem in the end celebrates a triumph of reasonable, universal order, represented by Jupiter on the transcendent level and by Aeneas in the world.

In these ancient texts we find models and foundations of what seems to be an aboriginal human impulse toward fantasy. The Egyptian "Tale of the Shipwrecked Sailor" is the earliest fantastic voyage, complete with serpent/dragon and a vanishing island; the Westcar Papyrus stresses the potency of magic and wizardry as well as the power of the word to bring an inanimate image to life, control the natural world and part the waters, and reanimate life; *Gilgamesh* introduces contrasting companion protagonists with its hero-king and savage, and together with the Sanskrit epics and the Bible the epic narrative stakes out the cosmic stage. *The Iliad* is the prototype of all great war tales; *The Odyssey*, the model for the hero on the road. The Roman *Aeneid* brings the raw, chaotic powers of the Greek epics under more civilized control in the story of the establishment of a glorious city (Rome) and its civilizing principles of order. Yet the verbal thrust for order finds its most compelling expression in the Old Testament Book of Genesis, in which the subjects are the first act of creation, the bringing of the world into being through the uttering of words, the unfolding of creation, and the relationship of creator and created. This emphasis on creation is echoed in personal terms through storytelling in *The Arabian Nights,* in which imaginative creation is essential to existence.[11] In each model of antiquity we find expression of the human imagination dealing with powers of infinity. These models are the roots and archetypes of fantasy.

We sense a purpose in these early works to cast the infinite in finite terms, to translate overwhelming and eternal forces into down-to-earth language and physical presences, to use the imagination and the containment, or expression, of words to control and comprehend the overwhelming forces. As the modern fantasy genre emerged in the nineteenth century, however, authors' instincts seemed to move in the opposite direction. The works from that time forward seem designed to reawaken imaginative faculties too long accustomed to control and command of the natural and created world, too long dominated and ruled by human reason. The authors seemed drawn toward the conjuring of primitive, unpredictable, infinite powers *beyond* comprehension.

Tributaries to the Fantasy Mainstream

Some other significant precursors of fantasy in folklore, classical literature, and myth should also be mentioned in passing. The Greek writer Hesiod in the eighth and early seventh centuries B.C.E. composed *Theogonia,* an organization of mythic tales into a history of the world in which violent power is eventually directed by reason. In his later *Works and Days* he presents a collection of myths of moral instruction, including a beast fable that predates those of Aesop. Many of the Greek plays of the golden age (fifth century B.C.E.) contain antirealistic elements, but the comedies of Aristophanes are especially rich in fantasy, perhaps most notably *The Birds*, in which a citizen of Athens, with assistance from the birds, challenges Zeus for control of the universe by building a city in the sky.

It is also with the Greeks that the earliest literary romances originate, and since modern fantasy is primarily a prose genre, these early prose romance forms were important influences. The Greek romances—such as Chariton's *Chaereas and Callirhoe* (ca. 245 C.E.), Xenophon's *Ephesiaca* (ca. 250 C.E.), and Heliodorus's *Ethiopica* (ca. 350 C.E.)—are tales of lovers' struggles that often feature pastoral settings and that usually involve travels over great distances and abundant strange adventures before the lovers can be united.

In Roman literature the most influential works in the fantasy tradition are Ovid's *Metamorphoses* and Lucius Apuleius's *Golden Ass*. Both demonstrate how the elements of myth can be woven in unique and personal ways, and by emphasizing the possibility of transformation, they perpetuate one of the key points of fantasy established in the earliest Egyptian texts: form is not fixed but changeable, and appearances can be altered by the power of magic and language.

At the same time that literary texts and techniques multiplied and diversified, the literacy of those who heard or read the texts continuously grew and changed. Most scholars now suggest that alphabets and writing first emerged for specific practical purposes, to record numbers and information necessary for economic transactions and exchanges. However, as both oral and written literatures appeared, they quickly and clearly came to be understood simultaneously on literal and figurative levels. The concept of symbolic, or metaphorical, meaning and its embodiment in parable, fable, allegory, drama, epic, and narrative modes soon followed. Both the pre-Christian writings of Plato and the Old and New Testament parables clearly reflect sophisticated nonliteral understandings of text and nonliteral principles of reading and writing that are fundamental to fantasy. The fantasy document is dependent on the simultaneous belief in the text's literal truth and the understanding of a nonliteral, numinous dimension. Dennis Kratz, one of the best critics to survey classical influences on fantasy, concludes that "the interaction of

Platonism with the literary imagination established fantasy as a medium for the exploration of philosophic concepts. This wedding of entertainment and idea in fantastic narrative was among the most significant contributions of the classical world to the Western literary tradition" (Kratz, 9). Kratz goes on to praise the way the impulse toward allegory preserved classical stories when medieval Christian scholarship held sway:

> It was a form of reading that proved useful to Christians confronted by the attractive yet dangerous literature of classical culture, enabling them to perceive beneath the surface narrative a deeper level of meaning—often unknown to the original author—consistent with Christian doctrine. Allegorizing in interpretation and creation is a consistent feature of not only medieval but also Renaissance literature. (11)

Not only did this mode of understanding help assure the survival of classical texts, "it enabled authors to employ fantastic scenes as a means of expressing deeper philosophic or religious truths" (11).

The last pregeneric flowering of the impulse toward fantasy occurred during the Dark Ages in Europe, when superstition and magic were as apt to be believed as truth as they were to be interpreted as metaphor or fiction. *The Arabian Nights* (ca. 1450), with its framing story of Scheherazade, who postpones her death by telling a different story each night, drew from Persian and Arabic sources to spin an intricate web of fantastic tales, including "Aladdin's Lamp," "Sinbad the Sailor," and "Ali Baba and the Forty Thieves," which are now firmly a part of the world fantasy tradition. As in Genesis, the core myth here is one of making, but it is a paradigm for the intangible constructions of imagination, for the infinity of narrative, and for the lifesaving power of storytelling.

On American soil, Native American oral storytelling similarly affirmed the value of myths of making, and generations of tale-tellers set down mythic roots that by the fifteenth century had become marvelously rich. Only relatively recently have these begun to bear literary fruits of contemporary fantasy, in such works as *Storyteller* by Leslie Marmon Silko and *Tracks* by Louise Erdrich, in which an old man literally survives by telling stories. Piers Anthony re-creates the tradition in his historical fantasy novel *Tatham Mound* and extends awareness of these sources in *Tales from the Great Turtle: Fantasy in the Native American Tradition.*[12]

Other early and medieval texts of great importance for fantasy internationally are *Beowulf* (ca. 725), the *Poetic Edda* (*Elder Edda,* ca. 800–1200), the French *Chanson de Roland* (*Song of Roland,* ca. 1100), the German *Nibelungenlied,* the Scandinavian *Volsungasaga* (ca. 1200), Snorri Sturluson's *Heimskringla* and *Prose Edda* (ca. 1220–1236), Gottfried von Strassburg's *Tristan* (ca. 1210), Dante Alighieri's *Divine Comedy* (ca. 1320), Geoffrey Chaucer's *Canterbury Tales* (ca. 1343–1400), *Sir Gawain and the Green Knight* (ca. 1370), *Grettir's Saga* (ca. 1375), and Sir Thomas Malory's *Morte d'Arthur* (1485) and the earlier Arthurian traditions preceding Malory that he collected from sources in France, England, and Ireland.

Victorian Revelations of Antiquity

Although most people in the nineteenth century looked to the future, toward the great advances applied science and technology would bring—an impulse toward science fiction—others put the science to different use. It was scientific methods, after all, that made possible the great nineteenth-century excavations and recoveries of the lost literatures of antiquity. In the eighteenth century, Antoine Galland had issued his 12-volume French translation of *The Arabian Nights* (1704–1717), introducing Europe to this text, and Alexander Pope had rendered important and influential English translations of *The Iliad* (1720) and *The Odyssey* (1725–1726), but the Victorians went further. In Germany the philologist and folklorist Jakob Grimm (1785–1863) published his popular collections of fairy tales with his brother Wilhelm between 1812 and 1815, founded the discipline of comparative philology, and established relationships between the various Indo-European languages in Grimm's law (1822). Philology and folklore have subsequently become cornerstones of the fantasy genre; it is more than mere coincidence that the greatest twentieth-century fantasy writer, J. R. R. Tolkien, was a philologist. A deep concern for language and for the act of naming is nearly universal in fantasy.

Part of the reason for the rediscovery of ancient Egyptian culture was the British capture of Alexandria in 1801. Among the treasures taken back to the British Museum in London was the Rosetta stone, which proved to be the key to deciphering hieroglyphics. The brilliant Frenchman Jean-François Champollion began studying a copy of it in Paris in 1808 and by 1824 was able to publish his *Description of the Hieroglyphic System of the Ancient Egyptians*. His decoding was the gateway to the Egyptian literature previously discussed. Edward Lane (1838–1842), John Payne (1882–1884), and Richard Burton (1885–1886) all published improved English translations of the *Thousand and One Nights*. By 1840 Austen Henry Layard was beginning excavations at Nineveh and Nimrud that would retrieve thousands of cuneiform tablets for deposit at the British Museum. His work was eventually brought to fruition by Henry Rawlinson, who had found the key to yet earlier forms of literature by his breakthrough decipherment of cuneiform writing on a rock in Behistun in Persia in 1833; Rawlinson's discovery of how to read the Behistun cuneiform led eventually to George Smith's announcement at the new Society of Biblical Archaeology in December 1872 that he had found, on an Assyrian tablet, an account of a cataclysmic flood; it was part of *The Epic of Gilgamesh*, eventually excavated on 12 clay tablets from the library at Nineveh. In another part of the world, Elias Lonnrott published the first version of the Finnish *Kalevala* in 1835, collecting from oral traditions the ancient stories of that northern people. The great medieval Welsh tales of *The Mabinogion* were first translated into English by Lady Charlotte Guest between 1838 and 1849. Translations and rediscoveries of more recent Roman and medieval works abounded.[13]

William Morris was among the major literary figures contributing to the trend. Not only did he translate Homer's *Iliad* and *Odyssey*, he brought into English substantial portions of northern saga literature in collaboration with Eiríkr Magnússon; they started with *The Saga of Gunnlaug Worm-Tongue* and *The Story of Grettir the Strong* in 1869 and followed in 1870 with *The Story of the Volsungs and Niblungs* (translations of *Volsungasaga* and songs from the *Elder Edda*). In addition, Morris popularized a central portion of Apuleius's *Golden Ass* in his own *Tale of Cupid and Psyche,* published his English versions of important Old French romances, and directed the attention of the modern age backward to the mists of a more golden time as he praised the triumphs of imagination in the so-called Dark Ages.

The Shaping of Modern Fantasy

William Morris and George MacDonald are the pioneers of fantasy as a modern literary genre. Morris published his first fantasy stories in 1856, and MacDonald's novel *Phantastes* appeared in 1858. They not only established radical, imaginative, antirealistic modes of fiction as antitheses to the realistic modes so popular at the time but recovered long-neglected vocabulary, syntax, and patterns of archetypal invention similar to many of the long-lost texts being rediscovered. Morris and MacDonald, an artist and a theologian, presented interesting philosophical alternatives in the early-fantasy genre through a marked contrast of values that emerged in their writing: radical, secular, idealist values (Marxist values) in the work of Morris; traditional, religious, spiritual values (Christian values) in the work of MacDonald. This polarity of divergent values was especially significant and set a thematic course for the genre, since fantasy was from the outset a more purely philosophic mode of writing than was realism. It was, after all, successor to the literary tradition primarily directed toward connecting finite existence with the infinite. It was less concerned with real, individual characters and situations than with embodying philosophical, intellectual, moral, and social discourse. Fantasy's philosophic orientation has been preserved, during the course of the genre's evolution, in the writing of some of its most popular practitioners, and with this evolution has come a lively dialectic of beliefs. There have been important subsequent fantasy writers, such as J. R. R. Tolkien, C. S. Lewis, and Orson Scott Card, whose fiction specifically exemplifies traditional religious values; on the other hand, such writers as David Lindsay, Anthony Burgess, and Stephen Donaldson have produced radical texts that, like the work of Morris, challenge traditional beliefs. There are also those, especially among contemporary writers, who push toward synthesis of the Christian/Marxist (spiritual/secular) dichotomies—Piers Anthony and William Gibson among them.

Shortly after Morris and MacDonald began their fantasy writing in the 1850s, the publication of Lewis Carroll's *Alice in Wonderland* (1865) enlarged the possibilities of fiction by introducing a kind of children's book that could be fully appreciated only by grown-ups and that became immensely popular. Beyond its rich, magical inventiveness, it embraced free association and nonsense and made fashionable the concept of doing "three impossible things before breakfast." Carroll's *Alice* and later *Through the Looking Glass* improved both the climate and the audience for fantasy. In fact, MacDonald had also written fantasies for children, including such stories as "The Light Princess" (1864) and "The Golden Key" (1867) and his novel *At the Back of the North Wind* (1871), which arguably can best be appreciated by adults. Hans Christian Andersen in Denmark was producing fairy tales so rich and multilayered that they seemed almost to have emerged from a folk tradition in some timeless past. His stories, including "The Little Mermaid" and "The Snow Queen," were translated and published in English in 1872. Carlo Collodi's *Pinocchio,* first published in Italy in 1882, was translated and issued in England 10 years later, in 1892. These works and others were influential in shaping adult fantasy not only because they were frequently read aloud and appreciated by adults as they shared them with their children but also because they cultivated and enhanced young people's appetite for fantasy. As these children in turn became mature readers, it was only natural that they desired to build on their rich, imaginative childhood literary experiences and continue to seek out adult books with similar motifs and devices.

In fact, children's literature has proven to be an enduring influence on adult fantasy. As a new century began, L. Frank Baum's landmark American fairy tale *The Wonderful Wizard of Oz,* published in 1900, and James M. Barrie's *Peter Pan,* published in 1904, were fantasy milestones that shaped both popular and literary perspectives. Many well-known authors, including Oscar Wilde, Walter De La Mare, Laurence Housman, James Thurber, J. R. R. Tolkien, C. S. Lewis, Lloyd Alexander, Andre Norton, Joy Chant, Jane Yolen, and Piers Anthony, have continued to explore the links between literature for children and adults. The interface between children's literature and adult fantasy is a fruitful continuum that has led many younger readers into adult fantasy and that has helped preserve childhood's pure delight in imagination well into adulthood for many readers and writers of fantasy.

The Savage and Dark Forces

Morris and MacDonald used the fantasy mode to create a type of high literary fantasy. Beginning in 1885 with *King Solomon's Mines*, H. Rider Haggard directed the popular imagination in a somewhat different direction as he established the pattern for "lost race" adventure fantasy with a more populist audience in mind. Haggard's hero, Allan Quatermain, a great white hunter exploring mysteries of the Dark Continent, was so popular with the public that he made Haggard famous and eventually appeared in 16 novels in plots that included supernatural events, Zulu wizards, ancient maps, and extraordinary adventures. Haggard also created a compelling female character, the deathless Ayesha, "She-Who-Must-Be-Obeyed," who appeared first in *She* in 1886 and later in three other books, including *She and Allan*, in which Ayesha shares the spotlight with Allan Quatermain. Haggard's Quatermain, the prototype for Edgar Rice Burroughs's Tarzan and Robert E. Howard's Conan, is the model for an approach to fantasy that is less self-consciously literary, built on elemental juxtapositions of advanced civilization with primitive, barbaric culture, and constructed in a series format to establish sustained, repeated contact with a broad, popular audience. Haggard, like Morris, drew directly from mythical sources; he wrote a sequel to Homer's *Odyssey* with fairy tale author Andrew Lang (*The World's Desire*, 1890) and used the Icelandic-saga backdrop in his *Eric Brighteyes* (1891).

One other significant innovation in fantasy during this early formative period was the emergence of dark fantasy that bordered on horror. Contributing influences included the gothic novel, occult lore, and many myths and superstitions. In some ways this mode was a development of the traditional ghost story, a long-standing source of the supernatural that had enjoyed great popularity. Charles Dickens had explored the possibilities of the modern ghost story to spectacular advantage in *A Christmas Carol* (1843), which utilizes the supernatural for effective didactic purposes and has become part of the popular mythology of Christmas. In the United States, Washington Irving, Nathaniel Hawthorne, and Edgar Allan Poe introduced the power of even darker forces in their writing. Irving's *The Sketch-Book of Geoffrey Crayon* (1819–1820) includes such classics as "Rip Van Winkle," "The Legend of Sleepy Hollow," and "The Spectre Bridegroom." Hawthorne's famous novels *The Scarlet Letter* (1850) and *The House of the Seven Gables* (1851) contain significant nonrealistic elements, and his stories are frequently infused with haunting presences and supernatural plot twists, as in "The Birth Mark" (1835), "Young Goodman Brown" (1835), "The Hall of Fantasy" (1843), "The Celestial Railroad" (1843), and "Feathertop" (1852)—whose scarecrow brought to life was surely an influence on Baum's more congenial scarecrow. In "The Fall of the House of Usher" (1839), Poe, who normally anchors his stories in reason, leads the reader to the very brink of fantasy, suggesting sinister powers beyond rational comprehension that transform the house itself into a powerful force in the story. The fear-inspiring side of fantasy in the early period is perhaps best represented, however, by Bram Stoker's *Dracula* (1897), a book that embodies the dark, supernatural aspects of the fantasy novel and prefigures many popular contemporary dark fantasy works, such as Stephen King's *The Mist* and *Salem's Lot*.

As the nineteenth century drew to a close, fantasy was attracting international attention from authors and readers alike. Other interesting British writers incorporating supernatural elements into their fiction included the spiritualist Marie Corelli (pseudonym of Minnie Mackay), in such novels as *A Romance of Two Worlds* (1886) and *The Sorrows of Satan* (1895); George du Maurier, in *Trilby* (1894); W. H. Hudson, in *A Crystal Age* (1887); and H. G. Wells, in *The Wonderful Visit* (1895) and *The Plattner Story and Others* (1897). In France, Gustave Flaubert's *Salammbô* (1863) and *The Temptation of St. Anthony* (1874); Pierre Louÿs's *Aphrodite* (1896); Théophile Gautier's tales, including "Clarimonde" (1836), "King Caudaules" (1844), and "Arria Marcella" (1852); and Gérard de Nerval's *Aurélia* (1855) explored the fantasy terrain through the spirit of romanticism, eroticism, and elements of surrealism and visionary madness. In Germany, Baron Friedrich de la Motte Fouqué had written three influential precursors of Morris: *The Magic Ring* (1813), a chivalric quest for a ring with strong allegorical resonances; *Sintram and His Companions* (1820), a novella inspired by Albrecht Dürer's engraving *The Knight, Death, and the Devil;* and *Undine* (1811), the story of a water sprite that was influenced by the *kunstmärchen* tradition and by the Grimms' *Kinder- und Hausmärchen* (1812–1813), in its turn helping to inspire a flowering of this type of writing.

Fantasy was, in fact, rapidly making its mark in national literatures throughout the world. Pedro Antonio de Alarcón in Spain (*El amigo de la muerte,* 1852), Guy Boothby in Australia (*Pharos the Egyptian,* 1899), James de Mille (*A Strange Manuscript Found in a Copper Cylinder,* 1888) in Canada, Fyodor Dostoyevsky (*The Dream of a Ridiculous Man; Another Man's Wife; A Meek Young Girl,* 1873–1874) and Nikolai Gogol (*Evenings on a Farm Near Dikanka,* 1831–1832; "Viy" and "The Nose," 1835; and "The Overcoat," 1842) in Russia, and even the playwright Henrik Ibsen (*Peer Gynt,* 1867) in Norway were demonstrating the global spread of literary fantasy.

Fantasy in a New Century (1900–1935)

By the start of the twentieth century, fantasy was an established mode for serious adult literature. Although it clearly enjoyed an international currency, it seems to have emerged most conspicuously *as a fully distinct genre* in England and the United States, to a large extent because literary realism was so dominant there. Both countries were at the forefront of the industrial revolution and at the cutting edge of scientific discovery at the very time when fantasy took shape. In many ways, science absorbed supernatural power; it evoked awe and wonder with its apparent magic. These factors, coupled with the relative absence of universal folkloric and mythic traditions in England and America, contributed to the formation of modern fantasy as a distinct literary form in these countries where the popular imagination was nearly starved for fantasy. In much of the rest of the world, where fantasy writing had been historically more integrally preserved through oral culture, myth, and a body of folklore and superstition, fantasy seems to have been more comfortably incorporated into mainstream literature, such as the work of E. T. A. Hoffmann, Franz Kafka, Italo Calvino, Jorge Luis Borges, and the contemporary magic realism of Gabriel García Márquez and others.

In England, William Morris devoted the last years of his literary life composing 10 novels that have served as solid grounding for the modern fantasy tradition. He dictated the final pages of his last novel, *The Sundering Flood,* from his deathbed in 1896, and it was published in 1897, the final accomplishment in a remarkable career of preservation, revival, and invention in the realm of the imagination. The genre Morris helped shape with materials from saga literature, Arthurian legend, Old French romances, Anglo-Saxon philology, utopian visions, and vigorous medieval and gothic scholarship rapidly evolved in the first few decades of the twentieth century. The popular author and editor Lin Carter, who, as editor of the Ballantine adult-fantasy series, has played an important role in the contemporary popularization of fantasy, commented in his 1970 preface to the paperback edition of *Phantastes* on one of Morris's most important generic contributions to fantasy:

> Morris' world is real, adventures therein are serious and the perils along the way are deadly; but the world of *Phantastes* is an imagined state of being and we are not meant to accept it as a real place. The adventures met by MacDonald's character Anodos are symbolic, and the dangers he faces allegorical.[14]

Carter articulates a defining characteristic of fantasy as a pure, distinct genre: it depicts adventures in a coherent and real fantasy world. The events and characters in the book cannot ambiguously be ascribed to a dream, a vision, or an aberration. Fantasy cannot be reduced to mere allegory or symbol; it is not a product of madness, superstition, or satire. Fantasy has a compelling and even dangerous reality.

Many writers during the next decades moved to imprint fantasy with their unique sensibilities, but with the publication of *The Gods of Pagana* by the Irish writer Lord Dunsany in 1905,[15] a major successor to Morris stepped onto the stage. Dunsany began creating his mythos from a map of an imaginary land he had drawn when he was 25, and his first book is a series of poetical pieces describing aspects of this world. The individual chapters, which are difficult to describe, have been variously referred to as sketches, prose poems, and stories. Somewhat biblical in inspiration and in form, they build up an invented mythology, a story of creation, and a coherent world with its own history. Dunsany continued in subsequent collections of stories to recount more sustained narratives of adventures in this world, but his unique style—a mixture of Celtic lyricism and King James Bible cadences—and sustained mythic invention became influential in the work of subsequent fantasy writers. He had particular impact on those who followed his example of constructing an elaborate invented mythos for an imaginary reality explored in several works, like his Pagana, a place he located on the world's "Third Hemisphere." James Branch Cabell and his Poictesme; Clark Ashton Smith and his linked stories of Hyborea and Zothique; H. P. Lovecraft and his Cthulhu mythos; Robert E. Howard and his tales of the Hyborean Age, and many others, both directly and indirectly, are inheritors of Lord Dunsany.

Dunsany's fellow Irishman James Stephens tapped into traditions of Irish folklore and fairy tale with humor and complexity. *The Crock of Gold* (1912) is his early masterpiece, though later books, including *Deirdre* (1923) and *In the Land of Youth* (1924), which contain stories based on ancient Irish legends, are also rich in poetry and depth. James Joyce (also born in Dublin and on the same day) admired Stephens to such an extent that he settled on the idea that Stephens should complete *Finnegans Wake,* though Joyce outlived him and the collaboration never came to pass. Stephens successfully shapes an adult fairy tale mode in fantasy that allows him great freedom of plot and character and ample opportunity for Irish cadences and the championing of Irish nationalism. He is direct about the extent of autobiography in his fantasy:

> I am Mary in the *Charwoman's Daughter,* and I am her mother and the Policeman—I am the Philosopher in the *Crock of Gold,* and I am the children, the leprechauns and the goat; so, in the *Demi-Gods,* I am the gods, and Patsy McCann and Eileen Ni Cooley, and whoever else goes through those pages.... My approach to humanity or life is through myself, and I try to cultivate the blessed cosmos inside my own head.[16]

On the heels of the Freudian revolution, Stephens, like Joyce, was acutely aware of how the conscious and unconscious mind could project itself in images, symbols, and fantasy.

G. K. Chesterton contributed to fantasy in a wide range of novels, essays, poetry, and plays that embody his deep religious concerns and foreshadow the work of C. S. Lewis and J. R. R. Tolkien. Today Chesterton may be best known popularly as the author of the Father Brown detective tales, but his fantasy classic, *The Man Who Was Thursday* (1908), incorporates elements of detective fiction, intellectual wit, comic irony, and theological depth. The author of other fantasy works as well, Chesterton is a multitalented literary figure who adds sophistication and depth to the allegorical, religious approach MacDonald first showed could work so effectively in fantasy.

Whereas Chesterton was a prolific and highly visible literary presence who earned his living as a writer and editor in the early twentieth century, David Lindsay remained largely unknown and impoverished. His father had deserted his family when Lindsay was just a young child, and despite showing himself to be an outstanding student Lindsay had no means to obtain a university education. He went to work with a London insurance broker when he was 16 and remained there for 22 years, until he left in 1916 to join the British grenadiers during World War I. After the war, living off of his savings and pension, he determined to express his complex philosophical insights in fiction, and his masterpiece, *A Voyage to Arcturus,* was published in 1920. It sold fewer than 600 copies. Two subsequent novels—*The Haunted Woman* (1922) and *Sphinx* (1923)—did no better, and his writing career went nowhere. At that time literary modernism was in vogue among the most thoughtful readers—those who had the kinds of literary minds Lindsay's complex fiction demands. Instead of reading fantasy, many of them were attracted by the new experimental realism of D. H. Lawrence, Gertrude Stein, Ernest Hemingway, James Joyce, Virginia Woolf, and T. S. Eliot. Lindsay tried his hand at writing in a more popular adventure format but never achieved real success or recognition during his lifetime. Only after his death have readers discovered in *Arcturus* a startlingly powerful, visionary novel about the nature of ultimate reality, a work that is intellectually, philosophically, and artistically challenging and inspiring. Lindsay acknowledged George MacDonald's *Phantastes* as one of his strongest influences, but he demonstrates the potential for theological fantasy much more complex than that of even Chesterton or Lewis, whose novels build allegorical structures from established religious doctrine. Lindsay's fiction expresses personal vision, and with its hallucinatory style leads readers toward challenging levels of philosophical and religious exploration of their own. Lindsay does not so much propound a coherent doctrine as present a process for gradually seeing into the deeper truths of things. At the same time he undergirds his writing with a sense that there *is* an ultimate reality to be grasped. He challenges the reader to undertake this mission and models in his book the kind of dangerous, personal voyage necessary to attain it.

A contemporary of Lindsay's, E. R. Eddison, published his first work of fiction in 1922. *The Worm Ouroboros* is a new novel of heroic fantasy in the tradition more of Morris than MacDonald. This may be due in part to the Homeric and Icelandic influences on Eddison, a lover of classics who became a scholar of Old Norse after reading *The Saga Library* of Icelandic translations by Morris and Eirikr Magnusson; though he earned his living as a civil servant, Eddison was an intellectual. His writing style also is indebted to Morris's archaic lyricism, though Eddison's archaism is more Elizabethan and Jacobean than gothic, and his novels have a more intellectual and metaphysical, less visceral grounding than those of Morris. Nonetheless, Eddison's books enrich that radical, secular, idealist strain of fantasy, which originated with Morris, and contribute innovations in mythic richness, language, and form.

Somewhat more commercially successful than Lindsay, Eddison wrote other notable fantasy books as extensions of his *Ouroboros* cosmos: his Zimiamvian trilogy—*Mistress of Mistresses* (1935), *A Fish Dinner in Memison* (1941), and *The Mezentian Gate* (1958)—is set in Zimiamvia, the legendary paradise of the earlier book. Eddison's writing is full of literary allusions; he develops archetypes as old as the Egyptian tales—the transmutation of identity, the worm Ouroboros itself, which Eddison takes from the ancient Greek name for the dragon, or serpent, that devours its own tail. The worm is a fascinating Gnostic symbol associated with the inscription *Hen to pan,* meaning "the one, the all," and that echoes the Eastern yin-yang symbol of the unity of opposing forces. It is an image of the wholeness of the natural cycle, in which things continuously return to their own beginnings. The ouroboros, in its alchemical associations with the cycle of earth-air-fire-water, its joining of the yin-yang's earthly, or dark, and heavenly, or light, principles (sometimes the ouroboros is rendered half in darkness, half in light), and its frequent depiction as winged serpent or dragon (serpentine as earthly, winged as heavenly), taps into archetypal symbology with a complexity best appreciated by readers enriched by the theories of Freud and Jung. In his foreword to the annotated 1991 Dell trade paperback edition of *Ouroboros*, critic Douglas E. Winter calls the book "the best single novel of fantasy ever written in the English language,"[17] and although this claim is largely an indication of personal taste, it does appropriately reflect Eddison's success in advancing the English fantasy novel in ways that fully appealed to the tastes of the modern reader.

American Innovations in the New Century

Simultaneously in America, fantasy's evolution was taking interesting twists. One strand is the thread interweaving humor and satire with the fabric of fantasy. Mark Twain may be seen in some ways as the progenitor of this American spin, particularly in his take on Arthurian fantasy, *A Connecticut Yankee in King Arthur's Court* (1889). In another book in the Twayne genre series, *Science Fiction Before 1900*, Paul Alkon makes a strong claim for Twain's novel as science fiction rather than fantasy and gives plausible arguments for doing so. Less plausibly, he observes that it is "the first story of travel to and from the past," adding that "this motif does not occur in previous literature or folklore."[18] The motif in fact *does* occur in the fantasy tradition in many forms earlier than Twain, including the relatively obscure novella by Max Adeler, *The Fortunate Island* (1882), which has been cited as one of Twain's sources for *Connecticut Yankee*. One of the most familiar earlier time-travel fantasies is Dickens's influential masterpiece *A Christmas Carol* (1843), in which the hero's visit to the past and return to the present are an essential part of his character transformation. Poe's "Tale of the Ragged Mountains" (1844) uses dream as the vehicle that allows the protagonist to experience the past through an avatar's body, and Morris's utopian fantasy *A Dream of John Ball* (1886) makes similar use of dream as the time-travel vehicle for exploring utopian ideas with the medieval preacher,

John Ball. However, the significance of travel to and from the past in the study of fantasy as a genre has less to do with which author first used the motif and more to do with the fundamental point that time travel is an archetypal impulse, inextricably woven into the inspiration and essence of modern fantasy. Antiquity—history—is one gateway to infinity. The impulse to explore and recover the past seems to be at the heart of the fantasy impulse, and I have suggested that the sciences of archaeology, anthropology, and philology (especially the translation of ancient texts) were of great importance in the formation of the genre. Morris's fantasy was intrinsically linked to time travel—perhaps most obviously in his two utopian novels but also in his protofantasy novels *The House of the Wolfings* and *The Roots of the Mountains*, both of which transport the reader into idealized medieval settings. In fantasy, visitation to the past is frequently an extrapolation from the tradition of the literary dream vision, and its symbology has been usefully explicated for critics in psychoanalytic terms beginning with Freudian and Jungian interpretations of dreams. In fact, as soon as it clearly emerges, the science of psychology also begins to color fantasy. The subconscious depths of the mind and the unknown riches of the past serve as "roots of the mountains" of fantasy. The ability to visit and return from explorations of the unconscious or undiscovered past is, in a sense, learned from scientific and historical study, from the recovery of ancient texts, from the reiteration of creation stories (the Book of Genesis in the Bible is surely an experience of time travel and has been a model for subcreation in fantasy), from exploration of the psychological past through personal history and archetypes in the mind. When Robert E. Howard takes his readers to the past in the partly real, partly mythic Hyborean Age, and when Tolkien later explores time travel in his posthumously published story "The Lost Road" or recounts the histories of creation and of lost civilizations in *The Silmarillion* and elsewhere, they are expressing the motif of exploring and returning from the past, which has been one of fantasy's recurring, essential aspects since its invention. In fact, implicit or explicit time travel seems to be as much at the heart of fantasy as space travel is at the core of science fiction.

Twain's *Connecticut Yankee* is a hybrid text that certainly can be claimed for science fiction, but it also has strong elements of satire, utopia, and fantasy. Its great originality lies in its ironic, hyperbolic use of Arthurian legend, so often viewed as a serious progenitor of fantasy for themes of chivalric, romantic, political, and spiritual idealism. Twain's comic exaggerations and juxtapositions question complacent notions about science and progress, and the ironic humor takes a turn toward black comedy as the plot unfolds.

Although *Connecticut Yankee* is not itself a milestone fantasy text, it is an influential transition novel on the road to American satiric and comic fantasy, subgenres most significantly developed in the work of James Branch Cabell. Beginning with *The Cream of the Jest* (1917), Cabell created an impressive interconnected mythos biographically related to himself and to his central character, Dom Manuel of Poictesme. Cabell explores the worlds of dream and fantasy as they relate to reality, intellect, and sexuality in a style at once elaborate, witty, and lyrical. He uses puns, anagrams, allegory, and irony to engage the reader's intellect and humor in the exercise of fantasy. Like Stephens and James Joyce, Cabell builds on the then-new psychological theories of Freud and Jung with language and imagination full of Rorschach and similar projective revelations. At another level, though, Cabell like Stephens makes explicit a submerged biographical subtext in fantasy. Some of the other noteworthy titles in his cycle of tales are *Jurgen* (1919), *Figures of Earth* (1921), and *The High Place* (1923). Cabell conceived these and other related books—from *The Eagle's Shadow* (1904) to *The Way of Ecben* (1929)—as one vast epic work, *The Biography of the Life of Manuel.* Critic Donald L. Lawler has said that the epic "is arguably the best and most ambitious work of fantasy conceived and carried out by an American writer."[19]

Also in the vein of American humorous fantasy are the gentler and more slapstick novels of Thorne Smith, including *The Stray Lamb* (1929), *The Glorious Pool* (1934), and of course his best-known creation, *Topper* (1926), in which a couple of fun-loving ghosts try to loosen up the life of the well-behaved middle-class suburbanite Cosmo Topper. Twain's treatment of Arthurian legend derived part of its humor through a process of deflating, bringing a myth of epic grandeur and heroism into a much more ordinary and mundane context, though in fact Twain's novel remains very much a tale of power, of the effect of great men and great deeds upon history. Smith's approach is antiheroic and individual. The events in Cosmo Topper's life will not disturb the cosmos. Smith allows fantasy to play itself out as primarily important to the ordinary individual and to the freeing of his spirit from the authority of habit and convention. His work is as much about the liberation of spirit as is Morris's, yet it has far less to do with the political and social order. *Topper* places the focus on the radical liberation through fantasy of the individual mind. It touts a genuine American individualism, as opposed, for instance, to the values of the commonwealth and Socialism in Morris's work. Smith also introduced the conflict between individual experience and society as a subject for fantasy, and much of *Topper*'s humor derives from the fact that the protagonist can see his two ghostly companions, George and Marion Kerby, whereas others cannot.

James Thurber polished and perfected many of Smith's motifs in the tales included in *Fables for Our Time and Famous Poems Illustrated* (1940), *The Thirteen Clocks* (1950), and *Further Fables for Our Time* (1956). He is a master of exploring what he refers to in *My Life and Hard Times* (1933) as "the manifestation of a twitchiness at once cosmic and mundane." His acclaimed story "The Secret Life of Walter Mitty" (1942) dramatizes the individual's dilemma as he dares to engage in fantasy, and Thurber raises similar issues in his purer fantasies, including his fables and fairy tales, in some of which the world of fantasy triumphs. Especially beautiful is *The White Deer* (1945), but many critics consider Thurber's genius to reside in his humorous presentation of fantasy's mundane edges and dilemmas, including an element of dark irony in which Thurber presents a complex balancing act an individual must perform in grappling with conventional reality and fantasy, and a recognition that one may easily fall into nightmare, madness, or suicide as a result.

A different American contribution evolved as an outgrowth of successful capitalism giving birth to a thriving circulation for pulp magazines, and an extension of some of the fantasy territory suggested by the work of H. Rider Haggard. Edgar Rice Burroughs and Robert E. Howard each made substantial contributions to the genre, both creating heroes who have assumed, like Sherlock Holmes, an enduring life beyond the pages of a book or the hand of a single author. Their influence was possible to a large extent because of the capitalistic innovation of American publisher Frank A. Munsey, whose *Argosy* magazine, begun in 1882, suffered financially. In 1896 Munsey came up with the idea of printing *Argosy* on cheap wood-pulp paper and cutting the cover price to 10¢ so it could compete with the popular dime novels. *Argosy's* fortunes quickly reversed; Munsey became a millionaire. He won a huge readership, and his new pulp magazine included fantasy fiction by James Branch Cabell and others. In 1906 he also began publishing *The All-Story* magazine, in which the first Tarzan story by Edgar Rice Burroughs appeared in October 1912. Munsey set an example other publishers could follow; in one truly unusual departure, J. C. Henneberger and J. M. Lansinger's Rural Publications issued an offbeat magazine called *Weird Tales* in March 1923. Here Robert E. Howard introduced his barbarian heroes and established the sword and sorcery fantasy mode, beginning with "Spear and Fang" in the July 1925 issue, continuing with stories featuring the barbarian King Kull (his first adventure, "The Shadow Kingdom," appeared in August 1929) and tales of the Pictish chief Bran Mak Morn in the late twenties and thirties, and culminating in stories of Conan the Barbarian (the first, "The Phoenix on the Sword," appeared in December 1932, and the series lasted until Howard's death in 1936). H. P. Lovecraft published fiction in *Weird Tales* that reshaped the ghost story, and on the magazine's pages, starting with "The Call of Cthulhu" in February 1928, he gradually revealed the Cthulhu mythos. And Ray Bradbury, whose work is a distinctive mixture of fantasy, horror, science fiction, and mainstream elements, first published many of the stories in his first collection, *Dark Carnival* (1947), in *Weird Tales*. With the publication in book form of *The Martian Chronicles* (1950) and *The Illustrated Man* (1951), Bradbury established himself as a unique American talent and subsequently broke out of the genre magazines to publish his stories in *Colliers, Esquire,* and *Saturday Evening Post.* Though Bradbury's name is popularly associated with science fiction, critic Peter Nicholls appropriately calls him "a fantasist, both whimsical and sombre, in an older, pastoral tradition."[20]

American pulps created a market that attracted more full-time writers—those who counted on earning a living through sales of their work. And as the pulps' solid circulation figures identified a nucleus of loyal readers and fans, the magazines helped create an opportunity for experimentation. Given a dedicated, interested consuming public as well as increased competition among magazines, there was a competitive advantage in publishing a writer who had a unique approach. The Clayton magazine chain launched a serious competitor to *Weird Tales* (which had to cut back to bimonthly publication during the Depression but still maintained a strong readership as a journal with high entertainment value and inexpensive escapism for a pre-TV generation) when it began issuing *Astounding Stories* (primarily science fiction) in 1930 and *Strange Tales* in 1931. Then in 1939 *Unknown* appeared, with John W. Campbell Jr. as editor. Already an acclaimed and influential science fiction editor, Campbell precipitated experimentation in the fantasy genre as he sought to publish stories that provided a context of logic similar to that Campbell demanded of the science fiction he chose for *Astounding Stories*. Among Campbell's authors who produced fantasy with unique mixtures of humor, logic, and even science fiction elements were L. Ron Hubbard, whose novella about travel to the world of *The Arabian Nights* appeared in April 1939, as well as L. Sprague de Camp, Robert Bloch, Raymond Chandler, and Fritz Leiber. Campbell's magazine gradually gained energy and readers, and other writers who published innovative fantasy there under his editorship include Robert Heinlein, Jack Williamson, and (collaboratively) L. Sprague de Camp and Fletcher Pratt. Fantasy pulps began to die out in the 1940s, and *Weird Tales,* one of the last survivors, published its last issue in September 1954.

The British Rebirth of Modern Fantasy

British writing, of course, did not stagnate during the American pulp magazine years. On the contrary, there continued to be lively markets for periodical publication in England and even some British emulators of the pulp magazine phenomenon (*Tales of Wonder*, 1937–1942; *Fantasy*, 1938–1939). Such long-established titles as *Strand* magazine, published between 1891 and 1950, featured stories by Jules Verne, H. G. Wells, Arthur Conan Doyle, and others. The *Idler* (1892–1911) published Doyle and Wells as well as Edwin Lester Arnold and William Hope Hodgson. *Strand* and the *Idler* were more traditional periodicals, aimed at better-educated and more affluent readers, and although they were not infused with the American flavor of novelty and fast-paced inventiveness, they sustained fantasy as a suitable mode within a general contemporary literary context.

The most resplendent blossoming of pure fantasy was, in fact, about to come from Britain, and from grafting on academic rather than on popular roots. Oxford University, where Morris and his friend and collaborator Edward Burne-Jones met and shaped the literary tastes that resulted in Morris's earliest fantasy stories and ultimately his watershed novels (some of which he published himself at his Kelmscott Press with illustrations by Burne-Jones), once again became the seedbed for fantasy when J. R. R. Tolkien, who first attended Exeter College, Morris's alma mater, in 1911, later returned to teach in 1925. At Oxford Tolkien became friends with C. S. Lewis, then 27, who had recently been appointed Fellow and Tutor in English Language and Literature at Oxford's Magdalen College. By 1927 the two were meeting to read Icelandic sagas aloud over beer with other friends in a group known as the Coalbiters (adapted from the Icelandic *kolbítar,* a word designating those who rest so near the winter fire they seem to "bite the coal"). Gradually the group shifted membership and purpose, and Tolkien and Lewis joined the Inklings, an informal student-faculty literary society begun about 1931 whose members read aloud and discussed their unpublished compositions. When the undergraduate founder of the Inklings moved on, Tolkien and Lewis became the continuing nucleus for the group, which met more or less regularly, often at Lewis's rooms. Other regular members included Lewis's brother, Major Warren Lewis (known as "Warnie"); Tolkien's and Lewis's Oxford physician, R. E. Harvard; Hugo Dyson; Lewis's London solicitor (and writer and philologist) Owen Barfield, who had already published his first fantasy novel, *The Silver Trumpet,* in 1925; and novelist Charles Williams, a published author of religious fantasy who worked for the Oxford University Press in London but was moved to Oxford in 1939 after war broke out. To this group Tolkien read drafts of tales from *The Silmarillion* and *The Hobbit.*

Beginning with the publication of *The Hobbit* in 1937, a great resurgence of fantasy occurred in England that was to establish the genre as a significant and serious literary mode. T. H. White followed rapidly on Tolkien's success with *The Sword in the Stone* the following year. From the Inklings circle came richly varied works of fantasy drawn toward the spiritual quest, most notably Lewis's space trilogy, a hybrid of science fiction and fantasy (*Out of the Silent Planet*, 1938; *Perelandra*, 1943; and *That Hideous Strength*, 1945), *The Screwtape Letters* (1942), *The Great Divorce: A Dream* (1946), and his Narnia series for younger readers (beginning with *The Lion, the Witch, and the Wardrobe* in 1950). Also well received were Williams's *All Hallows Eve* (1945) and his pre-Inklings novels.

Global Experiments and Innovations

The sixties is widely recognized as a time of countercultural change and innovation. Global culture was having an increasing impact, and radical, iconoclastic writers forged challenging new shapes for fantasy. In the United States William S. Burroughs, whose difficult-to-classify work is usually placed somewhere between mainstream fringe fiction and science fiction, began writing autobiographical books about drugs and sexuality, including *Junkie* (1953), *Queer* (written in the 1950s but not published until 1985), and his stylistically and conceptually groundbreaking novel, *Naked Lunch* (1959). These and other writings by Burroughs became widely known in the literary underground associated with the Beat movement of the fifties well before they were published. Using "cut-up" techniques of splicing together discontinuous images and syntax, motifs from avant-garde cinema, metaphors of drug addiction and the political paranoia of underground culture, as well as science fiction terminology and biological and sexual fantasy, he created peculiar, surrealistic mental landscapes that place paramount importance on interior perceptual realities. Novels that employ these techniques include *The Soft Machine* (1961), *The Ticket That Exploded* (1962), *Nova Express* (1964), *The Wild Boys* (1971), and *Exterminator* (1973). Recent works by Burroughs even more overtly subvert and cut up the genre itself, as in the trilogy *Port of Saints* (1973), *Cities of the Red Night* (1981), and *The Place of Dead Roads* (1984). *Interzone* (1989) conveys in its very title the hybrid fantastical soft space that he creates in his fiction.

Cuban-born Italian writer Italo Calvino experimented with surrealistic, comic elements in such philosophically and intellectually engaging works as *Il Visconte dimezzato* (1952) and *Il Cavaliere inesistente* (1959, translated into English as *The Non-Existent Knight & The Cloven Viscount* in 1962), *Il Barone rampante* (1957, translated as *Baron of the Trees,* 1959), *Le Cosmicomiche* (1965, translated as *Cosmicomics,* 1969), and *Ti con zero* (1967, translated as *t zero,* 1969). Like Burroughs, Calvino has been called a science fiction writer, but his surreal and mythic fables, especially those in the latter two volumes of linked stories from the narrative perspective of Qfwfq, an entity whose consciousness began at the moment of the birth of the universe, clearly embrace and extend the fantasy genre.

In Germany, Günter Grass's *Die Blechtrommel* (1959, translated as *The Tin Drum,* 1962), which became an international literary success, is an experimental mainstream work that embraces fantasy through wildly imaginative narrative techniques and through the ironic, updated Peter Pan figure of its protagonist, Oskar, a child who wills himself not to grow up in protest against the absurdity, injustice, and suffering in the world surrounding him. Caribbean and South American authors made notable contributions to fantasy with vivid imagery and characteristics we have come to call magic realism, a point on the generic continuum where fantasy and realism richly intermingle. The remarkable, labyrinthine fictions of Argentina's Jorge Luis Borges include *Ficciones, 1935–1944* (1944, translated as *Fictions,* 1962) and *El Aleph* (1949, translated in a somewhat different, enlarged format as *The Aleph and Other Stories,* 1978), and other volumes that established him as an original and provocative philosophical writer who continues to be an international influence. Gene Wolfe's *Peace* (1975), *Book of the New Sun* (1980–1983), which is science fiction at the edge of fantasy, and other writings are notable examples. Adolfo Bioy Cesares, a close friend and collaborator of Borges's, also contributed to the magic-realist tradition, in such early and influential experimental works as the surreal *Prólogo* (1929) and *El sueño del los héroes* (1954, translated as *The Dream of the Heroes,* 1987), as did Mexico's Carlos Fuentes and Julio Cortázar.

But the masterwork that defined magic realism is Gabriel García Márquez's *Cien Años de Soledad* (1967, translated as *One Hun-*

dred Years of Solitude, 1970). This and subsequent stunning literary works by this Nobel laureate further defined this new fantasy subgenre. Among the more arresting works of purer fantasy from the same geographical region are the stories by Cuba's Felix Marti-Ibanez collected in *All the Wonders We Seek* (1963); Brazil's Moacyr Scliar's comic story of a Jewish centaur born in Brazil to a family of Russian immigrants, *O centauro no jardin* (1960, translated and published in the United States as *The Centaur in the Garden,* 1985); and another unique South American treatment of a traditional fantasy creature in a medieval setting by Argentinian writer Manuel Mujica Láinez, *El unicornio* (1965, translated as *The Wandering Unicorn,* 1982).

In Ireland came James Joyce's experiments with language and style in *A Portrait of the Artist as a Young Man* (1916), *Ulysses* (partially serialized in the *Little Review,* 1918; published in book form in Paris, 1922), and *Finnegans Wake* (1939). Irish writer Flann O'Brien tamed and adapted Joyce with stronger fantasy elements in *At Swim-Two-Birds* (1939) and *The Third Policeman* (1967). In the United States Thomas Pynchon's experimental post-Joycean, postmodernist novels integrated imagery of rock music, political conspiracy, hallucinatory drugs, and secret realities in *The Crying of Lot 49* (1966) and *Gravity's Rainbow* (1973), essentially mainstream experimental literary works with strong elements of fantasy that influenced such subsequent fantasy writers as John Crowley, Rudy Rucker, and R. A. Lafferty. And John Updike, with *The Centaur* (1963) and later with *The Witches of Eastwick* (1984), together with John Barth, in such works as *Giles Goat-Boy* (1966), *Lost in the Funhouse* (1968), *Chimera* (1972), and *The Last Voyage of Somebody the Sailor* (1991), affirmed that American writers who had received the critical nod as the leading novelists of their generation could fruitfully till the rich soil of fable, myth, and fantasy. Other innovative authors affirming and extending the genre's reach include Donald Barthelme, Richard Brautigan, Anthony Burgess, Angela Carter, Robert Coover, Michael Moorcock, Salman Rushdie, and Kurt Vonnegut, each of whom is worthy of careful reading.

In realms of purer fantasy, impressive writing from authors including Michael Moorcock, Jack Vance, Andre Norton, Stephen R. Donaldson, Alan Garner, R. A. Lafferty, Tanith Lee, Patricia McKillip, and Richard Matheson in the seventies and eighties demonstrated that fantasy as a genre had the range and flexibility to continue to attract first-rate authors and readers alike without exhausting its potential. Roger Zelazny drew from Arthurian legends and Tarot imagery in his Amber series, beginning with *Nine Princes in Amber* in 1970. Robert Holdstock created fantasy that mixed poetic style and sensitivity with startlingly ordinary contexts in *Mythago Wood* (1984) and its sequel, *Lavondyss* (1988). John Crowley combined science fiction and fantasy elements in his first novel, *The Deep* (1975), and then moved on to purer, innovative, landmark fantasy with what may be the best fantasy novel of these decades, *Little, Big* (1981), and later *Aegypt* (1987) and its sequel *Love and Sleep* (1994).

America's most popular contemporary fantasy writer, Piers Anthony, employs elements of sword and sorcery combined with some of the linguistic and satiric impulses of Twain and Cabell in pun-rich prose scattered with scatological humor. Anthony also uses the American landscape and geography as the locus for his fantasy world of Xanth, which is modeled on Florida. Moreover, he pushes on toward dialectical synthesis of both genre and philosophy in his Gods and Tarot and Robot Adept series, which integrate science fiction and fantasy elements. Stephen R. Donaldson mixes elements of dark humor with heroic fantasy to create his new type of contemporary antihero, Thomas Covenant, the Unbeliever. William Gibson moves in yet another direction, toward synthesis, finding in the metaphors of the computer matrix and cyberspace places for the supernatural elements of voodoo and black magic to mix with the science of the computer chip and create a new fantasy environment.

One of the most influential critics of the twentieth century, Northrop Frye, provides a ground-breaking theoretical analysis of literary form in his *Anatomy of Criticism*. A literary scholar with a profound grasp of Freudian and Jungian psychology and a pioneer of archetypal approaches to literature, Frye's perspectives are particularly helpful for the study of fantasy. His *Anatomy* sets forth a "theory of genres" to describe literature in four basic categories—novel, romance, confession, and anatomy.[21] Although he does not specifically describe fantasy as a genre, it seems to blend elements of all four categories, both thematically and structurally. As works in the mythical mode, works of fantasy partake in the "analogy of revelation," and as encyclopedic forms, such as the Bible, they tend toward the creation of "definitive myth, a single archetypal structure extending from creation to apocalypse" (Frye 1967, 315). Fantasy has preserved romantic, mythic, and philosophic/theologic discourse in the fiction of an essentially pragmatic, scientific age. Fantasy is fiction that employs "myth extending over time and space, over invisible and visible orders of reality" (325). Its reach encompasses both antiquity and infinity,

> a gigantic cycle from creation to apocalypse, within which is the heroic quest of the Messiah from incarnation to apotheosis. Within this again are three other cyclical movements, expressed or implied: individual from birth to salvation; sexual from Adam and Eve to the apocalyptic wedding; social from the giving of the law to the established kingdom of the law, the rebuilt Zion of the Old Testament and the millennium of the New. (316–17)

Though Frye is speaking here of the Bible, he also describes the structural aspirations of fantasy to grasp antiquity (Old Testament creation, captivity, and loss) and reach infinity (New Testament resurrection, recovery, and consolation). Some authors offer us, as do the Gospels of the New Testament, "a sequence of epiphanies, a discontinuous but rightly ordered series of significant moments of apprehension or vision" (326), whereas other authors offer more comprehensive structures that encompass the "gigantic cycle"—"a parabolic dramatic structure of which the five acts are creation, fall, exile, redemption, and restoration" (325). Whether through epiphany or full cycle, each author tries a key to loose Blake's "mind-forged manacles" as fantasy aspires to liberation.

Chapter 2

FORGING FANTASY PARADIGMS: SWORD TEMPERED BY WATER

William Morris published his first experiments with fantasy in 1856 in the *Oxford and Cambridge Magazine,* a little literary journal he and his friends—Edward Jones (Edward Burne-Jones), William Fulford, Richard Watson Dixon, Cormell Price, and Charles Faulkner—established as a public expression of artistic brotherhood. Dixon had the idea, and Morris provided the funds and served as editor of the first issue, but he quickly turned that duty over to Fulford, claiming he couldn't stand reading proofs. As its name implies, the *Oxford and Cambridge Magazine* was a college effort, and it reflected the experimentalism, intellectual energy, and creative idealism engendered through close undergraduate friendships. It is appropriate that the earliest fantasy writing was published in a university magazine. As a genre, fantasy has appealed to and nourished the experimental and idealistic minds of young people, and it was the enthusiasm of a new generation of college students committed to liberation a century later in the 1960s that turned fantasy into one of the most popular genres of fiction, beginning with the nearly rock-star popularity on college campuses of Tolkien's *Lord of the Rings*.

As university students, Morris and Burne-Jones were the nucleus of an informal brotherhood that embraced the then still avant-garde countercultural art of Dante Gabriel Rossetti and the Pre-Raphaelites, the Gothic ideals of essayist John Ruskin, the spiritual vigor of John Henry Newman and the Oxford movement, and a select range of ancient and contemporary literature they read aloud to one another: Chaucer, Malory, Shakespeare, Tennyson, Keats, and others. During the course of 12 issues, the *Oxford and Cambridge Magazine* showcased the creative talents and aesthetic values of students from two universities. Tennyson praised it for its "truthfulness and earnestness," Rossetti contributed three poems, and Ruskin promised to send an article (which, unfortunately, never appeared).

Though the magazine's contents were unsigned, Morris and Fulford were the most frequent contributors. Among Morris's works are the seven pieces of short fiction that are his first excursions into prose fantasy. These are "The Story of the Unknown Church," "Lindenborg Pool," "A Dream," "Gertha's Lovers," "Svend and his Brethren," "The Hollow Land," and "Golden Wings." These stories contain many characteristics that have come to be permanently identified with fantasy. There is intrinsic value placed on ancient ways of life, which in Morris were usually exemplified in medieval trappings, but he also sought other connections to roots of culture and myth in antiquity. "The Story of the Unknown Church" is told by a deceased first-person narrator who was master mason of a medieval church, a personification of how the past speaks to the present. "Lindenborg Pool" is spun off of a tale from Thorpe's *Northern Mythology* and begins with a reference to that work; "The Hollow Land" starts with an epigraph from the *Niebelungen Lied*. In these narratives we find Morris's earliest explicit efforts to embrace the mythic heritage of the North as well as the gothic traditions of Britain to recover ancient stories and clothe them in fresh imagination. Frye praises this enterprise, which Morris continued to pursue throughout his life: "William Morris is to me the most interesting figure in this tradition for many reasons, one of them being his encyclopedic approach to romance, his ambition to collect every major story in literature and retell or translate it."[1] Morris's early stories also exemplify another quality of the fantasy genre he developed: geography and setting have a numinous value and function almost as characters and symbols in the work. The technique is an extension of the one Poe uses in "The Fall of the House of Usher." Morris, by cultivating the device consistently starting with these early tales and extending it into his later novels, was among the first to stake out the special role of setting and geography in fantasy that has been amplified and developed in the work of nearly all the major writers since, from Haggard to Tolkien to Le Guin.

Morris's recent biographer Fiona MacCarthy traces the sources of his particular landscape sensibility to his childhood. As a youngster Morris spent countless hours roaming Epping Forest and developed an almost mystic understanding of the natural environment. She observes that "in Morris's iconography of nature a forest was a place where you both lost and found yourself."[2] This experience of loss and recovery is archetypal and is one of the undergirding patterns of fantasy, as it is for Christianity and other religions. Morris experienced profound loss personally, through the death of his father when Morris was 13 and about to leave for boarding school. Morris, the eldest son and at a particularly impressionable age, must have keenly felt this unexpected death. Though the family was financially secure, the loss of the breadwinner also meant the loss of their palatial home at Woodford Hall, which Morris Sr. had worked his way up to through his enterprising brokering business. Morris's mother relocated the family to more modest accommodations, an eighteenth-century home in Walthamstow called Water House (now the William Morris Gallery). The house was surrounded by a moat and forests, an ideal site for a youth whose imagination was already drawn to tales of knightly valor, and Morris's rambles in the woods and make-believe adventures around the moat, complete with bouts of "single-stick," were diversions from the losses he experienced. Here Morris found solace in nature, and MacCarthy writes that he "understood the movement of water through the country" and that "the river for him was a spiritual investment, an essential human link back to antiquity and history" (MacCarthy, 15–16). She also notes in examining the biographical origins of his response to the natural world that "he always saw his role as the defender of the mystery" and that "he believed there was a certain morality in wildness, a recuperative power" (15). These personal attitudes formed in childhood and nurtured and refined throughout his life found particularly apt expression in his fantasy fiction, in which the invention of a geography could convey mystical force, connection to antiquity, recuperative power, and morality. Morris senses in the world and includes in even his earliest fiction a vision of a clear and unending struggle for values and the need for a fiction to address it. Moral and ethical principles become central to the purpose of fantasy, overriding characterization, social reform (specifically, targeting debtors' prisons, poor laws, the courts, and the like in the manner of Dickens and other Victorian novelists), and the correction of manners.

Given its special use of geography and setting—symbolic, numinous, nearly allegorical—fantasy brought a shift away from focus on individuals. Complex personality, which had become so essential to realistic fiction, was often only an incidental detail in the context of the geography of fantasy. Character in fantasy is frequently generalized or idealized, but as in myth, the concept and quality of the hero are of great importance. The realistic novel was following a literary path of individualism that would eventually lead to the depiction of unique characters, frequently isolated from their society and history, who ultimately tended toward solipsism and despair. Morris, who would later become a socialist, was from the first concerned with brotherhood, commonwealth, the individual whose identity was linked to a history, a people, a project greater than the self. This led Morris to develop protagonists whose stories had a large moral significance and affirmed human purpose within a natural geographic setting. The approach to plot in this context naturally again evokes myths, symbols, and archetypes. Action usually includes confrontation with large-scale evil forces—a plot conflict seen in terms not of individual conflict but of a dialectic of good and evil. Morris's desire to "defend the mystery" suggests an overt goal to create a sense of wonder in the reader; this amazement begins the turn toward mythic belief that occurs when reading fantasy.

Two final qualities that emerge in Morris's early stories and come to fruition in the later novels have to do, first, with the high value of invention and imagination nurtured in the reader and manifest by the author in the integrity of the created world; and, second, with the special importance of language—the creation of a privileged text, apart from the language of ordinary life, that affirms poetry and linguistic magic—the power of language for its own sake. One finds rudimentary examples of these qualities in the characters' names in the early stories: Lady Swanhilda, Red Harald, Siur, Cissela, and Leuchnar. They are also present in the diction and syntax, sometimes borrowed from the language of chivalry, the language of saga, the King James Bible, or invented by Morris for lyrical effect. Words catch our attention throughout the stories, as Morris points out, for example, in "Svend and his Brethren," in which Richard is identified as one "who drew men's hearts from their bodies, with the words that swung to and fro in his glorious rhymes."[3] It wasn't until three decades later, when Morris began to write novels at the end of his life, that he was able fully to create a special language for fantasy, yet even in the early stories he writes with a consciously crafted, elevated style, using language wrenched and reworked into an artificial beauty all its own, as distinct from prosaic speech as fantasy is from mundane reality.

By the time Morris again turned to prose fantasy, in the influential novels he wrote toward the end of his life, he had already established himself as a versatile artist, translator, and poet. In fact, his poetry had contributed a great deal to the mythic imagination of the age. In *The Earthly Paradise* his Wanderers, seafarers from northern Europe, exchanged poetic stories with survivors of a Greek colony in the Atlantic, one classical and one medieval tale for each month of the year. The monumental work made him one of England's best-known poets. Following Alfred, Lord Tennyson's death in 1892, Morris was approached as the leading candidate for poet laureate, but he turned aside the idea, finding it impossible to imagine himself "sitting down in crimson plush breeches and white stockings to write birthday odes" in honor of nobility.[4] In addition to his literary and artistic work, Morris became an activist for social and political change, declaring himself a Socialist in 1883. He lectured, demonstrated, and published widely on behalf of social revolution. An appointment as poet laureate would have made him a figurehead and mouthpiece for the establishment, a part of the very political order he sought to overthrow. He was far too committed to his ideals to entertain that possibility seriously.

Morris began delivering political lectures in 1883, and as he gained confidence in his effectiveness he sought out more and more opportunities to speak. In 1887 alone he delivered more than 100 talks.[5] He wrote for the Social Democratic Federation journal *Justice* starting in 1884, helped form the Socialist League in 1885, and edited and financially supported the league's new journal, *Commonweal,* which started in 1885. It was for that journal that he wrote his first full-length utopian fantasy, *A Dream of John Ball,* which was published serially beginning in 1886. *John Ball* employed time travel, through dream, to transport the reader back to medieval England. Here Morris repudiated temporal ethnocentrism—the complacent Victorian faith in progress and its rejection of the "unscientific," "unenlightened," or "dark" Middle Ages.

In the opening pages of *John Ball* Morris establishes, through numerous paradoxes, a fundamental premise of fantasy: that dreaming is awakening. The book seeks to recover the best values and lost utopian themes of antiquity through the character of the radical preacher John Ball, a neglected English historical figure who helped instigate the Peasants' Revolt under Wat Tyler in the fourteenth century in the days of Richard II.[6] Both in the book's structure and in Ball's character Morris refutes the premise that logical empiricism is sufficient to meet humanity's highest needs. He is clearly setting his novel against the utilitarianism of John Stuart Mill, rejecting Mill's method of pure induction, and suggesting that the idea of history as progress is a case of inductive illusion. Morris had articulated the idea in an 1884 lecture on the Gothic Revival; he rejected contemporary paradigms derived from Mill that tried to justify the social inequities and exploitation of labor associated with the industrial revolution. Morris believed instead that industrialism and utilitarianism together were stripping meaningful work and art from life, leaving "history a despised desert behind us, with a blank prospect of mere utilitarianism before us."[7] In this and other lectures, Morris formulates some of fantasy's underlying theoretical assumptions—patterns characterized later by another of its most influential critics and practitioners, J. R. R. Tolkien, as "Escape, Recovery, Consolation."[8]

While writing *John Ball,* Morris also completed his translation of *The Odyssey* (1887), which nurtured his mastery of epic and mythic storytelling. With *The House of the Wolfings* (1888) he took up the path to fantasy he had begun with his *Oxford and Cambridge Magazine* stories, this time without the mediation of a dream. His hero, Thiodolf, struggles to protect his fellow Wolfings' way of life, as they are on the verge of conquest by the "civilized" Romans. Although the invented world has a semihistorical setting, its tribe, its characters, and its magic and beliefs are an invented, coherent alternative reality. The story's affirmation of communal values and its symbolic presentation of a strong feminine principle of identity linked to that of the tribe through Mother Earth and the magical Hall-Sun begin to stake out the territory and techniques that Morris claims for fantasy. This book meets the test for fantasy proposed by Lin Carter: it drops the reader into a fully created "real" world, in which "adventures . . . are serious and the perils along the way are deadly" (Carter, vii). There is no explanation or transition mediation through dream (a device used in both of Morris's utopian fantasies); Morris's storytelling places the reader amidst an imaginary tribe in a more or less recognizable historical period, as Roman "civilization" systematically wipes out tribal cultures.

Morris's narration begins, "The tale tells that in times long past," a variant on "Once upon a time" that signals this fiction's unusual temporal and generic displacement. The novel also shows complementary stylistic displacement in its unique vocabulary and syntax for the telling of the tale. The writing is at once antique and immediate; its language is direct and plain but full of unfamiliar idioms and locutions. Morris mixes poetry and prose, and in his prose he incorporates many of the sounds and cadences he worked toward in his narrative poetry, especially in his *Odyssey* translation. These stylistic innovations continue in a second, related work, *The Roots of the Mountains,* published in 1889. This work is set in a slightly later, less well-defined time period in a world consistent with the lifestyles and geography of *House of the Wolfings.* In fact, as its title implies, *Roots of the Mountains* pioneers the use of the imagined landscape as an important symbolic and creative element of fantasy that places even greater importance on geography and on elemental symbols—water, wood, mountain, plain.

Morris's second utopian fantasy, *News from Nowhere* (1890), sets forth in even clearer fictional terms the communal and social ideals toward which he worked. In it he offers a vigorous alternative to Edward Bellamy's American socialist utopia, *Looking Backward* (1888). Bellamy had imagined just the sort of mechanistic, technological future Morris fought to prevent. In *News*, he exemplifies the ideals set forth in John Ball's rebellion. As Frye explains, Morris believes the true contribution of the Middle Ages becomes clear when we see it "as a creation of artists, not in its reflected or projected form as a hierarchy; when we realize that the genuine creators of medieval culture were the builders and painters and romancers, not the warriors or priests" (Frye 1976, 178). Morris's utopian vision projects "an equal society of creative workers. They have not returned to the fourteenth century: they have turned it inside out" (178). Although *News from Nowhere* is more purely a utopia than a fantasy, it takes its place beside Morris's other early novels as a milestone on the path to modern fantasy. Considered as a whole, the 10 novels Morris wrote during the last eight years of his life distill and recapitulate the work of a lifetime and also suggest new paradigms for literature. Morris brought to fantasy a rich visual, philosophical, poetical, philological, and revolutionary sensibility that enlarged the concept of fiction to shape a new genre.

Morris nicknamed *The Well at the World's End* (1896) "The Interminable"; he worked on it for nearly two years and spent another two years finishing the designs and typesetting for his beautiful Kelmscott Press edition—a great deal of time for a man accustomed to completing his work quickly. It is the lengthiest of his fantasy novels, probably the longest in the genre before J. R. R. Tolkien's *Lord of the Rings* (1954–1955), and it remains one of the most complex and beautiful fantasy quests ever written. Although its publication date is 1896, it was actually written during 1892 and 1893, following the composition of *News from Nowhere* and *The Story of the Glittering Plain or the Land of Living Men* (serialized in 1890 in the *English Illustrated Magazine* and published in book form by the Kelmscott Press in 1891). In fact, by October of 1892, Morris's secretary Sydney Cockerell, who would later become T. H. White's close friend and advisor, was able to read 200 proof pages already set in type, so the book was well under way before *The Wood Beyond the World* (written in 1893, published in 1894) and *Child Christopher and Goldilind the Fair* (written and published in 1895).[9] In addition to these two fantasy novels written and published while "The Interminable" was being drafted, Morris drew on his experiments with fantasy in *Wolfings* (1888), *Roots* (1889), and *Glittering Plain* (1891). Reading these novels in sequence reveals an impressive, rapid sophistication and mastery of a new form. His experience working through style and plot techniques that could unite utopian ideals with the literary imagination reached fruition in *The Well,* an entertaining and unified masterpiece.

The title of *The Well at the World's End,* as with most of Morris's novels, evokes the central theme and focus. The "well" is a pun that points toward the object of the hero's quest in at least two senses: on the one hand, he seeks a literal well, which contains magic, revitalizing water; and on the other hand, he seeks a general condition of well-being and human welfare, the happy ending that the reader knows will be the culmination of his quest for the literal well. "World" refers, of course, to the planet on which man lives, but it also retains its meaning as the Anglo-Saxon compound *weoruld* or *weorold—weor-*, or *were-*, as in *werewolf,* meaning "man," *-old* meaning "old," or "the age of"; thus *weorold* means "the age of man," a human temporal context on a cosmic or geologic scale. The world's meaning in this book is one of the relationship between human and physical place. "End" refers literally in the story to "a boundary or extremity," a place at the outermost edge where a well of water is found, but it also carries apocalyptic overtones, hints of pending death or destruction or salvation at world's end (at the end of human time). The book sets forth in its title multiple ways in which the story will be directed toward "well-ness," which is the object of human endeavor. Its emphasis is on and in the created world, not on heaven or an otherworldly place where mankind should seek happiness. Yet it remains apocalyptic in its ultimate vision of the world's end. Morris makes what Frye calls "the first great move from projection to the recovery of myth, from return to recreation," in which

> the focus of interest shifts from heroes and other elements of narrative toward the process of creating them. The real hero becomes the poet, not the agent of force or cunning whom the poet may celebrate. In proportion as this happens, the inherently revolutionary quality in romance begins to emerge. (Frye 1976, 178)

Morris is writing about the shaping of a revolutionary hero/poet, a curious precursor of Joyce's *Portrait of the Artist as a Young Man.*

The puns in Morris's title alert the reader to the language of the book, a poet's prose with close attention to the multidimensional significance of words' language and their roots. One other important detail is that key words are of Saxon rather than Latin derivation. In fact, Morris adopts this unusual Saxon-based vocabulary in all his fantasy novels. Anglo-Saxon, with its Germanic-Nordic origins, has a vocabulary primarily of short, active, colloquial words (including many of the familiar "four-letter" words, for example) and a different sound and rhythm than the Frenchified and Latinate language that dominated upper-class and scholarly vocabulary. Through his choice of words, which sound quaint and almost awkward to modern ears, Morris affirms philosophical and linguistic roots within a tribal, "uncivilized" past that values a more active, communal, nonhierarchical, noncompetitive lifestyle. The language helps to create a different reality and sets Morris's world apart from the inheritors of the road-building Romans, the hierarchical, artificial Latin of the Church, or even the romantic French, the refined language of society and diplomacy.

The story begins in the idyllic country of King Peter, where the hero, Ralph, is the youngest of the king's four sons. Their little land of Upmeads is bordered on one side by the Wood Debateable and on the other by the lands of a bishop and baron of the Holy Church. Since Saint Peter is the founder of the Christian Church, the patriarchal kingdom of King Peter (the father and four sons) carries overtones of a male Christian mythos, though Morris stipulates that the scattered churches are goodly and that the "good canons . . . knew not the road to Rome."[10] Ralph lives in a near-utopian condition, though he has no experience of other ways of living, and does not possess much in the way of material goods or money. Naive and uninitiated, he has nothing to compare to his own situation and so is discontented. King Peter knows his sons well and loves them; seeing their desire to leave, he allows them to draw lots to decide which three will be allowed to explore the world. He feels the need to keep one at home who can be raised as a future king. Ralph loses and must, if he accepts the hand of fate, remain with his aging father and administer the business of the kingdom. But his desire for the unknown is so strong that he cannot bear to stay behind and leaves secretly the next morning to begin his own quest for adventure.

As Ralph steps beyond his father's kingdom, he begins to shed his role in a male-dominated society (which espouses the patriarchal orientation of the Christian religion and its Holy Fathers). His journey becomes more and more female oriented and culminates symbolically with Ralph drinking deeply from the waters that bubble forth from Mother Earth. Throughout the book there is a symbolic association of males with rationality and physical forcefulness and of women with creativity, intuition, and emotion. Ralph is the unspoiled youth, whose social and sexual identity is not yet clear. At this stage, for instance, Ralph is studied closely by an old man, who finally declares, "His beard is sprouting, else might ye have taken him for a maid" (*Well,* 45). Morris's novel is full of sexual exploration, and its metaphors underscore the need for an equal integration of male and female natures to attain the well-being of the book's end. By the end, Ralph has attained more of the masculine qualities of strength and reason, but he also affirms his intuitions and emotions. He also symbolically joins the male and female principles in his marriage at the story's end.

At first, Ralph's journey has no defined objective, but he hears about mysterious water "beyond the Dry Tree" that is so potent that it can heal all wounds; strengthen body, mind, and spirit; win love from all; and extend one's life many times over. To find this water seems more than sufficient reason for a quest, and Ralph determines he will seek it. Before leaving the house of a nearby merchant, where he has spent the night, Ralph receives special gifts from a woman, an echo of a familiar narrative pattern from fairy tales in which the bestowal of charmed gifts plays an important role. The kindly and beautiful merchant's wife gives Ralph some gold coins so he will not set off penniless and a mysterious necklace of Saracen beads, an unusual amulet that she urges him to wear constantly, promising that it will aid and protect him on his journey. The necklace is only the first of several conventionally feminine aspects this male hero gradually embraces. As the quest comes into focus, its iconography seems to suggest a traditional religious pilgrimage in search of the Holy Grail. Ralph's beads resemble a rosary; the Dry Tree connotes crucifixion and sacrifice; the well at the end, at which there is even a chalice, promises salvation.

But the details of Ralph's quest form a step-by-step reversal of the traditional Christian one. Ralph's beads so little resemble the rosary that when he suggests he will have them blessed by the first holy man he meets, Dame Katherine replies emphatically, "[T]hat shall he not!" implying dire consequences should the Church become involved. (We might recall that these are Saracen beads, and in the Middle Ages Saracens were the Muslim opponents of the Crusades.) When Ralph asks if there is wizardry in the necklace, the dame replies sarcastically, "[H]ow like unto a man he speaketh; if there were a brawl in the street, he would strike in and ask no word thereof, not even which were the better side" (12). Ralph heads not toward the bishop but into the forest. At the waystop in the Abbey of St. Mary, he rejects the monk's religious life outright (as well as his male-dominated lifestyle) and follows instead the "feminine" impulses toward love and intuition.

The Dry Tree and the well are identified as icons of earth, not of heaven, and Ralph's drink from the chalice does not bring about salvation of the soul in heaven but long, physically healthy life and love on earth. Morris transfers spiritual impulses from the religious to the secular dimension. He advocates traditional ideals of love, goodness, decency, and forgiveness, but he suggests that the most profound expression of these ideals must take place on earth during human life. In fact, Morris implies that Christianity has done a disservice to mankind by limiting humanity's mythic and mystical options, narrowing its imaginative vision, and distracting its attention from the here to the hereafter. Christianity has displaced fantasy, not only through its dogmas, which have become excuses for individuals to avoid exploring other imaginative ideals, but also through its justification of suffering and emphasis on an afterlife; it has made existence merely a fantasy, a temporary trial to be endured and at last left behind by entering an eternal reality. At nearly every turn in Morris's story, elements of older, religiously oriented quests are redirected toward improving tangible life in the world. It is clear that the quest as a whole, its imagery and iconography, and its male and female characters revise and update archetypes from ancient quest in literature to practical humanistic social and political idealism. This is an important quality of fantasy to recognize in Morris's work; far from being escapist, his fiction takes us temporarily away from the ordinary and familiar in order to draw our attention to fresh possibilities in the real world.

The quest pattern is traditionally associated with rites of passage, particularly initiation rites, which represent in ritual the transformation of the quester into a new state of being and symbolize his rebirth. Studies of myths and rituals by Mircea Eliade and others have shown some of the archetypal elements of these primitive rites, and many of them are repeated in the course of Morris's narrative. Various key events can be interpreted in light of these rites, which affirm tribal roots in the cultural past and reaffirm customs and traditions that predate Christianity. Of particular importance in this regard are the tale's elements of androgyny, the changing seasons, the cave where Ursula and Ralph pass the winter, and Ursula's and Ralph's sexual initiations, all of which mark crucial stages of the narrative.

Nearly every event in the quest involves Ralph in some relation with a woman. Early in his journey, he saves a lady in the forest who has been captured by warriors from the Burg of the Four Friths. She later helps Ralph escape from that city, which is shown to be materialistic and self-serving, an evil and undesirable place. In the burg, Ralph is sought out by Roger of the Ropewalk, who pretends to be Ralph's servant. Ralph slowly realizes that the man is not what he appears to be but is associated with the Fellowship of the Dry Tree. Upon his escape from the burg, Ralph learns that the lady he has helped and who now has helped him is the Lady of Abundance, and he accompanies Roger to the Castle of Abundance to await a meeting with her, growing to love her more each day he waits.

When she finally arrives, Ralph finds she is a captive of the Knight of the Sun (an oxymoronic pun that is one of the more conspicuous reminders of Morris's sophisticated language play, accomplished through simple, one-syllable words, throughout this work), who has compelled her to accept him as her husband. The knight overcomes Ralph in combat. Only because of the lady's pleading is Ralph's life spared, and while the knight sleeps, Ralph and the lady escape together. She has tasted the water from the Well and promises to go there once again with Ralph. They consummate their love in the forest and enjoy a brief but perfect idyll, until the Knight of the Sun discovers them, kills the lady, and is finally killed by Ralph.

The Knight of the Sun, whose oxymoronic name suggests the obliterating *lack* of enlightenment in the purely masculine psyche, marks a crucial point in Ralph's movement away from a stereotyped male role and from the patriarchal backgrounds of the book. Ralph is saved in this instance by the Lady of Abundance, perhaps the book's strongest feminine presence, embodying intuitive and nonrational knowledge and profound sexuality. It is appropriate that she saves Ralph and initiates him into sexual experience, but she is also clearly his superior—she is older, wiser, more experienced—and Ralph's ultimate union is saved for an equal, Ursula. Ursula is no less strong in her femininity, and she, too, will save Ralph at a crucial point, when he starts to drink the poisonous water of the Dry Tree. By the end of the book, she participates fully with Ralph as an equal, and their union symbolizes an integration of the male and female aspects of the psyche rather than a rite of passage.

In a state of numbness and despair at losing the Lady of Abundance, his first and perfect love, Ralph presses forward. He meets his brother Blaise (who has become a wealthy merchant), Clement Chapman, and the old family servant, Richard the Red, so Ralph is at last comforted by the presence of family and friends, but he is still aimless and genuinely at a loss. The lady appears to Ralph in a dream to say farewell. She fades from his dream and is replaced by a woman who says she has been sent by the Lady of Abundance, for Ralph should not attempt his quest alone. She tells him that her name is Dorothea and that Ralph should seek her to share his journey.

Richard the Red helps Ralph on the next leg of the journey when he comes back from his home village of Swevenham with the information that the Dry Tree, a sure signpost on the way to the Well, is on the near side of the mountains called Wall of the World. Ralph sets off with Clement Chapman, who is bound in the same direction to conduct business in the city of Goldburg. They are attacked by thieves, but the robbers are beaten off and Ralph takes for himself a thrall, Bull Shockhead, who is grateful that his life has been spared and tells Ralph that the Dorothea he seeks has been captured by his band and taken to Goldburg to be sold as a slave. Ralph is greatly encouraged, but his hopes are dashed when he discovers that the maid has not been sold and that the man who holds her has evidently taken her to the Lord of Utterbol, "the worst of the tyrants who vex this land." Finally, they come upon Bull Shockhead's brother, who turns out to be the maiden's captor; he has been viciously slain, and there is no trace of the maid.

The direction of Ralph's journey from the beginning has been toward the east, where the Well rests at the "end of the world." It is therefore a journey toward beginnings, in the direction of the sunrise rather than toward its setting; it is a trip toward the origins of life. The civilizations that Ralph encounters seem increasingly primitive, as though he is simultaneously traveling back in history, leaving the Christian feudal realm of King Peter to encounter cities ruled by individual warring tyrants, barbaric tribal societies along the trail where he meets Bull Shockhead, and finally the Innocent People, who will lead him and his eventual bride (Dorothea/Ursula) beyond the Wall of the World. Morris suggests through this movement that future time is redeemed and reclaimed only by overcoming and finally transforming human history. The narrative is a repudiation of human history, fallen and corrupt, which can be redeemed only by looking beyond it to its source.

Ralph finally arrives in Goldburg, where the queen is kind to him but is unable to direct him to Dorothea. Ralph concludes that he must travel on to seek Gandolf, Lord of Utterbol, who is likely to have the maid. At this juncture, Ralph is approached by a minstrel, a eunuch called Morfinn the Unmanned, who says he has a pass from Gandolf that will assure their safety and offers to guide Ralph to Utterbol. Ralph accompanies him but finds he has been led into a trap, for he is taken captive by the Lord of Utterbol to be used as a lover for the lord's lady. After proving his valor in a tournament, Ralph is given some freedom and manages to escape. In the forest, he encounters the maid Dorothea, who tells Ralph that her real name is Ursula. She has been a captive in Utterbol, but she too has broken free. United at last, they pursue the quest and seek the Sage of Swevenham, whom the Lady of Abundance has promised will prepare them for the final journey.

They pass the Dry Tree, where Ralph is saved by Ursula as he is nearly hypnotized by the lure of the poisonous water, and they then proceed to find the Well itself and to drink its restorative water. Their quest complete, they retrace their steps. During their return, they discover that either the previous evils have been overturned or that things have set themselves right. Utterbol, the very epitome of evil, has been liberated by Bull Shockhead, who avenged his brother's death by killing the Lord of Utterbol and marrying his lady. The wicked rulers of the Burg of the Four Friths have been exiled. Ralph and Ursula return to Upmeads in time to save it from invasion and to assure a long reign of peace and happiness for Upmeads and the surrounding kingdoms.

Morris's book has been criticized for the long return journey, since the tale's climax is the drinking of the Well's water. Morris insists throughout the book, however, that the quest avails only those who love the earth and the world and will strive to be happy in it. By showing the reader the lengthy sequence of events after Ralph and Ursula have attained their quest, Morris concretely embodies the idea that the Well is not an end but a means; Ralph and Ursula drink not for themselves but for the sake of the world and of life, and their quest is finally complete and meaningful only if it increases happiness and beauty beyond themselves. This tale should ultimately be seen not as a story about a hero and heroine but as an affirmation of the possibility of noble human vision, which can transcend the individual to effect a greater well-being.

Morris's visionary purpose is perhaps his most substantial contribution to the fantasy genre. By creating a fully consistent and coherent fantasy reality, he in effect provides a parallel world, a world of correspondences in a medieval sense but one where potential and possibility are unleashed—a world no longer constrained by the actual, where imagination can shape alternative ideals. Other significant and enduring contributions include his invented language, syntax, and style; his semimedieval settings; his liberation of the feminine, or anima; his validation of *both* male and female as equally strong and heroic; and his shaping of a romantic heroic model. Morris's novels in his day were spoken of as "prose romances"; most critics were puzzled by them and frequently dismissed them as idle works of a purely decorative nature—daydream, escapist books to wile away the hours but little more. Although they do escape the trap of confinement in one's own mundane reality, Morris's novels are far more about liberation than about escapist avoidance. The books found a readership that refused to let them be forgotten. Gradually they helped create a path for a new type of literature as the trail blazed ahead in the works of H. Rider Haggard, W. H. Hudson, Lord Dunsany, David Lindsay, James Branch Cabell, Charles Williams, and J. R. R. Tolkien.

Chapter 3

SHAPING MODERN FANTASY: COSMIC LIGHT AND DARK

J. R. R. Tolkien breathed new life into fantasy in the mid-1950s when he published *The Lord of the Rings,* the twentieth century's most influential work in the genre. Its immense popularity, its consummate literary craftsmanship, and the depth and complexity of its vision prompted the general public and critics alike to take fantasy more seriously. In contrast to Morris, Tolkien placed his literary oeuvre firmly within a Christian context, adding to the early religious fantasy of George MacDonald a body of work with greater richness and subtlety. He moved beyond allegory and symbolic moral fable to show that fantasy was fully capable of treating complex, sophisticated modern Christian issues.

A teacher and scholar from one of the world's most esteemed universities, Tolkien bestowed a kind of academic blessing upon fantasy, and his lectures and critical writings were substantive contributions to literary theory about the genre. He helped explain its traditions and aesthetics. He brought philology, history, and a trained theoretical mind to his writing, but he was certainly more than academic. His natural love of storytelling was rehearsed and enriched, as he shared his tales aloud with his children and his Oxford friends. Drawing themes from his own experiences and observations, Tolkien enlarged their implications to address universal moral issues and to express his deep religious convictions.

Like Morris, Tolkien wrote from a personal background of displacement and loss. Born in 1892 in Bloemfontein, South Africa, not far from Cape Town, Tolkien lost his home and both his parents at an early age. His father, Arthur, a man of modest means, had moved from Birmingham, England, to South Africa to try to advance himself as a foreign manager for Lloyds Bank. Tolkien's earliest childhood experiences exposed him to Africa's rugged beauty and intense conditions of geography and climate, and the African heat proved to be hard on young Tolkien's health.[1] When he was three, his mother, Mabel, took him with his younger brother Hilary on a trip back to England to escape the heat and to visit Mabel's family in Birmingham, where Arthur was to join them. Tolkien's health improved, but his father wrote in November to say he had contracted rheumatic fever and could not make the trip until he had completely recovered. The family stayed to celebrate Christmas with Mabel's parents, John and Emily Suffield, but early in the new year, as the children prepared for the long voyage home to their slowly recuperating father, they received word that he had died suddenly of a severe hemorrhage on 15 February 1896. He was buried in South Africa, and Mabel and the children were left on their own with next to no financial resources.

Unable to live permanently with her parents, Mabel relocated her family to a small rented cottage on the outskirts of the city. She had found comfort and strength during her time of grief attending services regularly at a "high" Anglican church, but eventually her convictions led her to convert to Catholicism, not such a big step from the rites and beliefs of the Church of England, but her decision to accept the Church of Rome and papal authority turned her parents and most of the rest of her firmly Protestant family, and the Tolkien Baptist side as well, against her. She lost what little financial help they had been able to supply, and the children were effectively cut off from their grandparents.

Mabel struggled, but she managed to get by, even tutoring the boys at home to prepare them for advanced studies. One generous Tolkien uncle agreed to pay Ronald's tuition at Birmingham's finest private school, King Edward's, in 1900, and Mabel found a house to rent near the school, but the expenses and living conditions were a great strain, and in 1902 Mabel moved the boys again, to a cheaper house and school, the Catholic grammar school St. Philip's, associated with Birmingham Oratory. There in a house "only one degree better than a slum" (Carpenter, 27), they made the fortunate acquaintance of Father Francis Xavier Morgan, a parish priest who came to welcome them and who soon became a lifelong friend. Tolkien and his brother rapidly outgrew their classmates at the less expensive, less rigorous school, so Mabel had Ronald apply for a scholarship to King Edward's and began teaching Hilary again at home. Then early in 1904, the year after Tolkien had earned the scholarship enabling him to return to King Edward's, where his father had once been a student, Mabel was diagnosed with diabetes, an especially serious illness at that time. She died in November of that year, and the boys, ages 10 and 12, were left with Father Francis Morgan as their guardian.

Father Francis could not house the children at the oratory. He rented them a room for a time with their widowed aunt Beatrice, but that did not prove a satisfactory arrangement, and they were eventually settled in a nearby boardinghouse where they could be checked on frequently and continue to serve at masses for Father Francis at the oratory church. Certainly things could have been much worse, but Tolkien's sense of dislocation from the compounded loss of his home and of both parents must have become subconsciously almost a personal analog for Edenic loss and fall from grace. It must have been natural for Tolkien to internalize these feelings conjointly with those about his mother's adopted Catholic religion, a belief so important to her that it had divided her and the boys from the rest of their family. Father Morgan was a conscientious and well-intentioned guardian, assuring the boys' safety and education, but he could not replace mother, father, and home.

With this background of loss, similar to Morris's loss of his father at an almost identical age, it is little wonder that Tolkien concluded his description of the unique functions of fantasy in his influential treatise "On Fairy-Stories" with emphasis on its ability to offer "Recovery" and "Consolation."[2] Tolkien provides one of the earliest, clearest, and most influential critical descriptions of fantasy in this lecture, and it is worth pausing to discuss a few key points. He observes that by the early twentieth century, the literary imagination had been restricted to the ability to give idealized images the "inner consistency of reality," but he describes fantasy as an "older and higher" form of imagination that is liberated from the tyranny of reality and that possesses "freedom from the domination of observed 'fact' " ("FS," 45). He asserts that fantasy may deal with things that are not even found in the real, or "primary," world and that this endows it with a power of "arresting strangeness," making it "not a lower but a higher form of Art, indeed the most nearly pure form, and so . . . the most potent" (45).

He emphasizes that fantasy is not avoidance of the actual but a means of more complete understanding. In describing the genre's ability to offer "Recovery," Tolkien suggests that fantasy helps us regain the fresh, clear vision of childhood, the ability "to clean our windows; so that the things seen clearly may be freed from the drab blur of triteness or familiarity—from possessiveness. . . . [W]e laid hands on them, and then locked them in our hoard, acquired them, and acquiring them ceased to look at them" (53–54). Escape follows as a liberation from the prison of habits and conventions of the contemporary real world, and as the cultivation of the ability to imagine possibilities beyond all our limits—that we could communicate completely enough to speak with animals, elude the shoddy march and stench of technology, swim like fish, fly like birds, and escape even "hunger, thirst, poverty, pain, sorrow, injustice, death" (60). Tolkien speaks of the last as "the oldest, deepest desire, the Great Escape: the Escape from Death" (61). Lastly, he speaks of fantasy as offering "Consolation," something like the opposite of the feelings of tragedy, which Tolkien sees as the "highest form" of drama. He invents a word for the profound "Consolation of the Happy Ending" in fantasy: *eucatastrophe*—"the good catastrophe, the sudden joyous 'turn.' . . . a sudden and miraculous grace: never to be counted on to recur" (62). This moment is dependent for its effect on the universal recurrence of "sorrow and failure" but allows "a fleeting glimpse of Joy, Joy beyond the walls of the world, poignant as grief" (62). These principles are most revealing as they express the particular aims of Tolkien's writing, but they ring true for much of the best writing in the genre. Fantasy resonates with moments of joy amid darkness. Tolkien's eloquent assertion is an expression of profound faith: "Fantasy remains a human right: we make in our measure and in our derivative mode, because we are made: and not only made, but made in the image and likeness of a Maker" (52).

Tolkien first delivered these points at St. Andrews University in 1939 in the Andrew Lang Lecture, an address given in honor of the famous folklorist and collector of fairy tales, whose books, including *The Red Fairy Book* and *The Green Fairy Book,* were part of childhood for Tolkien and countless other British children. In his paper, Tolkien suggests one continuing link between fairy tales and adult fantasy when he says that the love of Faërie should not be dismissed as a childish fancy. He argues that fairy stories actually constitute a heightened form of writing, for they involve the author in an act of "sub-creation"—inventing an independent, self-consistent world (25). The making of such a "Secondary World" is, at heart, a religious act undertaken in reverence. Subcreation can reveal humanity's godlike potential, for, as Tolkien says, human beings are made in the image and likeness of a Maker. Tolkien's claims for literary fantasy are great, but they hold up well when applied to his own work and to most of the other acknowledged masterpieces of fantasy. They also square well with the romantic tradition, echoing Coleridge's conclusion in chapter 13 of the *Biographia Literaria* that the "primary imagination" is analogous to "the eternal act of creation in the infinite I AM."

Language, Imagination, and Loss

Given Tolkien's high valuation of imaginative creation and his love of the language that made the creation of fantasy literature possible, it is not surprising that his teaching and scholarship took a creative direction as well. During university appointments at Leeds and Oxford, Tolkien undertook the revision of the curriculum for English graduates. He is credited with achieving a more balanced relationship between literature and linguistics and with broadening the understanding of philology to encompass not mere mechanical description of language and its history but a love for its use and invention in literary contexts. Critic T. A. Shippey suggests that Tolkien's broad view of *philology* embraced the word's "old vague sense of 'love of learning' " and its newer associations with scientific practice inspired partly by Jakob Grimm, "the greatest of all philologists and responsible in true philological style for both 'Grimm's Law of Consonants' and *Grimm's Fairy Tales.*" Grimm helped establish nineteenth-century philology as a discipline that involved the "study of texts leading to comparative study of language leading to comprehension of its evolution."[3] Tolkien's curricular bridge building led philology away from years of isolation to connect its insights with those of other modes of critical and creative English inquiry.

Tolkien published influential studies in linguistics and criticism of Middle English and Old English texts, most notably his 1936 essay, "*Beowulf:* The Monsters and the Critics."[4] In Oxford he was stimulated by students and colleagues but most significantly by his family and by his fellow Inklings. Tolkien had read his early tales of Middle-earth to his wife and family, particularly the hobbit stories, which he read aloud to his children in various drafts as early as 1930. He also began reading *The Hobbit* (1937) in manuscript form to the Inklings as he worked on it. Originally he had composed the story for personal and family amusement, but it was so well received by both family and friends that word of it eventually reached a publisher, and Tolkien was persuaded to revise the book for publication.

The Hobbit is a book for younger readers, but it draws on a beautiful, comprehensive invented world that Tolkien had been writing about for many years in drafts of grown-up tales that have now been published in *The Silmarillion, Unfinished Tales, The Book of Lost Tales,* and other volumes. Partly because of this deep mythopoeic background, *The Hobbit* is rich enough to be appreciated most completely by adults. It serves now, as it did historically, as a prelude to attract readers to a more demanding fantasy world in *The Lord of the Rings* and other Tolkien writings. The charming hobbit Tolkien invented has been described by Shippey as a "mediator" for a modern audience between the ancient world of heroic legend and the ironic sensibility of the contemporary reader (Shippey, 55). Bilbo Baggins can express "modern opinions, modern incapacities" (55), but by the end of the tale he also finds his opinions and capacities enlarged, as the reader's sensibilities, too, are similarly stretched to embrace the potential for genuinely heroic and mythic actions of which even the lowliest unworthy character is capable.

Rosemary Jackson has observed that fantasy as a genre is a mode of oxymoron.[5] Tolkien's hobbit hero is a case in point. In fact, Tolkien is in many ways an exemplar for this modern genre that thrives on oxymoron and paradox. He is simultaneously an abstruse academic scholar and a popular-culture icon. He writes literature in a mode that appeals to both the child and the adult. He inspires responses from critics in academic journals and from devoted fans in photocopied fanzines. His contemporary, invented languages reflect linguistic history and ancient literatures, scientific scholarship and creative imagination. And his creations have a tendency to move off the page, into oral literature or real life, as in the form of the costumed faithful in procession at the annual meetings of the Mythopoeic Society. *The Hobbit*'s enduring appeal to children of all ages is exceptional; it is a book with ample craftsmanship and depth to reward repeated readings and a nearly perfect lure into the larger mythos of Middle-earth.

With *The Hobbit*'s popular success in print, the publisher was eager for a sequel. Tolkien offered "The Book of Lost Tales," a collection of related mythic adult fantasy stories in a serious, somewhat Morrisian style, but the tone and structure of that writing was so radically different from his well-received children's book that the publisher could not imagine an audience for it. Tolkien had nothing else on hand that he considered publishable, and there followed a 17-year period of gestation and creation (a time span that puts Morris's two years spent on "The Interminable" into perspective!).

In the meantime, World War II erupted. Tolkien's son Michael became an antiaircraft gunner, and Christopher was called into the Royal Air Force. Tolkien himself took his turn as an Oxford air raid warden while his family, like all the British, coped with the century's most horrific conflict. The rise of the Nazi empire and the Holocaust—an "Evil Empire" and "Dark Forces" in the real world—and the answering Allied resistance that ultimately ushered in the nuclear era and horrific weapons of mass destruction: all this violence, human suffering, and technological terror had a part in shaping the masterpiece Tolkien published at last in 1954 and 1955, *The Lord of the Rings*. It was a work so large the publisher insisted that it be divided and issued as three separate volumes. Its sales success created tremendous popularity for the trilogy, as it came to be known, and set a fashion for trilogies in fantasy that has existed ever since.

The struggle to survive and recover from loss is the background for all the major actions in Tolkien's works. Against this backdrop, characters apply various moral, technological, rational, and magical strategies. *The Lord of the Rings* plays out one power struggle so encompassing that it involves the very survival of geographical, social, political, and moral systems; the source of the struggle is glimpsed only gradually, in bits and pieces. In fact, the full story has become clear only with publication of *The Silmarillion* and other posthumous writings edited by Christopher Tolkien. These drafts, fragments, and other more polished tales together show the monumental accomplishment of Tolkien's creative invention, a depth of subcreation so complete that it offers layer after layer of language, history, and myth beneath the narrative surfaces of ample beauty, conflict, and engagement.

Tolkien's evolution as a writer is complex and fascinating but too complicated to explore here in detail. Briefly stated, the year after he earned a degree from Oxford University at age 23, he married the girl he had known and loved since he was 15, Edith Bratt, and then embarked for France, where he served in battle as a second lieutenant with the Lancashire Fusiliers. He returned to England in late 1916 suffering from "trench fever," and while recuperating early in 1917, he began writing "The Book of Lost Tales," which contained parts of an increasingly coherent mythology and history for several ages of the imaginary world that would eventually become *The Silmarillion*. With Edith as his audience, he invented languages, writing systems, and literary works for its invented cultures. Thus began a lifetime of creation that evolved during years of teaching and scholarly productivity at Leeds University and at Oxford and of parenting four children: John, Michael, Christopher, and Priscilla.

Tolkien's lifelong mythopoeic impulse stemmed from experiences of personal loss compounded by his exposure to catastrophic destruction and loss of friends to war, so that the act of writing was part of his "Recovery"—that critical attribute he would describe in his 1939 essay. Yet despite his tremendous energy of invention, Tolkien does not imagine a "paradise regained," as John Milton does to compensate for humanity's epic loss in *Paradise Lost*. Tolkien's "eucatastrophe" is more modest than Milton's and more traditionally Christian than Morris's *Earthly Paradise*. In *The Silmarillion* we learn that the original splendor of creation—the wondrous beauty of the Two Trees that grew in ancient days near the city of Valar in the Undying Lands and bestowed a glowing silver and gold light of immortality—is irredeemably lost. A High-elven craftsman named Feanor had fashioned three jewels called "Silmarils" and in them captured the light of the Two Trees. Unfortunately, the great beauty of this creation awakened possessiveness in one of the Valar, who poisoned the Two Trees and stole the jewels. After the destruction of the trees, the jewels contained the only remnant of their light. The thief came to be known as Morgoth the Enemy, and he plunged the world toward darkness.

Despite the prospect that "Consolation" is attainable through fantasy, Tolkien, unlike Milton, sees loss as irremediable. As a consequence, Tolkien's conception of the qualities a hero should have and the scale of victory he can hope to attain are far more modest than Milton's. Tolkien does not imagine a "paradise regained" but a struggle against evil that must continue endlessly. The mythic background for the theme of loss is detailed in *The Silmarillion* (1977), but it is important to keep in mind that this book was compiled before and during the writing of *The Lord of the Rings* though not published until after Tolkien's death. *The Silmarillion* serves as a kind of bible for Middle-earth, containing stories about its creation and fall. Like the account of the Fall of Adam in the Bible, Tolkien's story of the Two Trees shows that the radiance of the Simarils (like biblical apples) tempts even the Valar, the guardians of the world. This fallen one became known as Morgoth the Enemy. By poisoning the trees, Morgoth deprived the world of their light for all eternity and defined creation's capacity for acts of purest evil.

In *The Silmarillion* Tolkien created an imaginary history that reaches back into antiquity in the manner of the real ancient texts and oral traditions that originally gave birth to fantasy. He even made similar forms for his background texts: fragments of old manuscripts, some of which he calligraphed as documents complete with burned edges and holes that obliterated portions of the text. Some stories were presented as retellings of earlier tales that had been lost, or as translations of still older texts, the originals of which had been lost: his books of lost tales are so convincing they could take their place alongside extant world myth. In this totally invented mythic context, Tolkien demonstrated a scope for the imagination entirely new to fantasy, and his work, some of which still remains to be published, is the standard against which all subcreation is tested.

In Tolkien's history, Morgoth precipitated a war that devastated Middle-earth and finally ended the First Age. But at last the darkness was somewhat thrust back, and a seed of the Eldest of Trees, Telperion, survived to grow again and shed its silver light in Middle-earth. The golden light of Laurelin, the other Tree, however, was permanently extinguished by Morgoth. This loss without possibility of recovery lies behind *The Lord of the Rings.* The epic efforts depicted in the trilogy are to preserve what little of the precious light remains.

The Rings involved in the story possess a history parallel to the tale of the Two Trees. The making of the Rings of Power was the greatest work of the Second Age. They were made by Fëanor's descendants, the Elven-smiths of Eregion. The Second Age incarnation of evil is Sauron of Mordor—said to have once been a High Elf fallen to serve Morgoth. Pretending to help the Elven-smiths, Sauron steals certain of their secrets and simultaneously taints the Rings with evil. Sauron then forges a single ring of his own, the One Ring that can control them all. The story of the Rings, like the tale of the Two Trees, is in one sense a fable of how advanced technology and craft produce artifacts of great power and temptation but induce theft and war. It is an illustration of the "possessiveness" Tolkien condemns in his essay on fairy stories.

At last, the One Ring is cut from Sauron's hand by Isildur when the Alliance of Free Peoples (Elves, Dwarves, Ents, Men, and Hobbits) conquers him. At the beginning of the Third Age, however, Isildur is ambushed and loses the Ring, which rests on a riverbed for more than 2,000 years until it is found by Gollum and eventually acquired by the hobbit Bilbo Baggins.

The Ruling Ring undoes the good powers of the lesser Rings, just as the Silmarils extinguish the blended light of the Two

Trees. When the One Ring is consumed in the fires of Mount Doom at the end of the trilogy, it simultaneously destroys all the other Rings and dissolves all the good works that the Rings brought about during the preceding ages.

One final element of background must be mentioned to complete the context of *The Lord of the Rings*. In his 1936 lecture "*Beowulf:* The Monsters and the Critics" (published in 1937), Tolkien argues that the great strength of this early English masterpiece lies in its mythological embodiment of radical evil in the dragon, a malevolent force so great that man can never expect complete victory over it. Tolkien shows that heroism is defined by the strength of the adversary the hero faces. Our human ability to imagine evil is therefore central to our capacity to work for good. This and other points Tolkien raises in his essay on the sixth-century *Beowulf* poet radically altered prevailing critical approaches. Tolkien's fascinating discussion of the dragon also illuminates the mythological implications of the dragon he introduced in *The Hobbit* and of the monsters that appear in the trilogy. The essay is an example of the extent to which Tolkien's scholarly and creative work combined to form a single, unifying literary vision.

The Lord of the Rings

The Fellowship of the Ring, the first volume of *The Lord of the Rings*, begins, like *The Hobbit*, with a party. It is a celebration of the birthday of Bilbo Baggins, the hobbit hero of the earlier book. This birthday party—traditionally a time for friendship, joy, and camaraderie—receives many ironic touches in Tolkien's hands. Ownership of the Ring has made Bilbo virtually ageless, and the idea of observing a birthday for a hobbit who, at 111 years of age, shows no signs of getting older seems pointless. Furthermore, the whole party is a sham. Bilbo is staging it as a dramatic setting for his own planned disappearance. His possession of the Ring has not increased his fellowship with his neighbors and friends; rather, it has fostered his separation and isolation from them. He does share some rapport with his nephew Frodo, but Frodo, too, is essentially alone. He is an orphan, destined to be separated even from his guardian Bilbo as he pursues a quest to separate himself from the Ring, to isolate it from its maker, and to destroy forever the tempting lure of its technology. Finally, at the end of the book, as the Free Peoples celebrate the birth of a new age, Frodo, Bilbo, and Gandalf the Grey sail off into the unknown, at last separated from Middle-earth itself.

Gandalf is likewise a loner, though his concern for the welfare of others and his careful research have brought him into communication and frequent contact with the folk of Middle-earth. He meets Bilbo at his home at the start of the story to be sure that Bilbo really does give up the Ring. Later, Gandalf returns to assist Frodo in learning about the Ring and to set him on his mission to try to destroy it. To characterize those who make up this quest as a "Fellowship of the Ring" is, like the birthday party, ironic, for their actions as individuals increasingly form the basis for the story, and their paths lead them apart so that the visible fellowship rapidly dissolves. Through Gandalf's example (and in the tale's later action), Tolkien creates isolated characters who are able to transcend their isolation through the understanding of and participation in a moral and natural order. Gandalf also clearly perceives from the start that this order must be constantly defended.

Gandalf, Bilbo, Frodo, and Samwise Gamgee exemplify qualities of mind and heart that Tolkien approved of and tried to embody. He knew what it meant to be an orphan, and he shows through Frodo how a single, lowly orphan spirit can attain heroic heights. Although Tolkien does present acute separations and isolations in *The Lord of the Rings*, he also shows a lasting fellowship of purpose, perhaps best represented in characters who do scholarly research and make literature, two "Consolations" he discovered in his own life. Gandalf is often depicted in the role of a scholar of ancient lore and languages. In fact, his research is what leads him to understand the powers and dangers of the Ring. Through his study of history, his special research of hobbit behavior, and his mastery of linguistics (shown, for example, in his ability to translate the runes inscribed on the Ring), Gandalf comprehends experience larger than his own and attains wisdom and goodness. He shares his learning freely with others and becomes a model for both Bilbo and Frodo, who later become scholars, poets, and chroniclers themselves. One of Frye's premises applies even more explicitly to Tolkien's narrative than to Morris's: "the focus of interest shifts from heroes and other elements of narrative toward the process of creating them. The real hero becomes the poet" (Frye 1976, 178). Tolkien, the linguist and scholar, conveys from first to last the conviction that dedicated study and creative expression can enable one to overcome isolation. Through Gandalf's example especially, he shows how depth of knowledge can lead in turn to freedom of choice and action.

Free will is of great importance in Tolkien's moral scheme, and here again his literary attitudes are consistent with his Catholic beliefs. The connection between knowledge and free will is one of the profound relationships defined in the Christian story of man's paradoxically fortunate fall from paradise when he chose to eat the fruit of the tree of knowledge. Freedom of choice is possible only through knowledge, and it is partly for this reason that Gandalf relates the Ring's history to Frodo.

The Elven-smiths of Eregion, Gandalf explains, forged—with the treacherous help of Sauron—seven Rings of the Dwarf-Kings, nine Rings of Mortal Men, and the lesser Rings of Power. Sauron's part in their creation bent the Elves' good intentions, and Sauron made all the Rings subject to control by the One Ring he planned to forge. Fortunately, Celebrimbor, chief of the Elven-smiths, secretly made three Rings of his own, which Sauron never touched. Known as the Three Rings of the Elven-kings, these were more powerful than the rest, enabling the Elves to heal, create, and preserve. The Three Rings were forces for good for about 10 years, until, in Mordor's Chambers of Fire, Sauron forged his controlling Ring, the One Ring, which is the focus of *The Lord of the Rings*. Celebrimbor instantly was aware of what had happened and hid the Three, but the Seven and the Nine, which had already been given to Dwarves and Men, fell under Sauron's spell. Sauron was able to rule the bearers of the Nine completely, but the Dwarves, who were always strong in resistance, were more difficult to master. Sauron at last lost the One Ring at the end of the Second Age, when Isildur cut it from his hand. This lifted the restriction on the Three Rings, which could be brought out of hiding and used for good works once again; however, Gandalf concludes, the One Ring still exists, and if Sauron regains it, not only will the good works be destroyed but the minds of those who bear the other Rings will be open to Sauron's control.

Clearly, there is a vast scale of powers associated with these Rings in Middle-earth, but Gandalf also indicates that there is yet another transcendent power that plays a role in the world's events. He assures Frodo that Bilbo was meant by someone other than its evil creator to find the Ring and that Frodo, in turn, was meant to have it. This information encourages Frodo to accept responsibility for the Ring, but the final choice must be his. The opportunity and responsibility of this choice are in marked contrast to Bilbo's lack of choice in *The Hobbit*. Bilbo was tricked into helping the Dwarves, but Frodo is a more mature hero, facing and accepting moral decision making from the outset of his story.

Although he does not know where to go or what lies ahead of him, Frodo does clearly understand that the nature of his journey is markedly different from Bilbo's. He states his situation to Gandalf succinctly: "Bilbo went to find a treasure, there and back again; but I go to lose one, and not return, as far as I can see."[6] Gandalf does not dispute the statement, and it stands as a fair summary of the book's action. *The Lord of the Rings* is a mythic embodiment of the Christian paradox that one must lose one's life to save it. It is a narrative of loss—a loss that is echoed on many levels: Bilbo first gives up the Ring and his life in the Shire; Frodo gives up the home and community he has found after the loss of his parents and finally relinquishes and destroys the Ring itself, which he can accomplish only by consigning it to the fires of the Cracks of Doom in the depths of the Fire-mountain, Orodruin.

At Gandalf's suggestion, Frodo sets his immediate sights on reaching Rivendell, and he readily accepts the further suggestion that he need not depart alone. Accompanied by Samwise Gamgee, Meriadoc "Merry" Brandybuck, and Peregrin "Pippin" Took, the small hobbit Frodo sets out to do what he can to prevent evil from encompassing the cosmos. The opening scenes are set mostly in familiar geographies, homey interiors, and inns or pubs. The looming threat of mysterious shadowy riders adds an ominous quality to Frodo's departure, but in the first book of *The Fellowship of the Ring* (the first book alone contains 12 chapters), there is far less entrapment and trickery than in *The Hobbit.*

In addition, most of the action of the first two books takes place on the earth's surface, again in contrast to *The Hobbit*, which is characterized by a womblike atmosphere, many of its scenes taking place in caves or in holes in the earth. Trees, rather than burrows or caves, are very much in evidence early in *The Fellowship of the Ring*. Frodo hides inside a hollow tree at the start of his journey, and as the company enters the Old Forest, Merry and Pippin are trapped inside a willow tree. The tree is a complex symbol for Tolkien, as it has definite Christian echoes of both the tree of knowledge and the tree of sacrifice, the cross. The symbol becomes more important later in the trilogy, but at this point the tree symbolically embraces all three dimensions of the universe— its roots are deep in the earth, its trunk stands on the earth's surface, and its branches reach toward the heavens.

The hobbits are saved from their tree trap when Tom Bombadil comes along, singing a song that opens the tree. This is the first of many episodes that stress the power of the word, especially of poetry and song, to restore harmony and order to the natural world. Bombadil, one of Tolkien's most winning characters, is exuberant and uplifting in every aspect of his nature. He frees the hobbits and leads them to his home. His merry song is echoed there by his wife, whose voice is "as young and as ancient as Spring, like the song of a glad water flowing down into the night from a bright morning in the hills . . . falling like silver to meet them" (*LOTR*, 1:133). The writing in this passage is the most beautiful in the book thus far, and "with that song the hobbits stood upon the threshold, and a golden light was all about them" (133). When one recalls that the light lost to the world when the great tree Laurelin was killed was also golden, the light bathing the hobbits in this scene gains added significance.

It is never clear exactly who Tom is. He says he is "Eldest" (142) and that he knew darkness even before it was associated with evil. He is like a man, though not tall enough to be one, and his face is "red as a ripe apple" (131), creased into hundreds of wrinkles of laughter. Here is the image of the fruit of the ancient tree of knowledge, wrinkled with joy rather than with care and worry. Not only does Tom liberate the trapped hobbits, but he also brings a clear breath of joy and hope into the journey, which he conveys in his treatment of the Ring. He asks to see it, laughs, and tosses it about playfully. He slips it on his finger, and to everyone's surprise he does not disappear. Finally, Tom tosses the Ring into the air, and it vanishes in a flash. Frodo is astounded, but then Tom leans forward and hands it back to

Frodo, plucking it out of nowhere with a smile. Here is an altogether hopeful foreshadowing. Tom clearly has control over the Ring, and his treatment of it suggests for the first time that it may be possible for the Ring and not its bearer to disappear.

With Tom's help, the travelers resume their journey, managing to escape the living/dead clutches of the Barrow-wights, and they reach a resting place, the inn at Bree. There, caught up in a holiday spirit, Frodo gives in to an impulse to try on the Ring, and he vanishes at once, causing quite a stir among the guests. The incident leads to a meeting with a dark stranger, Strider—later identified as Aragorn. Fortunately, Strider understands enough about the dark forces in pursuit of the group to help the hobbits along toward Rivendell, but the tone of the narrative, in contrast to that describing the visit with Bombadil, darkens considerably as Black Riders surround the party.

Frodo again gives way to the urge to slip the Ring on his finger. Instantly, he is able to see the terrible faces and merciless eyes of the Riders, but the Ring also makes him clearly visible to the enemy. They stab him and he is overcome by pain that resembles "poisoned ice" and finally lapses into unconsciousness (208). Book 1 ends, then, with Frodo's symbolic death. The seriousness of the danger he faces is brought home to the reader and to Frodo, and the sphere of action expands from the earth's surface to include the shadowy plane the Black Riders inhabit and the oblivion of Frodo's swoon.

Book 2 begins happily, with Frodo regaining consciousness; his symbolic death is followed by his rebirth in Rivendell, where the company has carried him. The death-rebirth cycle is another reflection of Tolkien's Christian conviction that one *can* recover from loss. When Frodo awakens in the house of Elrond, the first cycle of the tale has been completed. Frodo has been tested, strengthened, and reborn, rising in a spiral so that his next cycle in the quest will take place at a higher level. Recalling Christ's Resurrection, Frodo's death and resurrection after three days may suggest he is a savior figure. He has allowed himself to be sacrificed, and he has *chosen* this path consciously.

Rivendell is a timeless realm, like heaven on earth, because Elrond, son of Earendil the Mariner, bears the Great Ring Vilya, strongest of the Three, and holds the earth's chaos at bay. The real challenge in *The Lord of the Rings,* however, is not how to be reborn into heavenly bliss but rather how to sustain a fallen world and, through sacrifice, partially redeem it. The past can never be fully recovered, but consistent with his own Catholicism, Tolkien shows in his story that great faith and sacrifice in a fallen world can indeed limit the power of evil. Indeed, one *must* work constantly to prevent its triumph, and no price is too great to prevent its victory. Tolkien denies any conventional view of progress, instead placing a clear golden age (shown in Bombadil's golden light and in Laurelin's lost golden radiance) in the past. The purpose of present existence is not to build an improved city of God but merely to prevent the fragments and ruins of the old city from disappearing completely.

In the Council of Elrond, the whole story of the Ring is told for the first time. This is appropriate, for the House of Rivendell is a center of art and learning where ancient knowledge is preserved and where scholarly activity is highly prized. Here Bilbo becomes a fine poet-scholar, and Gandalf makes use of Elrond's library to deepen his knowledge before facing the final conflict. Through these examples, Tolkien repeats the message he introduced in Bombadil's symbolic apple face—that knowledge per se is not the reason for the fall. Knowledge can be allied with joy and freedom, and it can be applied artistically through the process of "sub-creation." It is, in fact, through knowledge, free choice, and the support of all the cultures of their past that the Free Peoples of Middle-earth will win victory at last.

The Council at Elrond determines that a group of nine should accompany Frodo, including representatives from all the Free Peoples of Middle-earth—Dwarves, Ents, Men, Elves, and Hobbits. They also agree that no better Ring-bearer can be found than Frodo himself, who has chosen to accept its awesome charge in full knowledge of the significance of doing so. The fellowship of nine members of the Free Peoples will balance the "Nine Riders who are evil" who oppose the company (289).

The fellowship sets out toward the fires of the Cracks of Doom by the route judged most strategic and heads toward Moria, a vast underground city the Dwarves call Khazad-dum. When they reach their destination, they begin a descent in both space and time, and the surface travel that has characterized the narrative is broken. Bilbo refers to this new movement as he and Frodo speak together for the last time, and he assures Frodo that even though he looks like a mere hobbit, there is "more about you than appears on the surface" (291). Henceforth the narrative ranges above and below the surface in action and moral dimension. The company descends and ascends to perspectives that afford new points of view, always returning to the level pattern of their journey and bearing in mind the final descent they must make to the fires beneath the mountain where the Ring must be destroyed.

The fellowship's first descent proves painful and destructive. Moria, the name of the great pit, means "given without love" in the Elvish tongue. It is a non-Christian backdrop against which fate is unredeemed by love and sacrifice. Here, however, the fellowship *is* redeemed by sacrifice, as Gandalf urges the company to escape across the bridge of Khazad-dum and turns alone to face the monstrous Balrog. Gandalf appears momentarily victorious when his staff breaks the bridge beneath the Balrog, but the creature entangles him in its whip and together they fall into oblivion. The fellowship is broken and grief overcomes those remaining, yet Frodo and the others have survived this place of no love through Gandalf's loving sacrifice. Redemption in Tolkien's works is always linked to love, and Gandalf's sacrifice shows that his love for the Free People is a bond of great strength, as is the love between Sam and Frodo, and that between Beren and Luthien in *The Silmarillion*.

Love, for Tolkien, assumes an ideal, medieval, Christian quality—it is a beatific *caritas*. *The Lord of the Rings* is practically unique in twentieth-century literature for its epic depiction of this central value, linked closely, as previously stated, to free choice and increasing in significance during the course of the quest. He presents his idealized love as an idea or an instinct totally lacking any overtone of sexual passion, and this too distinguishes him from most other modern writers. It is not accidental that the moral importance of love and sacrifice increases at the very time that the external fellowship begins to dissolve. It affirms a nonmaterial power of great strength, which will preserve the Fellowship of the Free Peoples despite the separation time imposes.

The remaining eight companions find their way to Lothlórien, and there they are given a more complex perspective on their mission. Their senses are sharpened, and they glimpse the remnants of the golden past as well as glimmers of the future when they gaze into the Mirror of Galadriel. The Lady of the Galadhrim offers another measure of the outer limits of choice, for even she is not free from the necessity of choosing. Frodo offers her the Ring, and she entertains for a moment the prospect of herself as a terrible goddess. As she considers the idea, she seems to Frodo to grow "tall beyond measurement" and unbearably beautiful, "terrible and worshipful." The lady laughs, making her choice and breaking the Ring's terrible power. Having met this test, she says simply, "Now we have chosen, and the tides of fate are flowing" (381).

The eight companions leave Lothlórien together, but soon they are separated, as the members individually face choices and challenges. Tolkien's reiteration of the choice motif suggests that he sees life as continuous choosing. Every minute of time represents a choice and thus a potential downfall or salvation that will affect not only the individual moral agent but also the delicate balance of good and evil in the world at large. *The Fellowship of the Ring* ends with a triad of rapid-fire and consequential choices: Boromir decides suddenly to attack Frodo and seize the Ring; Frodo chooses to leave the company and complete the mission on his own; and Sam decides suddenly to stay with his old friend. As Frodo and Sam set off together, their choices are tied to love, to *caritas,* and though the fellowship of nine is no more, their bond of fellowship is far deeper than any yet seen in the story.

The two central books of *The Lord of the Rings,* books 3 and 4 (published as *The Two Towers*), place great emphasis on symmetry and correspondence. Whereas the action in the first two books is largely confined to the earth's surface, book 3 focuses on the assault of a tower and book 4 tells of a descent into a cave. These symmetrical upward and downward directions of narrative focus illustrate the cosmic extension of the conflict Tolkien is depicting and complicate the conflicts already introduced.

Book 3 focuses on two towers, concentrating on Orthanc, Saruman's Tower at Isengard, in particular. Traditionally, towers are emblematic of aspirations to pride, an association epitomized in the biblical story of the Tower of Babel. True to tradition, the towers in Tolkien's tale stand as symbols of isolated, powerful ambitions that ultimately result in widespread disorder and disintegration. Orthanc and Barad-dûr, symbols of blasphemous aspirations and desire, stand for the profane pride of Sauron and Saruman, whose names, goals, and citadels are similar in malevolence but who can never work together. Sauron and Saruman stand in pitiful contrast to the fellowship, whose members share few superficial similarities but who work magnificently in coordination to preserve their moral order despite being hopelessly divided and scattered.

Tolkien understands the paradox of unity in division. Through the action of his tale, he characterizes the nature of any spiritual struggle as involving countless individual decisions and choices. Each isolated choice made by a member of the fellowship, because it is made for a principle larger than the self, can contribute ultimately to the triumph of a common cause. Sauron and Saruman are doomed to isolation and defeat by the nature of their decision-making process; each of their actions is dictated by pure self-interest and by the desire to accrue additional power for the self, so each action pursues its own course. The actions cannot cohere because they serve no larger purpose.

Just as the two towers present a symmetry, so the action of books 3 and 4 is symmetrical. Tolkien's structural use of symmetry in *The Two Towers* reflects the weighing of the forces of good and evil. Tolkien wanted to portray an enemy as strong and persistent as evil itself in order for the final victory of good to be significant; thus the Dark Legions of Sauron and Saruman are made unimaginably strong. The possibility of triumph for Frodo and his cause seems small indeed. One technique Tolkien employs, especially in these symmetrical central books, is the rhetorical and scenic use of comparison and contrast. Contrast between tower and cave is prominent, for example, as is the consistent imagistic contrast between light and darkness.

One particularly interesting contrast is that between the Orcs and Ents in book 3. The creatures are diametrical opposites in nearly every way except for the symmetry of their three-letter names. In their abduction of Merry and Pippin, the Orcs run tirelessly for hours as though they were machines; Tolkien even describes them as being made of "wire and horn" (*LOTR*, 2:55). The Ents, on the other hand, move agonizingly slowly, and their every aspect, from their appearance to their mission of tree herding, associates them with natural rather than technological images. The Orcs are killed off in droves during battles and raids, and they seem to take little notice of the loss of their fellows. Robbed of any individual significance, they have the quality of interchangeable parts. The Ents, in sharp distinction, live practically forever, and the loss of even one tree under their care grieves them deeply.

The Orcs, the reader learns, are a race created long ago by Morgoth for his foul purposes. Their very existence was contrived through technological manipulation of other living creatures. Morgoth turned his helpless victims into the Orcs and Ogres who now comprise the armies of the Dark Legions. They are extensions of the dark technology of the two towers. Resembling the sorcerous towers, the Ents and the trees they guard tower over the earth on their trunks but are clearly in harmony with it.

Even the languages of these two races reflect their differences. Tolkien does not reproduce the Orcs' language in great quantity, but what he does supply—such words as *Uglúk*, *Grishnákh*, *búbhosh*, and *skai*—is ugly and awkward. The Ents' language is open and full, especially in contrast with the Orcs' cramped gutturals. Treebeard the Ent is fond of saying, "*Hrum, Hoom*"—a pleasant exclamation with a humming sound. It suggests the *Om* that is chanted in prayerful meditation in the East and echoes the name of the universal tree of Eastern art called *hom*, which symbolizes the cosmos. Treebeard's characteristic language is open and full throated and contains *mmm* sounds of satisfaction. It is similar to Tom Bombadil's delightful rhymes. Compare the Ent's song, for example, with Tom's. Treebeard sings, "Hoom, hm; hoom, hm, how did it go? Room tum, room tum, roomty toom tum" (2:68). In spirit, rhythm, and the open *o* vowel sounds, it echoes Tom's "Hey dol! merry dol! ring a dong dillo! / Ring a dong! hop along! fal lal the willow!" (LOTR 1:130).

At the center of *The Lord of the Rings,* in books 3 and 4, the universe is in delicate balance. The Orcs are weighed against the Ents—technology is weighed against nature—and the forces of light and darkness seem for a time to be equally balanced. Indeed, sheer numbers and power suggest that the Dark Legions will overthrow the small challengers. Gradually, however, the balance of power begins to lean metaphorically toward the forces of light. In metaphor, symbol, and action, elements of rebirth and renewal proliferate. Gandalf, last seen falling into dark oblivion, returns in a glorious resurrection as the White Rider. Merry and Pippin escape what seemed to be certain death at the hands of the Orcs. The Ents are awakened from their trancelike hibernation, and Gandalf visits the Golden Hall at Edoras, casts out the evil Gríma Wormtongue, and awakens King Théoden from lethargy and illusion. These allied forces for renewal converge at the tower Orthanc, where the Orc armies are defeated. Saruman and Wormtongue are trapped in the tower, and in a fit of helpless rage Wormtongue throws away one of the few remaining treasures of evil technology, the magic crystal "palantir" that enabled Saruman to communicate with Sauron.

There is a metaphorical conflict between tree and tower, a dialectic of arrogant technology versus unpretentious organic nature. Technology, epitomized by the towers and personified in the Orcs' mindless slave fellowship, competes with the natural strength represented by the Old Forest and personified by the Ents' careful and univocal fellowship. One of Tolkien's strongest statements rests in the triumph of the Ents, for they emphatically make the point that nature is capable of throwing off technology with little more than a shrug.

Whereas book 3 shows a successful move upward to assault the tower, book 4 recounts how Frodo and Sam begin a descent into the earth as they enter Mordor, where they intend to throw the Ring into the Cracks of Doom. First, on their way toward the dark kingdom, they cross paths with Gollum, who is obsessed with regaining the Ring. Frodo knows about this treacherous creature from Bilbo's stories and is prepared to hate him. Unexpectedly, however, Frodo finds that he is overcome by "Pity and Mercy." He intuitively recognizes that Gollum is merely an ordinary, weak spirit overwhelmed by the Ring's lure. The reader is impressed not simply because this response is surprising but because of its contrast to the behavior of Saruman, Wormtongue, and Sauron. Frodo's ideally Christian acceptance of Gollum affords palpable relief from the concentrated monomania of the Dark Legions.

Critic Randel Helms has pointed out numerous parallels between books 3 and 4, showing that in each of the books a pair of hobbits (Merry and Pippin; Frodo and Sam, respectively) must cross a seemingly impossible distance or impassable area in a limited amount of time. In each case, the hobbits succeed because of the unexpectedly reversed effects of evil intentions on them (Saruman's and Gollum's). After making this near-miraculous journey, each hobbit pair meets an authority figure in a forbidden land (Treebeard in Fangorn; Faramir in Ithilien) who has come to the area because of rumors of an enemy's presence and has been led to the hobbits' specific location by the sign of smoke (the Orcs' cremation; Sam's cooking fire). In each book, the leader must decide whether to kill or to help the hobbits, and in each case he decides to help but only because an initial impulse toward killing gives way to a spirit of deliberation and reconsideration. After some useful exchange of information, both pairs of hobbits proceed with the authority figure to his cave, where they receive nourishing food after a long period of hunger and peaceful sleep. Rested and strengthened, the hobbit pairs then continue on their quests, and each pair eventually destroys a dark tower (Orthanc and Barad-dûr).[7]

Helms points out these and other instances of symmetry and parallelism in *The Lord of the Rings*. Through the very structure of his narrative, Tolkien presents a universe in which coherence and correspondence prevail. Appropriately enough, parallel but independent actions eventually triumph, whereas actions dictated by ruling authorities are impotent or briefly enforced only by mere threat. The dictators eventually disintegrate and fall. One of Tolkien's strengths is his ability to use form to give the reader tacit assumptions about the way the world operates and then reinforce a system of values the reader has already accepted because he believes in the fantasy. Because the narrative has a structure of great order and coherence, the reader more readily accepts the thematic point that the free choices of independent and eccentric individuals (such as those who make up the fellowship) result in far more positive outcomes than does the totalitarian imposition of uniform will on chaotic masses that Saruman and Sauron practice. One recognizes their machinations as prideful exercises of will, attempts to impose their own self-serving plans on an organic order that is far more complex, natural, and inevitably stronger than they.

At the same time the mighty battles are taking shape at Orthanc, Sam and Frodo move steadily if less spectacularly forward. They find the gate and the entrance to Mordor heavily guarded and impenetrable, but Gollum recalls a cave that leads into the land, an approach that might catch Sauron by surprise. It is the den of the great spider Shelob, who sucks the blood of living victims. Gollum has had dealings with this monstrous, ancient force of evil and intends to deliver Sam and Frodo to her as sweet morsels.

Shelob, the last of the Great Spiders that wrought terror in Middle-earth's First Age, voraciously saps life from the world, serving no cause but her own limitless appetite. She lives in utter darkness, her only visible feature being the glow of "evil purpose in her remorseless eyes" (LOTR 2:334). The struggle seems hopeless and is made worse when Gollum himself attacks Sam and gets a deadly grip on his neck. Sam manages to break Gollum's stranglehold, and the cowardly Gollum retreats. Sam turns to vanquish the spider with a last, unexpected resource, the phial from Galadriel that contains the light of Eärendil's star, the only surviving Silmaril, which shines as a beacon of hope from the waters of Galadriel's fountain. The light symbolizes the permanent illumination of good works, and the water is the source of all form and creation, the *fons et origo;* the light Sam releases in the very bowels of dark Mordor thus prefigures the ultimate victory of the forces of good.

Books 5 and 6, *The Return of the King,* depict the process of hope fulfilled through arduous effort (good works) and through a large measure of grace. The story does not conclude by singling out a hero, however. For example, although the return of King Aragorn embodies the restoration of harmony and justice in the sociopolitical order of Middle-earth, he cannot be said to be the hero, for his success rests on the past actions of others and on pure accident (the element of grace). The splendid *eucatastrophe,* the denouement's split-second timing, and the dire straits in which each of the characters has found himself elevate the cause of the final success beyond the single hero.

Great faith, deeply informed by Tolkien's Catholicism, is in evidence at the end of *The Lord of the Rings.* One of the qualities Tolkien must have found attractive in that religion was its hierarchical form. Here was a spiritual order that transcended history, politics, and commerce; it was a mirror of divine order in the universe. *The Lord of the Rings* narrates the restitution of Middle-earth's historic hierarchy and shows the difficulty of reestablishing order once it has been disrupted. Sauron attempts to supplant order with tyranny, a totalitarian hierarchy based on absolute power and the subjugation of everything to a single will. He would exchange ignorance for knowledge, servitude for choice, fear for faith, lust for love, and hopelessness for hope.

Tolkien's ideal society is not egalitarian, but it is free. He establishes a patriarchal hierarchy as the highest spiritual, social, and political ideal. The hope for social order clearly rests with the king, whose childhood name, Estel, is translated in Tolkien's appendix as "hope." The monarch's restoration at the novel's end seems politically anachronistic in the twentieth century; Tolkien's utopian vision is curiously neither democratic nor socialistic, but it is certainly Catholic, English, and even Arthurian. His New Age is like a reborn England in which divinely ordained kingship takes on its full significance. Although it is meet and right that the king assume his throne, his ascension is a matter of affirming form and structure rather than of rewarding a hero. His position as ruler promotes himself far less than it does the restitution of order, which has been accomplished through the convergence of all the eccentric individuals of the Free Peoples.

In the first four books, Tolkien explores surfaces, towers, and caves. In the last two books, he includes all these physical settings in his action but also places special emphasis on the nonmaterial dimension of time. Destruction of the Ring will reshape time itself. It will take with it all the other Rings and will end all of the orders that the Rings helped build and sustain. Galadriel, Elrond, and Gandalf carry the Three Elven Rings with them away from Middle-earth at the end of the age, and with those Rings pass forever the shining of Rivendell and Lothlórien; the struggle between good and evil will begin again with a clean slate. New Age future time is anticipated in a number of chronologies that Tolkien provides as appendices: "Annals of the Kings and Rulers," "The Tale of Years," "Family Trees," and the "Shire Calendar." There is also a detailed note on calendars in general.

In this last book, then, Tolkien's concern for human and moral order is emphasized in definite relationship to time. The end of the Third Age means a loss of good works as well as of evil ones. The glimpse of the future provided in the appendices is bound to be colored by loss, especially the loss of the friends who sail away from Middle-earth forever. The book is structured so that this final loss, which returns the reader to the sense of loss with which the story began, is bearable and the recognition of it ennobling. This is the experience of *eucatastrophe* masterfully evoked; the happy ending contains a heavy component of loss and holds it so fully that its presence makes the experience complete.

As the fifth book begins, Gandalf rides to Minas Tirith, chief city of the kingdom of Gondor, carrying Pippin with him on his great horse, Shadowfax. They go to enlist the support of Lord Denethor, but the lord is anxious to hear details of the death of his son Boromir and is suspicious of the wizard. Pippin adds credibility to the account, and when he impulsively kneels before the old man to offer his services, Pippin ensures that they will have Denethor's assistance. The veteran warrior is flattered, accepts the service as a noble gesture, and immediately begins counsels to prepare for battle. In the meantime, Aragorn, Gimli, and Legolas leave with Theoden to join the mustering of the Rohirrim. Aragorn looks more and more like a king leading mighty armies, and when his fellow Rangers arrive, they bring from Arwen a Royal Standard of Gondor's ancient kings. Aragorn decides to trust an old prophecy and cuts short his ride to Gondor by following the Paths of the Dead. He penetrates the black gloom of Dwimorberg, the Haunted Mountain, a strange realm in which the folk have been accursed for an ancient sin. In this episode, Tolkien again shows the fabric of time begin to tear. Aragorn's presence liberates the tortured spirits, and a shadowy company of the dead ride with him when he leaves.

War erupts suddenly in Gondor, under the deepening shadow of black sorcery. The first onslaught of the Legions of Darkness is finally broken, largely because of the power of Gandalf, mounted on Shadowfax, who banishes the Nazgûl with a blast of radiant light. The alliance suffers heavy casualties as well, however, including Faramir, the last surviving son of Denethor, who is mortally wounded. The forces of Rohan do not arrive to reinforce their efforts.

The Dark Legions continue to attack, breaking open the Gate of Gondor with a battering ram. As the Lord of the Nazgûl rides in to be confronted by Gandalf, dawn is breaking and horns begin to sound. It is the long-awaited arrival of the hosts of Rohan. The alliance enjoys a momentary victory as the Lord of the Nazgûl himself is dispatched, but even this does not stop Sauron's armies, and as their assault rebounds everything seems to be lost. A fleet of dark ships swiftly approaches, and with this added assault the Free Peoples think they will fall. Then a banner can be seen—a white tree and seven stars—and Aragorn, the rightful king, sails in with his Rangers of the North to save the day.

Tolkien orchestrates the battle scenes beautifully. He includes enough detail to make the wounding and dying real and maintains enough distance to depict the battle's tactical maneuverings and scope. The clashes of the mighty armies, however, serve merely to buy time. They will never resolve or alter the conditions of inequality under which they fight. They are part of the great structural plan of *The Lord of the Rings* and give the novel a firm place in the epic tradition, but the theological solutions, the thematic conclusions, must be finished on a smaller scale. Aragorn and his forces regroup on the fields of Pelennor to attack Mordor's full might at the Black Gate. Sauron's messenger informs them that Frodo, the Ring-bearer, has been captured. Gandalf knows that if this is true their quest has failed, but he will not surrender despite the implications of this news.

Book 6 contrasts in many ways with the epochal clashes of book 5. It is as though a camera has cut quickly to a quieter scene that features close-ups rather than distance shots. Inside the cave where he has chased away Shelob with the flash of light, Sam has impulsively put on the Ring. Under its invisibility, he penetrates the Orc fortress to discover Frodo still alive. Sam rescues Frodo, and they press on in a last desperate effort to complete their journey. Together they struggle across the harsh desert until they come to Mount Doom. Beneath this mountain are the fires that can consume the warped technology. They are near the end of their mission.

At the brink of the great chasm, Frodo is gripped by hesitation. He falls victim at last to the Ring's lure and is unable to surrender it. Sam yells at him to throw it in, but Frodo declares that he chooses not to relinquish it. Then Sam is knocked over as a dark shape, Gollum, springs toward Frodo, who has put the Ring on his finger and become invisible. They wrestle wildly, and suddenly Gollum bites Frodo's finger, and the Ring with it, from Frodo's hand. With a cry of triumph, he holds his prize aloft; but in that instant he loses his balance and falls together with the Ring into the fire. The flames roar; Mordor shakes and writhes, and mountains crumble as Sauron's power collapses. Sam carries Frodo outside into the air.

The destruction of the Ring occurs while the forces of the West are locked in terrible battle with the Dark Legions at the Field of Cormallen. With this lucky destruction of the Ring, the Dark Forces are undone and disperse. Gandalf mounts the great eagle Gwaihir and rescues the hobbits. Their act has transformed the material world and temporal reality and marks the start of a New Age. (This death and rebirth of Middle-earth after three ages was prefigured in book 2 by Frodo's symbolic death and resurrection.) March 25, the day Sauron falls, is the first day of the Annunciation in the Catholic calendar.

Time in *The Lord of the Rings* begins and ends with moral order, without which, Tolkien believes, time is meaningless. Moreover, time is not seen as linear or progressive but as cyclical. The reader witnesses the ending of one age *and* the beginning of a new one. The forces of evil have not been eliminated; Saruman and Wormtongue are still loose, prowling the Shire and perpetuating chaos, but Sam, Merry, Pippin, and the other hobbits now seem equal to the fight. Elrond, Galadriel, Gandalf, Frodo, and Bilbo board a ship to sail away from Middle-earth to the Undying Lands, and the reader, like Sam, quietly accepts their departure as inevitable. The book ends with a close focus on Sam and his family. Tolkien describes the simple, concrete fellowship of family life: "And Rose drew him in, and set him in his chair, and put little Elanor upon his lap. He drew a deep breath. 'Well, I'm back,' he said" (LOTR 3:311). The unassuming Sam Gamgee, king in his castle, has returned home at last.

Despite the colloquial and homey quality of the final words, the conclusion of *The Lord of the Rings* is rendered in a formal, rhetorical style that complements the epic scope of its titanic clashes and moral scheme. The rhetoric is highly conjunctive, rhythmical, and stately. The style itself is one of Tolkien's great achievements and is worth close attention and analysis, especially in the final books, in which the writing is Tolkien's most serious, elevated, and poetic.

Tolkien uses formal cadences to give measured and orderly development to the chaotic and sprawling events. He frequently uses inverted syntax, so that the weight of the actions tends to pile up impressively. This device and repetition are skillfully combined for rhetorical effect in, for example, the passage that announces the Dark Lord's entrance into Gondor:

> In rode the Lord of the Nazgûl. A great black shape against the fires beyond he loomed up, grown to a vast menace of despair. In rode the Lord of Nazgûl, under the archway that no enemy ever yet had passed, and all fled before his face. (3:102–3)

As Tolkien said of the author of *Beowulf,* the high tone and the sense of dignity alone are evidence of a lofty and thoughtful mind. The reader is aware of the "sub-creative" power at work in this description of the Dark Lord.

Tolkien also continues to punctuate the high style with richly colloquial and homey rhetoric, most often associated with the hobbits. A good example of this is found in book 5, in which the narrative concentrates on Merry while the armies mobilize for the final battle. Merry is feeling rather lonely and meditative, lying quietly wrapped up in his blanket, when suddenly somebody stumbles over him. The figure curses the tree roots that have tripped him. "I am not a tree-root, Sir," says Merry, "nor a bag, but a bruised hobbit" (3:105). It is a brief moment of comic relief delivered in ordinary language, but this casual exchange is skillfully interwoven with other narrative threads and themes. Even though he is an Oxford academic, Tolkien does not lose touch with ordinary sensibilities. His fiction embraces the full range of fantasy sources, from slapstick, folk, and oral aspects to classical and literary traditions.

By the end of the chapter, the tempo has changed; Merry's heart "beats slowly," and he is, in fact, about to become a great hero, playing a part in the slaying of the Chief of the Nazgûl himself. The somber beat is audible in the slow throb of war drums, and "[t]hen suddenly Merry felt it at last, beyond doubt: a change" (3:112). The language begins to roll like the climax of a grand symphony, like the stately elevation of the King James Bible:

> For morning came, morning and a wind from the sea; and darkness was removed, and the hosts of Mordor wailed, and error took them, and they fled, and died, and the hoofs of wrath rode over them. And

then all the host of Rohan burst into song, and they sang as they slew, for the joy of battle was on them, and the sound of their singing that was fair and terrible came even to the City. (3:113)

In marked contrast to the staccato exchanges of the early portion of the chapter, the sentences are long, stately, and linked by repeated conjunctions. Tolkien has not only achieved the epic's narrative scope and rhetorical grandeur but has also managed the nearly impossible task of expressing himself in a personal way through this vast, potentially impersonal narrative. Like Milton, Tolkien sustains a voice that is uniquely his own and creates both intimacy and delicacy as well without spoiling his work's monumental quality. One senses throughout the story Tolkien's human presence as father, as friend, and even as a slightly tongue-in-cheek professor.

In keeping with the lofty mission of "sub-creation" Tolkien delineates in his essay "On Fairy-Stories," *The Lord of the Rings* sustains the reader's belief in an intricate, imaginary world. The scenes, characters, and actions correspond to those in the familiar world, but they are at the same time separate and distinct from familiar reality; the reader's hopes and expectations are freshened once he is distanced from his jaded habits of response. Whereas the conventional realistic novel usually depicts a single central character struggling with circumstances, Tolkien's fiction portrays a struggle for cosmic order, an elemental conflict that encompasses and swallows up all space and time.

It is nearly impossible to overstate Tolkien's importance in the history of fantasy. His work's popularity led thousands of readers to rediscover the lost tradition of literary fantasy that originated with Morris and MacDonald. Author and editor Lin Carter helped guide this revival through his Adult Fantasy series for Ballantine Books, and new writers drew inspiration (and found an audience) for similar works. Among the most notable are Terry Brooks, whose *Sword of Shanarra* and its sequels are nearly a direct imitation; Piers Anthony, whose fantasy novels, which combine Tolkien's scale and inventiveness and his own style, humor, and theme, first put the genre on the *New York Times* best-seller list; and Ursula Le Guin, probably the most original and compelling writer in the Tolkien tradition, whose Earthsea series is discussed in a later chapter.

Tolkien's investment of himself in his books produced a distinction born of painstaking commitment and effort throughout a lifetime. *The Lord of the Rings* achieves genuine literary richness, not only of surface action and invention but also of underlying thematic and linguistic structure. It is a moving human statement that expresses an inspiring breadth of thought, feeling, and creative power. In short, it is a splendid "sub-creation."

Chapter 4

PLOTTING THE MODERN MYTHIC HERO: MORRIS AND TOLKIEN

Northrop Frye points out in *The Secular Scripture* that early nonrealistic texts—the very body of work that "forms the mainstream of Western literature until the Renaissance" (Kratz, 3)—provided rich mythic soil not only for the growth of later romance literature but for the eventual evolution of the popular realistic novel, which Frye says was "a realistic displacement of romance, and had few structural features peculiar to itself" (Frye 1976, 38). The similar dialectic with or displacement of the popular realistic novel that shaped modern fantasy was, as we have seen in chapter 1, both revolutionary and recursive. Frye observes that the structural shifting of fantasy

> assumed a more definite shape after the publication of Tolkien's *Lord of the Rings* in the mid-fifties. On the T. S. Eliot principle that every writer creates his own tradition, the success of Tolkien's book helped show that the tradition behind it, of George MacDonald and Lewis Carroll and William Morris, was, if not "the great" tradition, a tradition nonetheless. (43)

The modern tradition rapidly developed two complementary but distinct thematic branches—secular and religious—and the resulting differences may be more fully appreciated through a look at the archetypal modern mythic heroes that emerge as fundamentally different in the work of Morris and Tolkien.

For Tolkien, at least, the principle that every writer creates his own tradition was one he addressed directly. He documented that Morris was, for him, a pleasure and an inspiration. When Tolkien won the Skeat Prize for English at Oxford in the spring of 1914 he used the £5 of prize money to buy several works by Morris, including his translation of the *Volsungasaga, The Life and Death of Jason,* and *The House of the Wolfings* (Carpenter and Tolkien, 69). The fact that Morris, like Tolkien, had been an undergraduate at Oxford's Exeter College also helped to create the bond of "tradition" that Tolkien affirmed. It seems appropriate, then, that the first letter in Tolkien's published *Letters,* one written to Edith in October 1914 (when they were still engaged), tells of his project to adapt a tale from the Finnish *Kalevala* "into a short story somewhat on the lines of Morris' romances with chunks of poetry in between."[1] "The Story of Kullervo," as he called it, was Tolkien's first plunge into the crafting of modern legend in poetry and prose. Although he left it unfinished, it nonetheless established a literary tradition. Beginning where Morris had left off, Tolkien undertook his own mythopoeic project. Carpenter observes that Morris's influence continues in the "Book of Lost Tales" and in *The Silmarillion.* The influence of Morris's style is particularly evident in the first of Tolkien's tales about the First Age, "The Fall of Gondolin," written during his convalescence at Great Harwood early in 1917. The story was read aloud to the Exeter College Essay Club in 1920, and the minute book for Wednesday, March 10 reflects that the tradition was acknowledged by his audience as well:

> [T]he president passed to public business and called upon Mr. J. R. R. Tolkien to read his "Fall of Gondolin." As a discovery of a new mythological background Mr. Tolkien's matter was exceedingly illuminating and marked him as a staunch follower of tradition, a treatment indeed in the manner of such typical romantics as William Morris, George MacDonald . . . etc. (Carpenter and Tolkien, 445).

Tolkien himself clarified the influence in a letter about *The Lord of the Rings* to Professor L. W. Foster in 1960 when he wrote that he did not think that the world wars "had any influence upon either the plot or the manner of its unfolding," but he added that "They owe more to William Morris and his Huns and Romans, as in *The House of the Wolfings* or *The Roots of the Mountains*" (Carpenter and Tolkien, 303). Christopher Tolkien recently recalled that his father owned nearly all of Morris's works and said that he has a distant but clear recollection of having been read *The House of the Wolfings* by his father.[2] In a subsequent letter, he listed 11 titles of Morris's books of poems, translations, and fantasies that his father bequeathed to him, including *The House of the Wolfings, The Roots of the Mountains,* and *The Sundering Flood,* plus J. W. Mackail's two-volume *Life of William Morris* and A. Clutton-Brock's *William Morris: His Work and Influence.*[3] Tolkien had begun collecting and reading Morris—even reading Morris aloud to his son—at a time when his popularity and critical reputation were at an all-time low and his work had been eclipsed by World War I and the onward rush of technology and current events.[4]

Tolkien found in Morris something of a kindred spirit or inspiration; the spark or connection helped advance a new fantasy tradition. The Western romance tradition staunchly reasserted itself in Britain at the great watershed of the twentieth century, and the modern romance hero was first clearly shaped in the 10 fantasy novels Morris wrote between 1886 and 1896. A quarter century later Tolkien began to craft a related but original heroic pattern of his own. Morris and Tolkien approached the creation of their fantasy heroes at different times and with different assumptions, and the results are interestingly diverse and revealing. The two authors, sharing many influences and values, nonetheless developed markedly distinct heroic types, which have set the course for the ongoing stream of fantasy in the twentieth century.

The characters of their influential fantasy novels define themselves within three frames: (1) the transcendent supernatural or spiritual universe with its moral dimensions (atemporal or extratemporal); (2) the social order of tribe or nation in history; and (3) the individual mind, with its complex matrix of internal realities, conflicts between subject and object, self and other, thought and action.[5] By this yardstick the hero can be measured first against the gods in an infinite and atemporal reality, then in the finite and temporal order of history and society, and finally in the finite and contained universe of individual consciousness as it comes to know itself, the world, and others.

Morris's fantasy hero in *The House of the Wolfings*, Thiodolf, serves as the prototypical Morrisian hero, not only because he is the protagonist of Morris's earliest fantasy novel but also because the book has been singled out by Tolkien as such a significant influence. Thiodolf is a godlike man, which Morris makes clear in the character's name (theo=god). In fact, one can hear this same grandeur in the names of many Morrisian heroes—Face-of-God in *Roots of the Mountains*, Hallblithe in *The Glittering Plain*, Golden Walter in *The Wood Beyond the World*, even Ralph in *Water of the Wondrous Isles*; Ralph's uncharacteristically short name is derived from the Anglo-Saxon *Rædwulf* (*rede* + *wolf*, plus the influence of the French *Raoul*) and thus obliquely associates this hero with Thiodolf, the Wolfings, and Beowulf. The heroes are physically handsome, strong, courageous, virtuous, and innocent. Although they are clearly human, they transcend their humanity to measure themselves against the gods. Morris does not belittle Thiodolf in the comparison. Instead, he confers on the hero the necessity to create and affirm an atemporal moral framework, which, like a god, he will validate through both word and deed.

The Morrisian hero begins to establish a continuum between the transcendent supernatural, or spiritual, universe and the social order in history. The title *The House of the Wolfings* emphasizes the importance of the social order, for Thiodolf gains his identity as a member of the house of the tribe of the Wolfings— which is agrarian, ecological, communal. The novel is *not* named for a single character—or, as is the case in Tolkien, for a titled position in a hierarchy (*The Return of the King; The Lord of the Rings*).[6] The values are collective rather than individual; identity is conferred through ritual, history, and group identity, and the book takes its title from the Wolfings' communal dwelling hall.

Thiodolf, in effect, brings the gods to earth. In the novel he physically bridges the gap between infinite and finite as the lover of the goddess Wood-Sun and the father of a lovely daughter, Hall-Sun, a kind of tribal priestess whose task is to tend the glass lamp that illuminates their hall. The hero in Morris's tale, then, is defined on the first level in relation to the gods as being the very vessel of divinity itself, a match and mate for an actual goddess. In relation to the history and society of the tribe he is one of its champions and is responsible, as the others are, for the continuous creative application of its values. Finally, within the frame of the self, he once again demonstrates continuum rather than separation as the moral and social frames connect with his personal interactions with his mate, his daughter, and his mundane circumstances.

Thiodolf must confront a significant antagonistic force in the encroaching, road-building Romans whose hierarchic, urban society gradually makes inroads into the communal tribes. As he faces these hostile forces, both on the battlefield and in his mind, Thiodolf grows in complexity and depth. We see him in relation to a significant other as he struggles with his deep love for the female Wood-Sun and for the world's quality of life. She fears for his safety in battle and persuades him to wear a magic hauberk of gray rings, made by the Dwarfs in the ancient days, which will protect his life in battle through its nonhuman magic.

The novel's climax occurs as Thiodolf renounces the hauberk's magic, strips himself of its enchanted protection, and dies on the battlefield in defense of the tribe. In renouncing the supernatural power he affirms his human nature and his tribe's communal values. He is immortalized in the stories and legends of his people.

Morris has created a horizontal hero, a godlike man rooted to land and tribe. Frye speaks of "horizontal" and "vertical" metaphors for somewhat different purposes, but his comments may help extend the idea:

> The principle of action on two levels, neither of them corresponding very closely to the ordinary world of experience, is essential to romance, and shows us that romance presents a *vertical* perspective which realism, left to itself, would find it very difficult to achieve. The realist, with his sense of logical and horizontal continuity, leads us to the end of his story; the romancer, scrambling over a series of disconnected episodes, seems to be trying to get us to the top of it. (Frye 1976, 49–50)

He also speaks later of the vertical romance movement as "rising into wish fulfillment or sinking into anxiety and nightmare" (53). Though by this measure I would call Morris a realist and Tolkien a romancer, Frye's theory here is analogous to what I am trying to suggest with the contrast of horizontal and vertical fantasy hero. The one seeks a wholeness or synthesis of relationships in terms of *this world,* a *horizontal* continuity of community and history. The vertical hero seeks resolution by departing the world for heaven or hell. The horizontal hero struggles to know himself and to share himself in love with another, to affirm his tribe's rights, land, and values against encroachments of an enemy, and to assume, and later responsibly discard, the mantle of the supernatural, instead taking on a godlike prerogative for moral continuity himself. In other words, he tries on the clothes of the gods but feels uncomfortable in garments not his own. So in taking off the supernatural hauberk he paradoxically puts on the even more godlike identity of one who creates his own moral universe. He rejects the contrived supernatural force that would preserve his life, for it would at the same time separate him from his tribe and from his very identity as a man.[7]

In *The Lord of the Rings* Tolkien's hero is also asked to define himself by renouncing power and possessiveness. In the case of Frodo Baggins, however, the hero is unable to do so alone. The name Frodo itself lacks the grandeur and stature of Thiodolf, and the hero figure is hardly godlike. In fact, he is not even human but a hobbit, a diminutive creature, about half the size of a man, with skillful hands and hairy feet. Tolkien explains that hobbits

> are relatives of ours: far nearer to us than Elves, or even than Dwarves. Of old they spoke the languages of Men, after their own fashion, and liked and disliked much the same things as Men did. But what exactly our relationship is can no longer be discovered.[8]

Tolkien then begins to create his hero by setting him apart and by raising questions about him, stating that his relationship (a key word) to man "can no longer be discovered."

Frodo is placed from the outset in a questionable relationship to man and to the supernatural. His connections are intentionally uncertain, the hero's condition in a sense mirroring man's doubtful position in a traditional theological universe: is he a god or a beast? The supernatural and social histories provide clues but no answers.

Frodo's personal psychology reinforces his isolation. He is self-oriented rather than relational by inclination and habit, living as an outsider to hobbit society. Frodo and his ancient cousin Bilbo, who adopted Frodo when both his parents drowned in a boating accident, consciously shun society.[9] They choose to live privately, shut off from the shire's other hobbits, and share a reputation for eccentricity and adventurousness. Neither is married. But Bilbo is rich and famous for his role in the restoration of the Dwarf-kingship of Erebor and is set apart from all others when he gains possession of the One Ring, the burden of which Frodo bears in his turn. Both are also destined for lasting fame through the practice of their solitary craft of authorship.

Though Frodo is shown to be a "worthy vessel," circumstances force him to take a somewhat unwilling part in a cosmic struggle against evil. Unfortunately, the battlefield is dominated by a male society, which allows little opportunity for a significant relationship with a female other. Though Frodo encounters lovely, powerful, and wise women along his journey, his closest associate, Sam Gamgee, is the nearest approximation of a significant other, and with Sam he essentially re-creates the comfortable and reassuring male companionship he enjoyed with Bilbo. There is a celebration of detachment in this approach to heroism. It is clear that the hero will not, like Thiodolf (or Tolkien), fall in love, marry, and have children to carry on the communal, or tribal, values. Sam Gamgee follows that path, which seems ordinary, predictable, and decent but not heroic.

This hero, then, is not defined by rivaling the gods in grandeur or in power. He is not defined in relation to history or society (until later, when he himself writes a history showing how important he is!). Nor is his own finite consciousness explored and deepened through a relationship with a significant female other. Instead he comes to define himself internally in a moral struggle with the power of the Ring and externally through deeds and words (as author). Tolkien suggests that human identity springs from direct personal confrontation with the clashing cosmic forces of light and dark powers and that identity is created in the choices that result from this confrontation.

Throughout *The Lord of the Rings* it is largely outside forces that prompt and motivate Frodo to action for good or ill. In the end, when he must destroy the Ring of power, his internal resources give way and he puts on the Ring. Like a bolt of lightning from on high, Gollum lunges, gnaws the ring from Frodo's fingers, and plunges with it into the fire to destruction. Victory is achieved by an act of grace, leaving the hero to sail off into the West to depart Middle-earth, an image of the wounded king, the wounded Beowulf, or the dying Arthur.[10]

In contrast to Morris, Tolkien here favors a "vertical" hero whose actions move upward or downward as he is propelled toward or away from absolute good or evil, rather than one who struggles horizontally on a plain where values must be determined without the benefit of divine intervention, where the hero himself must be God. This observation then extends and makes sense of Frodo's outside motivation. His hero identity resides in trying to choose good in the face of clashing outside forces from which he remains separated; only later, when he is again isolated, can he express in writing the story of his choices.

Tolkien's fiction is a complete and self-contained reality. This is part of his great achievement as an author. And the self-contained quality of the fiction mirrors the self-containment of his characters. The many fascinating peoples of Middle-earth are separate and set apart from each other. They are fallen descendants of a golden age, locked in cosmic battle on a mortal stage, and even their history and lineage serve to illustrate a fall or separation, not a hard-won continuance of one tribe or culture.

The nature of the Tolkien hero, the hobbit's clearly unfamiliar diminutive stature, and the conscious exclusion of significant relationships with a female other further enhance this idea of separateness and considerably limit the fiction's psychological terrain. Tolkien's hero moves, then, toward alienation at the very time when the cosmic struggle demands the greatest cooperation and fellowship for victory. The battle with which Tolkien is most deeply concerned seems not to be collective or relational but isolated, solitary, and waged by an individual too weak to be victorious except by grace. It is probably as close as the romance hero can come to the sense of isolation and flaw found in the traditional tragic hero. In Frodo, Tolkien fully realizes a hero firmly in the tradition of Morris while reversing nearly all of the characteristics Morris affirms.

Morris's horizontal hero struggles to preserve community and communal values while moving toward psychological complexity through the encounter (i.e., love) with a significant other. The enchantments, deceptions, and corrupt forces he meets along the plain are fear-inspiring challenges—both emotionally and physically—

to which the hero is equal and over which he is ultimately victorious, but his strength comes from affirmation of the community and of his relationship to it and to the opposite sex, and from an internal godlike human potential for virtue, valor, and love.

Tolkien's vertical hero emerges not from communal hall but from hobbit hole and struggles upward to the peaks of a monumental cosmic battle of good and evil, surrounded by but ultimately cut off from others engaged in the struggle. He is essentially alone, deprived of a significant relationship with a female, not ultimately strong enough to renounce the Ring of power. Here is a modern, alienated hero, saved by grace or accident or by Gollum's paradoxically fortunate fall.

Yet as Verlyn Flieger points out brilliantly in her essay "Frodo and Aragorn: The Concept of Hero," there are *two* strong candidates for the hero title in *Lord of the Rings,* and Aragorn in many ways comes closer to the Morris model (Flieger 1981, 40). Here is a handsome and powerful man, destined to be king and to lead a people, who is in close touch with history and destiny and who possesses strength for battle and some ability to confront even the greatest supernatural forces unleashed in this war. In the end he even has a bride, Arwen, though their relationship is given short shrift in the narrative.[11] Tolkien's artistic finesse in creating these bookend heroes raises a host of fascinating points broached by Flieger, but Aragorn's presence does little to alter the fact that the essential character of Tolkien's vertical hero is different from that of the horizontal Morrisian one. If Tolkien's tale has two heroes—one high, one low—this only reinforces the divided or alienated nature of his mythic type. Tolkien's model is clearly not an integrated heroic character able to achieve desirable relationships simultaneously with the supernatural, society, and the self. Neither hero has much of a sexual dimension or much psychological development. Aragorn, too, is positioned above and separate from his people at the end, isolated from the society he is destined to rule. Frodo is the wounded king who in his isolation chronicles and immortalizes the events of which he has been a part. He sails off alone at the end toward eternity and the gods, toward a hoped-for supernatural union, his adventures and finale eclipsing the social and individual identities he has never really clarified. In marked contrast, Thiodolf's heroic deeds are recorded and preserved by others.

But of course Thiodolf is not the only hero type Morris presents, and because I have discussed both Frodo and Aragorn I also want to mention a second alternative present in Morris's work. True to the archetypal pattern of a *comic* rather than a tragic ending, often symbolized in marriage or union, the fortunate conclusions of each of Morris's romances involve the union of male and female, as with Ralph and Ursula. But Morris does not always cast the male as hero. The maiden Birdalone in *The Water of the Wondrous Isles* is a case in point. As a child, Birdalone is stolen away from her mother by a witch. She eventually escapes in a magic boat, experiences adventures in a series of wondrous isles, and is at last united in love with a handsome knight, Arthur. Together they set out to establish a new social order.

Birdalone differs from a male hero in the way that anima differs from animus in psychological terms, but the heroic standards are precisely parallel. Birdalone renounces the magic of the witch who raised her, comes to terms with physical sexuality and emotional love through her encounter with a significant other of the opposite sex, and together with her knight, to whom she is joined with bonds of love, seeks to perpetuate their newfound sense of moral order in the setting right of the social order in history. The supernatural, historic, and psychological frames are viewed not as isolated realms but as parts of a continuum. The hero is able to responsibly conjoin all three. Such an integration, Morris suggests, is capable of transforming not only a single psyche but an entire social order.

Morris and Tolkien offer two radically different heroic types. The Morrisian hero is rooted to the human community, charged with the task of becoming his own god, overflowing with the need to explore individual and psychological potential in relationship to the other of eternity, history, and sexuality. This is a horizontal hero wed to the "skin and surface of the earth," a secular, pre-existential hero with the potential to become whole in commitment to spouse and community. The Tolkien hero is dislocated in a fallen world, charged with the task of renouncing the temptations of human power, surrounded by others clearly different from himself and from whom he is destined to remain distant, finding his hope in creating from his sufferings an immortal written word and sailing off at last to seek peace in an eternity with the gods. This is a vertical hero who falls or rises according to his worthiness and to grace, a religious hero, painfully alienated, inspired to subcreation, destined, perhaps, to share immortality by dint of grace and virtuous intent.

The continuation of the mythopoeic romance hero in contemporary fantasy fiction suggests connections between Morris's Goldmane or Golden Walter and Stephen Donaldson's White Gold Wielder. Or we may find the *alienation* of Donaldson's wounded hero Thomas Covenant more directly foreshadowed in Tolkien's work. We can see clear traces of the horizontal hero Thiodolf or Face-of-God in Brother Paul of Piers Anthony's *God of Tarot* and in the Xanth books' earthy sexuality and heroic quests. But we can also find intriguing vertical parallels between Frodo, the lowly hero caught up in great matters, and Bink or Dor in Anthony's Xanth. Regardless of exactly how we draw the lines of influence in our emerging contemporary literary tradition, Morris and Tolkien have provided the horizontal and vertical axes on which the modern fantasy hero can be plotted.

Chapter 5

SHINING PAST AND FUTURE: THE PERSISTENCE OF CAMELOT

T. H. White, like Morris and Tolkien, began his life with personal separation and loss. He was born in India, the only child of parents who "loathed each other and were separated," and White adds that he spoke Hindustani before he spoke English.[1] He was brought to England in 1911, where he was raised by his maternal grandparents; his father, and later his mother, returned to India. He was educated at Cheltenham, an English public school (what would be called a private school in the United States), followed by a year of private tutoring to prepare him for Cambridge University, where he entered Queens' College in 1925. At Cheltenham, one special teacher, C. F. Scott, encouraged White as a writer and introduced him to *Morte d'Arthur*. At Cambridge he demonstrated his sustained interest in the book by submitting an essay on Malory as part of his Tripos exam, an essay that one of his teachers recalls as "clearly the germ of *The Sword in the Stone*" (Warner, 38). However, White was diagnosed during this time with TB and given possibly less than a year to live. He postponed his studies and left England for a sustained period of recovery in the warmer climate of Italy. There he regained his health, both his writing and thinking maturing in the process; he wrote and published a volume of poems and, in 1929, earned a First Class degree with Distinction from Cambridge.

His attraction to the Arthurian stories remained strong, fresh, and alive over the next years as White taught for a time at a prep school and wrote and published nine books, several under the name James Aston (a surname borrowed from his grandparents). Then in 1938, *The Sword in the Stone* was published in London by Collins. It appeared the following year in New York, issued by G. P. Putnam's Sons, and was chosen as a Book Club selection, which guaranteed a large initial sale. In addition, Disney immediately began negotiations for screen rights. White quickly completed his second book in the cycle, *The Witch in the Wood* (1939). The success of these two books cemented his commitment to tell the full story, to complete the series of novels that eventually became *The Once and Future King*.

Many aspects of this perennial fantasy classic are interesting to explore. First, there is the direct connection to ancient British literary sources. Malory himself wrote his great work as a compilation of oral and written sources that extended from the fifth-century Latin histories of Gildas, Bede, and Nennius through French and English texts of the Middle Ages. Among other essential sources is the great Welsh body of stories *The Mabinogion*, which has served as an important source of the fantastic for such other modern fantasists as Evangeline Walton and Lloyd Alexander. White also consciously affirms fantasy's significant linguistic roots, its primary concern with language. He sets his story in the England of "Gramayre," thereby making an explicit connection with Middle English and Old French vocabulary, which preserved the link between *gramma*, something written (*gramayre* was "knowledge"), and also magical knowledge, or occult learning.[2] In Arthur's Gramayre, learning becomes not only magical but utopian. The book, like all the best works in the fantasy genre, is driven by philosophical and utopian impulses. That White created it in the shadows of the terrors of World War II only adds complexity to its utopian attempts. It is a book that celebrates, in the midst of horrors, a bright and shining moment and the civilized fellowship for justice and right principles symbolized by the round table—the perfection of an unbroken circle.

And it mixes history and imagination, past and future, in intricate patterns suggested by the "Once and Future" of its title.

White wrote and published the work in stages, almost like a serial, in three separate books; the most magical, exuberant, and poetical fantasy is found in the first, *The Sword in the Stone*. The appeal of this first volume to young readers—the reason Disney so quickly optioned it—seems similar to that of Tolkien's *Hobbit*, which had been published successfully just the year before and in a sense helped to prepare an audience for White's book. White starts his story with the loss of a lunatic governess and the need for "eddication." Young Arthur is known as Wart, which is short for Art—itself short for Arthur and also a pun on art, which is emphasized again at the end of the book when a young literary artist is appointed to learn and retell the tale.

In a departure from the pioneering writing in the fantasy genre by Morris and MacDonald, White begins his work with a strong comic touch. Sir Ector and Sir Grummore Grummursum are bumpkin aristocrats whose manners and malapropisms offer charm and amusement. Although the appeal of the writing to youngsters is unmistakable, it is also ideal read-aloud fiction, for only adults can fully appreciate the wit and allusion at every turn. White's narrator's voice thrives on anachronisms, first establishing itself with tongue in cheek and a twinkle in the eye, as in the description of Sir Grummore speculating about sending the boys to Eton, then adding the narrative remarks

> It was not really Eton that he mentioned, for the College of Blessed Mary was not founded until 1440, but it was a place of the same sort. Also they were drinking Metheglyn, not port, but by mentioning the modern wine it is easier to give you the feel.[3]

Young Arthur's first real adventure beyond the bounds of the castle occurs as he follows Kay's hawk into the wilds of an ancient forest that White refers to as "the great jungle of Old England." But although there are real dangers there, the beasts are made to seem dwarfish and slightly comic: "There were even a few dragons, though these were small ones, which lived under stones and could hiss like a kettle" (*Once*, 18). When Wart has become truly lost, he meets King Pellinore, who is engaged in a lifelong pursuit of the Beast Glatisant, also known as the Questing Beast. Pellinore, who has inherited this quest as the "Burden of the Pellinores," tracks the thing by its "fewmets . . . the droppings of the beast pursued" (23). Pellinore's description of the monster only adds to the comic effect:

> this Beast has the head of a serpent, ah, and the body of a libbard, the haunches of a lion, and he is footed like a hart. Wherever this beast goes he makes a noise in his belly as it had been the noise of thirty couple of hounds questing. (23)

However much the Questing Beast is a creature of fantasy, Merlyn, whom Wart next stumbles upon, becomes the primary locus of the fantastic in "The Sword in the Stone."[4] He is befuddled, bumbling, and slovenly, and the narrator notes his scatological features:

> some large bird seemed to have been nesting in his hair. . . . The old man was streaked with droppings over his shoulders, among the stars and triangles of his gown, and a large spider was slowly lowering itself from the tip of his hat, as he gazed and slowly blinked at the little boy in front of him. (29)

This initial image of Merlyn "streaked with droppings . . . among the stars" encapsulates the oxymoronic ridiculous, sublime, and earthy transcendence of White's style and vision. Merlyn is absentminded, subject to particular confusion with regard to time, and sometimes gets his spells muddled. But he works *real* magic, no doubt about it. And his destiny to be Wart's tutor begins to shape the rest of the story. There is delight in clever realization as young Arthur becomes aware that he has found his teacher· "his eyes sparkled with excitement at the discovery. 'I must have been on a Quest!' " (37).

White elects to adopt a body of existing mythic material as the basis of a story in the modern fantasy mode. He skillfully employs the novel—and all the techniques of modern fiction—to relate an ancient tale with all the requisite fantastic elements. His sources include all of Malory's, especially the thirteenth-century French Vulgate cycle, plus history (to the extent that Arthur is a historical figure) and literature, including two prominent Victorian writers who themselves contributed to the store of Arthurian literature—Morris (of whom he approved) and Tennyson (whom he mocked). Morris's striking early poems in *The Defence of Guen-evere* (1858) were only part of the story of his immersion in the subject; his early paintings and sketches mostly interpreted scenes from Malory,[5] and he was planning to use the poems in *Guenevere* as "the basis for an epic on King Arthur and the Knights of the Round Table" until unenthusiastic critical response to Tennyson's *Idylls of the King,* published the following year in 1859, discouraged him (MacCarthy, 147). Still, it is right to see Malory in the background of all of Morris's novels and as a continuing locus for fantasy up to the present. White is writing from both sources and mythos Morris himself might have chosen to write about had Tennyson's *Idylls* not been published.

As the tale progresses, however, White develops a narrative voice of great originality. The narrator's confidence seems to increase, and the voice matures and expands. It is a literary voice conscious of telling a great and interesting story and of telling it in certain intentional ways, as is evident by the comic anachro-nisms and explanations in the early pages. But White uses the distance and narrative awareness to increasing advantage as the book continues. Even in this first section, there are serious asides: "for this part of the story is one which deals with troubled times" (*Once,* 40). The author (as well as Merlyn, since he is living back-ward through time) is aware of the tale's largeness and of how it fits into or links with contemporary experience. The anachro-nisms so frequent in the narrative serve to place the fantasy in a contemporary context—and ultimately to relate the whole story to the crisis of values, the idea that "right is might" raised by World War II. "People in those days had rather different ideas about the training of dogs to what we have today," the narrator tells us (42–43).

There is not the same attention to language that we find in Morris or in Tolkien, but White is consciously playful in and attentive to this dimension as well. For instance, Merlyn pro-nounces words backward as he transforms Wart evolutionarily backward into a fish to begin his education metamorphosed into a small perch. There is wittiness typical of White in the sort of magic of correspondences that would allow words said back-ward to cause one to devolve into a fish. Wart is able to speak with a giant perch, who is known as King of the Moat, his vast ironic mouth permanently drawn downward in a kind of melancholy, his lean, clean-shaven chops giving him an American expression, like that of Uncle Sam. He was remorseless, disillusioned, logical, predatory, fierce, pitiless—but his great jewel of an eye was that of a stricken deer, large, fearful, sensitive and full of griefs. (51–52)

This wonderful, complex description suggests something about evolutionary origins but also comments politically on the contemporary image of America on the brink of war. The lesson is simple: "Power of the body decides everything in the end, and only Might is Right" (52). And in a second, Wart almost loses his own will (and his life) as he is nearly swallowed by the giant fish whose mouth opens

horrible and vast, skin stretching ravenously from bone to bone and tooth to tooth. Inside there seemed to be nothing but teeth, sharp teeth like thorns in rows and ridges everywhere, like the nails in labourers' boots, and it was only at the last second that he was able to regain his own will, to pull himself together, to recollect his instructions and to escape. (53)

Particularly in this first section White presents an ecology of transformation. As in Ovid, form is not fixed but changeable, and the differences between apparently separate forms can be bridged by magic. The book moves simultaneously forward (Wart) and backward (Merlyn) in time; a creature's droppings, or "fewmets" (its past), may lead the hero toward his future destiny; Merlyn is first described as "streaked with droppings over his shoulders, among the stars and triangles of his gown" (29), so we see in the magician the waste and wonder of the universe, its excrement as well as its stars. King Pellinore is linked to his Questing Beast not only by its droppings but by a *need* for it as the object of a quest. It gives purpose to his life, and a sort of love extends between them that becomes apparent when the beast languishes whenever the king is distracted from his pursuit. Finally, the book's ecology is developed through White's incorporation of another great English myth, that of Robin Hood, the green man of the woods. He is drawn into the story when Wart is concerned that Kay's education is being shortchanged because all the adventures are being allotted to the Wart. The two of them share an excursion into the deep forest, where they come to know (and to aid) the outlaw Robin. In reality, we are told, his name is Robin Wood ("like the Wood that he is the spirit of," 118), and we learn that he, like the future king, struggles for justice, endeavoring to use might for right. In the forest they help defeat the evil Morgan le Fay, Kay slays her monster Griffin, taking its head as a trophy, and Wart takes home Wat in hopes that Merlyn may help him regain his wits—which he does through "analytical psychology and plastic surgery" (119).

Just prior to the Robin Hood excursion with Kay, Wart endures his first experience as a bird when he is transformed into a merlin (cf. Merlyn/merlin) to spend the night with the hunting birds. His courage is tested and he becomes acquainted with an even more lethal and literal pecking order than that which he observed as a perch. The chanted "Ordeal Hymn" affirms that "Life is blood, shed and offered / . . . Strength to the strong and the lordly and lonely. / *Timor Mortis Exultat Me*" and concludes, "*Timor Mortis are We*" (82–83). The most deadly of the hunting birds, Colonel Culley, strikes in "the terrible moonlight," but Wart stands his ground and proves himself courageous, escaping with a scratch, bloody lines from Shakespeare's *Macbeth,* anachronistically pronounced by the colonel, ringing in his ear.

In another solitary test after the Robin Hood experience, Wart becomes an ant—an episode interpolated from White's *Book of Merlyn*.[6] In contrast to the clear individuality and unique valor tested with the birds, Wart experiences here a kind of machine society in which no individual thought is allowed. Its correspondence to Hitler's fascist state is made explicit in the programmed broadcasts of "Antland, Antland Over All" together with specific justifications and preparations for war against other ants. Wart finds this experience terrible: "A question was a sign of insanity to them. Their life was not questionable: it was dictated" (128). Set in context in this first book, the ants accelerate the questioning of an existence that dictates that creatures destroy one another, particularly others of their own species.

White is inspired in his creation of a fantasy that combines the talking-animal tradition with the Arthurian mythos. By having his young hero Wart undergo metamorphoses White allows him

last and slept on his decision. And man says, "I think that You made me in the shape I now have for reasons best known to Yourselves, and that it would be rude to change" (192); man therefore remains a "defenseless embryo." God, delighted, says, "He is the only one who has guessed Our riddle, out of all of you, and We have great pleasure in conferring upon him the Order of Dominion" (193). This is an ironic echo of Tolkien's belief that "we are made: and not only made, but made in the image and likeness of a Maker" ("FS," 52), but for all its irony it rings true. White struggled personally with issues of the nature and existence of a creator, with belief in God, and with whether or not he should become active in a church. His friend and best biographer Sylvia Townsend Warner, also a fantasy author (*Lolly Willowes; or, The Loving Huntsman*, 1926; *Kingdoms of Elfin*, 1977), records his religious struggles throughout her biography. Though White never shared Tolkien's faith, neither did he have Morris's confidence in the vitality and significance of the real. He lives up to the "white" of his name in portraying the moment of bright hope and idealism but in the end moves into darkness with far more uncertainty than Tolkien does. Nonetheless, these three masters of fantasy—each an accomplished poet and prose writer (as is Le Guin)—affirm and uplift the act of creation, celebrated in the figure of the poet or writer and, in White's case, as previously stated, illustrated in the pleasure of the narrator's voice and in the poet's appearance in its concluding pages.

At this juncture, the badger storyteller seems shy about Wart's praise for the parable but confesses doubts about God's granting of dominion and about God's blessing, for he points out "that Homo Sapiens is almost the only animal which wages war. . . . There are five ants, one termite that I know of, and Man" (193–94). The Wart confesses that he would go to war were he a knight, for in the trial of battle are to be found the virtues of great deeds, courage, endurance, and comrades whom you love. Badger poses a question: "Which do you like best, . . . the ants or the wild geese?" (194). The question remains explicitly unanswered, but the questions and the choice remain: in this case the vertical low versus high is compounded by the individualism of the geese versus the collectivism and fascism of the arts.

The first section then rapidly closes with the departure of Merlyn, the announcement of the death of King Uther Pendragon,

young Arthur's drawing of the sword from the stone, his corona-
tion, and Merlyn's return as royal adviser to announce that King
Uther was his father and to address him as King Arthur.

Book 2, "The Queen of Air and Darkness," begins with a
glimpse of childhood that dramatically contrasts that of the first
book. The four brothers—Gawaine, Agravaine, Gaheris, and
Gareth—sons of Queen Morgause, recite the story of how Pendragon had his way with their Gaelic grandmother Igraine. The
resulting child was Arthur (it unfortunately slipped Merlyn's
mind to tell Arthur this fact). Meantime, Morgause is working
dark magic, boiling a cat alive in a caldron in the dead of night.
She is one of three sisters—Morgan le Fay, Morgause, Elaine—all
of them witches and daughters of Igraine and the Earl of Cornwall. The first chapter of book 2 recites a history of racial warfare
that pits Gall against Gael—Cornwall, Orkney, Lothian against
England—a seemingly endless history of revenge. Raised with
no father, the brothers, the narrator tells us, adored their mother
"dumbly and uncritically, because her character was stronger
than theirs" (213). She seems to have neglected them, however,
her attentions having been devoted instead to satisfying her own
appetites. The boys were therefore brought up "through indiffer-
ence or through laziness or even through some kind of posses-
sive cruelty—with an imperfect sense of right and wrong. It was
as if they could never know when they were being good or when
they were being bad" (214).

The tone of the second book is immediately more somber, its
view of children and of childhood more horrific. Here the children are immediately caught up in cycles of witchery, rape,
seduction, and revenge. The animal imagery so sensitively
wrought in Arthur's childhood now suddenly turns horrid—the
black cat boiled alive by Queen Morgause, the senseless slaying
and gruesome decapitation of an enchanted, innocent unicorn
by the boys (they had hoped to attract their mother's attention
and thus maybe something resembling love). Another gruesome
image is Morgause's horrifying spell for love, which calls for a
"Spancel"—

> a tape of human skin, cut from the silhouette of the dead man. . . . the
> cut had been begun at the right shoulder, and the knife—going care-
> fully in a double slit so as to make a tape—had gone down the out-

side of the right arm, round the outer edge of each finger as if along the seams of a glove, and up on the inside of the arm to the arm-pit. Then it had gone down the side of the body, down the leg and up it to the crotch, and so on until it had completed the circuit of the corpse's outline. . . . it made a long ribbon. (306)

It is this dark charm that Morgause throws around the sleeping Arthur to cause him to love her and that gives life to his illegitimate son Mordred.

The second book is about the darker fruits of love and its results. Merlyn warns Arthur about Gwenever and reveals his foreknowing also of the treacherous love that will result in his imprisonment by Nimue; King Pellinore languishes in love for the Queen of Flanders's daughter; and the Questing Beast, pathetically, falls in love with a costumed puppet beast constructed by Sir Palomides and Sir Grummore in their attempt to shake Pellinore from his lovelorn depression. At the end of the section, while Arthur and the guests celebrate during the wedding feast of King Pellinore and his queen, a young boy excels at games. He is Lancelot, son of King Ban of Benwick, Arthur's ally at Bedegraine. So the eventual rival for Gwenever's love has been brought into the story's action.

It is greatly ironic that in this book of revenge, deceit, and treacherous love Arthur should conceive the vision of his Round Table, at which no one serves as head. As Arthur envisions it, "we must catch them young" to break the old habits of warfare: "We must breed up a new generation of chivalry for the future" (265). Arthur has conceived with youthful idealism of man's perfectibility and is driven to carry out the reconception of civilized behavior that will allow him to move beyond his history of brutality and deception in the cycles of destiny. Merlyn tries to convey a parable about destiny and seeks to explain how cycles of time will be reconceived by Einstein (286), and though he sees no way to escape destiny, he does tell Arthur, "It will not happen for hundreds of years, but both of us are to come back" and explains that on Arthur's tombstone "the once and future king" will be inscribed in Latin (287). Only several chapters later, too late, does Merlyn awaken with a start to realize he has forgotten to tell Arthur an essential, simple thing—his mother's name, Igraine, "that very Igraine . . . that the Orkney children had been talking about in the Round Tower at the beginning of this book" (310). But Merlyn's thought escapes him, "the image of Nimue already weaving itself in his sleepy brain" (311). In a dramatically parallel scene, Arthur awakens with a start to see the "black-haired, blue-eyed beauty" Morgause standing over him with the Spancel tape in her hand, and nine months later this half-sister twice his age gives birth to Arthur's first son, Mordred.

White turns into explicit critic and lecturer at the end of book 2. He reproduces a genealogical chart drawn by Merlyn and urges it on the reader: "Even if you have to read it twice, like something in a history lesson, this pedigree is a vital part of the tragedy of King Arthur." Then he concludes his lecture:

> It is the tragedy, the Aristotelian and comprehensive tragedy, of sin coming home to roost. That is why we have to take note of the parentage of Arthur's son Mordred, and to remember, when the time comes, that the king had slept with his own sister. He did not know he was doing so, and perhaps it may have been due to her, but it seems, in tragedy, that innocence is not enough. (312)

Book 3 begins once more in childhood, this time with the 15-year-old Lancelot, but now the story is weighted with tragedy. Lancelot is not the handsome hero of storybooks; White tells us he "looked like an African ape" (317). But Arthur had spoken briefly to the boy at the King Pellinore's feast, and Lancelot seemed to understand Arthur's vision immediately: "You want to put an end to the Strong Arm by having a band of knights who believe in justice rather than strength. Yes, I would like to be one of those very much. I must grow up first" (316). Now at 15 Lancelot is training and "thinking of Arthur with all his might. He was in love with him" (315).

Having set the story moving, it is almost as though White steps back to watch it unfold; he comments on it and interprets it for the reader, playing a role greater than that of storyteller. Merlyn, on a sort of honeymoon with Nimue, materializes in the French court at King Ban's castle to declare that Lancelot "will get the hope of his heart thirty years from now, and he will be the best knight in the world" (325). He also brings the boy news of Arthur's marriage and of the Round Table before he and Nimue abruptly depart.

Typical of White's interpretive distance as narrator, he observes,

> There was a feature about the great families which centered round
> the doom of Arthur. All three had a resident genius of the family,
> half-way between a tutor and a confidant, who affected the charac-
> ters of the children in each. At Sir Ector's castle there had been Mer-
> lyn, who was the main influence in Arthur's life. In lonely and distant
> Lothian there had been St. Toirdealbhach, whose warlike philosophy
> must have had something to do with the clannishness of Gawaine
> and his brothers. In King Ban's castle there was an uncle of
> Lancelot's, whose name was Gwenbors. . . . known to everybody as
> Uncle Dap. (323)

Upon Merlyn's departure, Lancelot, now 18 years old, determines to go at once to Camelot. He departs with Uncle Dap, who,
because he is a wise, humane man and a scholar of chivalry,
knows "that he had taught the finest knight in Europe" (328).

Once on English soil, young Lancelot does not wait long to
prove himself. He chances upon a black knight with whom he
jousts and delivers him a skillful fall. The knight removes his
helm to reveal himself as Arthur and immediately recognizes and
welcomes Lancelot, then takes him to Camelot, where he knights
him and presents him to Gwenever with the prediction, "He is
going to be the best knight I have" (331). White recounts some of
Lancelot's deeds that quickly earn him great fame and respect,
but he also leaves part of the telling to his literary sources: "There
is no need to give a long description of the tourney. Malory gives
it" (349). Increasingly, White extends the realm of his fantasy by
referring to literary and actual history, past and recent. The
anachronistic allusions present from the first have helped to
build these connections, and as the book moves toward its conclusion, White places ever greater emphasis on these links to various other points in temporal reality. Many authors in the fantasy
genre use this technique to place their works more firmly in a
familiar context. Although many elements of the created fantasy
detach characters and text from reality, most of the best authors
in the genre use techniques such as this to provide alternative
connections.

White accomplishes this also through increasing emphasis on
his narrator's interpretation and analysis. For example, White

uses the utopian aspects in his book to place Arthur within a real context in the history of ideas:

> He was a kind of conscientious, peace-loving fellow, who had been afflicted in his youth by a tutor of genius. Between the two of them they had worked out their theory that killing people, and being a tyrant over them, was wrong. To stop this sort of thing they had invented the idea of the Table—a vague idea like democracy, or sportsmanship, or morals—and now, in the effort to impose a world of peace, he found himself up to the elbows in blood. . . . He was one of the first Nordic men who had invented civilization, or who had desired to do otherwise than Attila the Hun had done, and the battle against chaos sometimes did not seem to be worth fighting. (364)

Arthur suffers an internal conflict as he realizes the difficulty of his struggle and as he ultimately comes to sense that he must choose sides in his assumptions about man's innate impulses toward goodness or evil. Since evidence of treachery and injustice abounds, he recognizes frequently that even "civilization" may be bad, and when he sees the deaths, greed, and suffering it has wrought he laments, "I wish I had never invented honour, or sportsmanship, or civilization" (366).[9]

The book's two most heroic characters—Arthur and Lancelot —both suffer from this type of double vision. In Lancelot's case, he faces this frightening double reality in himself and in external action. It is perhaps most dramatically presented in his encounter with a lady and her husband, a knight who is trying to cut her head off. Lancelot interposes himself in the quarrel to try to exact a promise from the knight that he will not kill the woman. He won't promise, and the lady states that he would not keep his promise even if he gave it. The knight will not fight with Lancelot, whom he has recognized by his argent as Arthur's most valiant knight, but he distracts Lancelot's attention for a moment by calling for him to look behind him at pursuing soldiers (there are none), and "at the same moment the knight leaned over to his near side and swapped off the lady's head" (360). Lancelot turns white with fury, but when he threatens to kill the murderer, the knight immediately throws himself on the ground and begs for mercy: "Lancelot put up his sword and went back from the knight, as if he were going back from his own soul. He felt in his heart cruelty and cowardice, the things which made him brave and kind" (361). Recognizing these very qualities in himself, Lancelot has tried to create their opposite in his character and actions, just as Arthur has tried to do on a larger scale with civilization. Lancelot embodies the struggle at a more personal and emotional level; Arthur personifies it in the political and philosophical sphere.

Perhaps the difference between Arthur and Lancelot is their difference in foreknowledge, for however imperfectly Merlyn has prepared the king, he has at least forewarned him of the tragic aura that will surround his life. Lancelot is no less filled from birth with the seeds of tragedy, but he is more the innocent than is Arthur, for his education has shown him less of the world's power, cruelty, and temptations. He experiences those things step-by-step, as do ordinary humans who lack wizard tutors. So in an act of valor in which he rescues Elaine from consignment to eternal torture in a boiling cauldron, he is robbed of his virginity—through deception and the sorcery of a secretly administered love potion he is doomed—by the very one he saves. He makes the point himself as he realizes what has happened:

> When I was little, . . . I prayed to God that he would let me work a miracle. Only virgins can work miracles. I wanted to be the best knight in the world. I was ugly and lonely. The people of your village said that I was the best knight of the world, and I did work my Miracle when I got you out of the water. I did not know it would be my last as well as my first. (376)

White's task as author becomes increasingly to explain his characters' psychology. He has brought the cast of Malory's *Morte d'Arthur* vividly to life, and now he gives us an explanation of their psyches, their visions and ideals, the significance of their lives. White is a master of this unusual narrative technique. The opening of chapter 16, for example (386–89), discusses the various states of mind of Gwenever, Elaine, Lancelot, and Arthur as Elaine prepares to descend on the court at Camelot with Galahad, Lancelot's son. The readers now are surely no longer the children who would easily enjoy "The Sword in the Stone." Book 3 is, in a sense, an act of scholarship performed on Malory, a work of interpretation, almost an extension of White's Cambridge undergraduate essay on Malory. Yet White creates in his narrator a point of view even more complex than that of Merlyn, who in living backward through time knows much more than the characters he passes; he derives considerable wisdom and insight from this knowledge, however befuddled it may sometimes be. Regardless of his peculiar path through time, Merlyn is still a magician, in touch with the supernatural and able to control and command natural forces. Interestingly, however, he is no more free than mortals of destiny, which encircles even magic with its tragic forces. White as author and narrator does not lay claim to magic or to control over nature (except to the extent that we as readers are aware that he is the creator of all that we behold), yet he is a tremendous force of reason and explanation, seeking always to clarify the actions he describes. Like the scholar, he seeks through logic and articulation to illuminate and set in context the significance of people and events.

In explaining Gwenever's state of mind, White offers a representative lecture from the point of view of a literary sensibility far beyond Malory's England. Interestingly, it is also a reference to a masterpiece of literary realism, Tolstoy's *Anna Karenina:*

> Yet the thought [of unfaithfulness] was probably there, unconscious and undetectable except to women. The great Anna Karenina, for instance, forced Cronsky into a certain position by the causeless jealousy of a maniac—yet that position was the only real solution to their problem, and it was the inevitable solution. Seeing so much further into the future than he did, she pressed towards it with passionate tread, wrecking the present because the future was bound to be a wreck. So with Gwenever. (388)

White treats this anachronistic character as though she were a real person and in the process directly compares his own book and its characters with the international literary mainstream.

Besieged by temporal pressure, Arthur concludes that he has made a mistake in attaching the Round Table to a "temporal ideal" and concludes, "If we are to save it, it must be made into a spiritual one. I forgot about God" (434). He decides to change the emphasis of his knights' quest from goals of justice in this world to a search for spiritual perfection, manifest in the quest for the Grail. This reach beyond the world, a typical feature of the fantasy genre, seems to have been at the heart of the book from the first. After all, Merlyn, the sword, the transcendent perspectives on time, the inevitable purity and tragedy of Lancelot's love—all of these have moved toward the nonmaterial. Yet White, like Arthur, seeks to grasp the symbol of transcendence within time.

Arthur articulates the goal; his knights set forth to achieve it. Lancelot, who knows his tragic loss of purity will keep him from this end, still enacts an extraordinary miracle. A knight from Hungary, Sir Urre, has been suffering enchanted wounds that will not heal "until the best knight in the world had tended them and salved them with his hands" (511). Arthur allows each of his knights to try, and Lancelot moves forward last of all, knowing his guilt and imperfections, believing himself incapable of miracles. But when he dresses the wounds the impossible happens, and the crowds erupt in celebration as Arthur exclaims, "It shut like a box! It shut like a box!" (513). White creates a scene full of vitality and exuberance, in extreme dramatic contrast to Lancelot's internal state of mind: "This lonely and motionless figure," White writes, "knew a secret which was hidden from the others. The miracle was that he had been allowed to do a miracle." Then White quotes Malory: "And ever Sir Lancelot wept, as he had been a child that had been beaten" (514).

This closing of the hemophiliac knight's wounds is a true miracle, a work of magic realism, since its accomplishment is dependent on the belief of all in the very definition of the enchantment. It is perhaps a minor miracle by comparison to the attainment of the Grail but a purer one in terms of consequence than the tragic, miraculous rescue of Elaine. And as White points out, the real miracle is that he has been allowed to perform a miracle. Lancelot enacts the Grail's very message—forgiveness of imperfection, grace to accomplish the impossible. And in closing the open wounds of knighthood, Lancelot in a sense heals the gaping sore that Arthur's withdrawal of the sword from the stone (however unintentionally) has promoted.

The fourth and final book of *The Once and Future King* turns toward the dark winds that blow against the vulnerable light of a single candle lit in darkness. Mordred's treachery is the inverse of Lancelot's miracle of healing and of Arthur's quest for honor, law, and spirit. Mordred is incapable of forgiveness. He distills and reenacts a strand of vengeance more ancient and unshakable than the faint light of Arthur's chivalry or law:

He became, on this matter, everything which Arthur was not—the irreconcilable opposite of the Englishman. He became the invincible Gael, the scion of desperate races more ancient than Arthur's, and more subtle. Now, when he was on fire with his Cause, Arthur's justice seemed *bourgeois* and obtuse beside him. (518)

The final pages unfold a dark drapery of destiny. The utopian flames of Camelot flicker and are extinguished as desperate, ancient impulses toward conquest, power, and revenge overtake the history whose outcome is foreknown to reader and narrator alike. Arthur's enemies will turn his very laws against him and his ideals of justice upside down. Still, in a narrative voice fully mature and reflective, White takes control as artist, shaping the final book with an artistic and patient editorial hand. The narrative voice, now far from the youthful, comic tone of the first book, portrays the very qualities of patience, forgiveness, insight, and perspective that the villains lack. Thus the young Arthur, once referred to in the shorthand "Art" and "Wart," gives place to "art" and "author" as the book concludes. King Arthur's final act is to find a boy, young Tom Mallory, whom he sends away from the final battle charged with the telling of the tale: "you are a kind of vessel to carry on the idea, when things go wrong, and . . . the whole hope depends on you alive" (637). Arthur makes explicit to the 13-year-old page that his "idea of those knights was a sort of candle . . . I have carried for many years with a hand to shield it from the wind. . . . you won't let it go out?" (637). The boy assures him he will keep it burning, and White's story deftly folds itself into art as it becomes part of literary history, for we know that Thomas Malory did keep the candle burning by creating a compelling and enduring vision that has been reinvigorated in the fresh text we are completing.

A twentieth-century writer, White created a sort of cyclic, mythical time travel. Compounded of Merlyn's backward temporality, the text's historical, linguistic, and literary anachronisms, and the prophetic "once and future" motif, the book's temporal perspective is nonlinear. Like Tolkien in his posthumously published time-travel story *The Lost Road,* White suggests that time travel is not only fully appropriate to fantasy but that unlike in science fiction, the time traveler in fantasy requires no machine to perform the task. Thus at the end of the book, as Arthur thinks about and re-creates his life in his imagination, "[t]he old King felt refreshed, clear-headed, almost ready to begin again." The book's conclusion is biblical in its paradox of alpha and omega, its end as its beginning: "Explicit Liber Regis Quondam / Regisque Futuri / The Beginning" (639).

White, finally more like Morris than like Tolkien, imagines his king as a mythopoeic, horizontal hero, one who seeks to establish a continuum between the transcendent supernatural, or spiritual, universe and the social order within history. He makes the point through the narrator's editorial comments, through Arthur's final reflections as he insists on the illusory futility of wars fought over "political geography"; such wars are particularly senseless because "the imaginary lines on the earth's surface only needed to be unimagined". White explained his understanding of his political and social message in a letter to his former tutor at Cambridge: "You see, I have suddenly discovered that (1) the central theme of Morte d'Arthur is to find an antidote to war, [and] (2) that the best way to examine the politics of man is to observe him, with Aristotle, as a political animal" (*Merlyn*, xvi). The difficulty of finding a plausible utopian model in the face of World War II is immense, but as Arthur faces his final war, he imagines his new Round Table:

> a table without boundaries between the nations who would sit to feast there. The hope of making it would lie in culture. If people could be persuaded to read and write, not just to eat and make love, there was still a chance that they might come to reason. (*Once*, 639)

For White as for Morris, the hero is not a king who rules from above, handing down his edicts from a position of authority, but a mutually acknowledged leader among brothers—the Round Table is surely a symbol of equality and commonwealth as well as of the cyclic nature of alpha and omega, or the eternal ideal— and the path through fantasy and magic leads paradoxically to reason. The world they imagined through the fantastic seemed driven by the hope "that they might come to reason."

Chapter 6

DARKENING ANTIQUITY:
SWORD AND SORCERY

Not all kings in fantasy are predictably regal. One of the most famous fantasy heroes, Conan the Barbarian, worked his way from thief to king, yet his appeal as a character is certainly not rooted in the traditional hierarchical valuation of kingship based on lineage and virtue that we find in Tolkien, or the utopian impulses of a preordained king in Arthurian legend, or even the ability to reach beyond self to anima and commonwealth, as in the case of Ralph, the king's son. Robert E. Howard reversed the path to the throne by choosing a brute as hero, thereby creating a model of barbaric superman for heroic fantasy, a path to power through muscle and might, with little affirmation of civilization or philosophy along the way. Robert E. Howard is the American prototype for a bottom-up approach to fantasy and one of the strongest influences in defining the modern subgenre known as sword and sorcery.

Beginning in 1925 with his first story, "Spear and Fang," published in the magazine *Weird Tales,* Howard explored a world of primitive, sudden violence. His fiction depicts the harsh realities of savage life that William Morris also took as a worthy literary subject in some of his treatments of the tribal Middle Ages. Morris wrote about medieval violence most vividly in his early poetry in *The Defence of Guenevere and Other Poems,* such as in "Sir Peter Harpdon's End" and "The Haystack in the Floods," and in his 1856 fantasy stories, perhaps most notably in "Golden Wings." He explored tribal life on the verge of Roman conquest in *The House of the Wolfings* and in this and other writings echoed a similarly violent, heroic model he found in the northern saga traditions. But Howard moved decisively beyond mere Gothic tribalism and northern European sagas, setting his stories in a wild, unexplored ancient world. He literally redrew the map, by placing his stories in the "Hyborian World," which exists some 10,000 years back in time. In this world, the African continent is still joined with Europe, the area of the Mediterranean Sea is dry lowlands, and what is today modern Africa is framed by the River Styx (Dante's river of hell); the land of Stygia is roughly parallel to an enlarged Egypt, and Zimbabwe, and the Black Kingdoms lie to the south. It is an oddly familiar, yet unfamiliar and untamed geography appropriate for bringing an American frontier mentality into fantasy.

Howard carried forward many of the aspects of the modern fantasy tradition as it was being developed by British authors, including Morris and H. Rider Haggard, who was one of Howard's personal favorites (his collection of books, bequeathed to Howard Payne College after his death, includes *Allan Quatermain* (1887), *The People of the Mist* (1894), and *The Ancient Allan* (1920)[1], but he elevated primitive power and brute force to new importance. Howard's development of the popular pulp-fiction, beefy model for heroic fantasy—King Kull, Bran Mak Morn, Solomon Kane, and Conan—has exerted a lasting influence, even though he was not the first to depict such characters.

Under Haggard's influence, the American writer Edgar Rice Burroughs invented a savage African setting for *Tarzan of the Apes,* which was first serialized in the magazine *All-Story* in 1912 and was published in book form in 1914. Tarzan, whom critic David Pringle has called "a remarkable creation, and the best-known fictional character of the century,"[2] was a primitive hero uniquely at home in the jungle. Adopted by apes, he had developed his instincts, strength, and senses to the fullest. The concept of an

English aristocrat's son raised in the jungle by apes offered a model for a new direction of heroic fantasy, building on the British precedents and making them even more wild and primitive. In the 23 sequels Burroughs eventually wrote, Tarzan visits the earth's core, is shrunk like Gulliver to a diminutive size, and rediscovers lost cities and species, including dinosaurs. Burroughs seems to have used Haggard's fiction as a starting point, but Burroughs made his stories more fantastic. Yet as Brian Attebery points out, Burroughs seems to celebrate as a theme the basic metaphor of "conquest, of Western man expanding his territory," and the suggestion "that man—white, male, American man—is the measure of all things."[3] Attebery faults him for his failure to probe ideas and for "embryonic Fascism" but adds that he

> had neither the insight nor the inclination to direct his fantasy toward dogmatic ends, and so any philosophical pitfalls beneath the surface of his adventures are so deeply buried as to be of danger to no one. (Attebery 1980, 118)[4]

Howard's Conan is even more physical and brutal than Tarzan, and his environment is more permeated by the dark fantastic than the worlds Tarzan explores. Howard's fiction also has more thematic density. Though Conan is the hero of more than two dozen stories by Howard and has been adopted for dozens of other books written by L. Sprague de Camp, Lin Carter, Robert Jordan, and others, *The Hour of the Dragon,* published as *Conan the Conqueror* in the version edited by L. Sprague de Camp,[5] is the only novel-length fiction with Conan as hero that Howard completed before his death by suicide at age 30. It is remarkable that this only child, born at the turn of the century in a small town in Texas, a high school graduate who had only a little college training in typing, shorthand, and bookkeeping, should have had such popular success with his short stories; it is also remarkable that a writer of short pulp fiction should deliver such a strong performance in his single Conan novel.[6]

Like Morris and Tolkien, Howard acknowledges an intuitive attraction for the distant past, a feeling that Howard said had its origins in his childhood. He recalled reading a book during a brief visit to New Orleans when he was 12 and seeing a reference to "the small dark people which first settled Britain, . . . referred to as Picts." Though the author cast them as "altogether inferior to the races which followed[,] . . . I felt a strong sympathy for this people, and then and there adopted them as a medium of connection with ancient times." [7] He came to see their name on maps at the edges of the Roman empire, and the very position of these tribesmen

> suggested terrific wars—savage attacks and ferocious resistance—valor and heroism and ferocity. I was an instinctive enemy of Rome: what more natural than that I should instinctively ally myself with her enemies, more especially as these enemies had resisted all attempts at subjugation. (Cerasini, 17)

These sympathies place him squarely yet independently in a position parallel to that of Morris in *The House of the Wolfings*. But in Howard's work, the fascination is not so much with the communal life and tribal values as with the *battles*, the opportunity for "valor and heroism and ferocity," and with the resistance to "all attempts at subjugation," a fierce dedication to freedom.

The dramatic opening scene of *The Hour of the Dragon* is an invocation of fantasy's traditions—there are a mummy case, cryptic hieroglyphics, a jewel like "a ball of living fire" known as "The Heart of Ahriman," and "an incantation that was old when Atlantis sank" (*Dragon*, 18). In the "weird greenish light" of candles a ceremony of necromancy resurrects the demon Xaltotun from a lifeless mummy:

> In the jade sarcophagus lay a living man: a tall, lusty man, naked, white of skin, and dark of hair and beard . . . his eyes wide open, and blank and unknowing as a newborn babe's. (20)

The scene is reminiscent of Mary Shelley's animation of the monster in *Frankenstein*, but the creation (or in this case resurrection) is achieved through black magic and sorcery rather than through science.[8] The blackness of the book's opening scene remains a major motif, which Howard refers to in his poetic epigram:

> And deep in the haunted mountains, the lost, black gods awake.
> Dead hands grope in the shadows, the stars turn pale with fright,
> For this is the Dragon's Hour, the triumph of Fear and Night. (17)

Orastes, who presides over the resurrection of Xaltotun, acknowledges that "we have been close to the open gates of hell this night" (20), and given the presence of the River Styx, the Stygian gloom, and the Black Kingdoms, the force of evil magic is unmistakable from the start. When Xaltotun has carried out Orastes's plan to bring plague on the people until the present king is killed and a puppet ruler in the person of Tarascus installed, Conan learns it is a stranger from Stygia who is giving counsel there and replies, "A stranger from Hell, more like!" (36).

As the Nemedian army led by Tarascus assembles to attack the Aquilonians, Conan is assaulted in his tent by a demon (Xaltotun) only he can see. Conan is a loner. Why is it that only he can see this supernatural force against him? He partially rallies himself from his paralysis in order to make himself understood. Pallantides finds an officer to don Conan's armor and ride in his stead. Chapter 2 ends with Conan wishing for the stand-in Valannus to bring him the head of Tarascus:

> In the stress of his anguish Conan's veneer of civilization had fallen from him. His eyes flamed, he ground his teeth in fury and bloodlust, as barbaric as any tribesman in the Cimmerian hills. (41)

The Aquilonians battle ferociously and eventually win the upper hand, but as they rout the Nemedian invaders on the opposite shore of the river, black magic comes into play and the cliffs collapse on nearly 5,000 men, including the impostor king. The Aquilonians flee in despair at their king's death. Conan is urged to surrender "with the dignity becoming one of royal blood" and replies, "I have no royal blood. . . . I am a barbarian and the son of a blacksmith" (48). The very idea of a barbaric king is, particularly in the context of modern history, oxymoronic: Conan is a paradoxically "uncivilized" head of a civil society. There is no doubt an implicit American rejection of the European model of monarchy, particularly all traditions of rarefied, dandified, inherited courtly royalty that are so strongly associated in cultural terms with the monarchy. But by ensconcing Conan as king—and one with clear virtues at that—Howard turns his fantasy toward recovery of another part of the lost past, a time when one led by virtue of strength, action, and example.

Whatever his shortcomings, Conan possesses many clearcut virtues. In addition to his spectacular physical prowess and courage, he has patience, stoicism, a painful, childlike honesty, and a clarity of understanding that allows him easily to reject the Faustian bargain (which drives the book's basic evil characters), in which he is offered the prospect of being restored to the throne by Xaltotun. Conan immediately asks, "What's your price?" Hearing that it is absolute obedience to Xaltotun, Conan, at the moment physically a helpless prisoner, replies,

> Go to hell with your offer! . . . I'm no figurehead. I won my crown with my sword. Besides, it's beyond your power to buy and sell the throne of Aquilonia at your will. The kingdom's not conquered; one battle doesn't decide a war. (56)

As he is carried off in chains, Conan exhibits the strength of stoicism. Howard writes, "The Cimmerian did not curse, scream, weep or rave as a civilized man might have done" (65). Instead, he draws on an independent, internal strength sufficient to prevent him from losing his freedom, whatever physical circumstances might bring. Still, as he is taken in chains deep into maze-like dungeons, the situation seems literally at its darkest. Zenobia, the first of several important women in the book, provides the means of escape. She has loved the barbarian from her first glimpse of him from afar and arranges to deliver him keys and a knife to allow him a chance at freedom. On the one hand, she is depicted as a male-fantasy stereotype of the doting female—Howard actually has her say to Conan, "The very feel of your arm about me, even in menace, is as the fulfillment of a dream" (76)—yet on the other, she and other women in the book possess resourcefulness, self-sufficiency, independence, and strength in some ways similar to Conan's. The women have a habit of coming along at just the right time to save the hero, as if the hero *needed* a woman to stay free. And they are certainly more admirable characters than most others in the book.

Though Conan's escape is made possible by a woman, it is realized only through his heroic strength. First he battles a man-eating gray ape: "half mythical and altogether horrible, these apes were the goblins of Hyborian legendry, and were in reality ogres of the natural world, cannibals and murderers of the nighted forests" (72). Yielding to "unchained blood-lust," Conan makes the mistake of attacking Tarascus in the palace and again is rescued by Zenobia, who shows him a way out. He flees by night across the countryside, then stops to drink at a well, where he encounters a Nemedian Adventurer in chain mail who recognizes him. Conan springs "with the desperate quickness that lurks in barbaric sinews" to catch the guard unawares:

> Before he could either strike or parry, the king's poniard sheathed itself in his throat, above the gorget, slanting downward into his heart. With a choked gurgle he reeled and went down, and Conan ruthlessly tore his blade free as his victim fell. (88)

Morris uses similar violence in his early story "Golden Wings":

> I turned and caught him by the ribs with my left hand, and with my right, by sheer strength, I tore off his helm and part of his nose with it, and then swinging him round about, dashed his brains out against the castle-walls. (*Golden,* 146)

The emphasis on violence, which is described in precise, gruesome detail, seems partly a reaction against the blandness of nineteenth-century life, in England represented by the bourgeois Victorians, in the United States by the quiet agrarians or middle-class tradesmen after the taming of the wild West and the collapse of authentic frontier experience. In Morris's depiction of elemental, physical confrontation and in Howard's often more elaborate use of force and violence, we are graphically reminded of our bodies, of our vulnerable flesh and blood, of the precarious and unpredictable play of life and death—and the moral decisiveness of life-and-death choices. In "civilized" routine, both today and in the times of Morris and Howard, it is easy to lose track of moral consequence when so many individual decisions have no apparent or immediate connection to simple survival.

Fantasy's natural and architectural settings for both Morris and Howard serve a similar purpose. Interior and exterior settings are not mere backgrounds; attention to their details can free us from routine perception and suggest the moral implications of environment. In Morris's early stories Gothic ruins most frequently provide the architectural context, and the creative mark of the craftsman's or artist's hand is conspicuously in evidence; his natural environment is nearly surreal and is filled with eerily precise details like those in John Everett Millais's Pre-Raphaelite painting of *Ophelia* and Holman Hunt's *The Scapegoat*. The landscape of "Lindenborg Pool," for example, contains

> steep banks of dripping yellow clay, striped horribly here and there with ghastly uncertain green and blue . . . a rank crop of dreary reeds and segs, some round, some flat, but none ever flowering as other things flowered, never dying and being renewed, but always the same stiff array of unbroken reeds and segs, some round, some flat. (*Golden*, 10–11)

In Howard's stories the architectural settings are frequently subterranean, in ancient, complex palaces, tombs, or pyramids. The architecture below and above ground is vague but complicated, representative of builders who have both great technical mastery and vast deviousness: there are traps and dungeons, secret entrances and exits, mazelike constructions that seem designed to confound as much as to enlighten or convenience those within. The natural environment in Howard's fiction is only slightly less disturbing. The world is full of creatures of violence and treachery, like the man-eating gray apes or the raven who tracks Conan in his flight from the dungeon. And the landscape ranges from "shapes in black reeking jungles" (*Dragon*, 23) to vistas of fertile, rolling farmland, the very geography stamped with the shape of man's good and bad intentions. At the beginning of *Dragon*, for example, a black plague is loosed upon the land, there is a horrifying battle in the river in which men die in shallow water, as their armor prevents their rising, and the Nemedians loose the crumbling cliffs, apparently crushing Conan and his bravest knights (46).

After Zenobia facilitates Conan's escape from the palace, the hero soon turns to a woman in the natural world to facilitate his efforts there. Zelata, an old female magician, has been rejected by the male establishment and lives in the mountains. She is able to call forth a wolf to help Conan clinch the battle with his pursuers and summon an eagle to destroy the demon raven who has tracked him. This is Conan's second deliverance at the hands of a woman, this time a figure of wisdom rather than of beauty. He looks to her for further answers, but she explains,

> I cannot save you, though I would if I might. Man must, at last, work out his own salvation. Yet perhaps wisdom may come to me in

dreams, and in the morn I may be able to give you the clue to the enigma. (102)

When she tells him the results of her dream the next morning, her advice is full of resonance: " 'Find the heart of your kingdom,' she said at last. 'There lies your defeat and your power' " (103). The reader recalls the jewel of power, the Heart of Ahriman, though Conan does not seem to understand the advice. As is typical of Howard, the statement is literal but figurative as well, since Conan's leadership *is* the heart of the kingdom, a pulse of fierce individualism, a steady refusal to yield to servitude.

Conan profits from a series of realizations in the course of the novel. Though Howard is not known as a philosophical writer, he speaks very directly about meanings from time to time: wisdom in dreams, the heart of one's kingdom. And Conan as a character benefits from lessons he learns not only through actions and advice but through his self-reflections. As he travels west through Aquilonia, he laments that the country has surrendered so easily. Because of the action at the beginning of the book, his countrymen think he is dead, yet he knows that under his leadership

> the invading army would have been forced to buy every foot they gained with their blood. This bitter realization permeated his soul; he was not the representative of a dynasty. He was only a lone adventurer. Even the drop of dynastic blood Valerius boasted had more hold on the minds of men than the memory of Conan and the freedom and power he had given the kingdom. (104–5)

Conan's insight stems from the conflict represented in the concept of the vertical and horizontal hero. And Howard's answer is different from either Morris's or Tolkien's. Morris's ideal is of radical equality, fellowship, and/or communal heroism; Tolkien affirms the conservative hierarchy of a king who should be returned to the throne, and his dynastic-blood metaphor draws on the traditional Christian rituals of salvation, which validate the shared body and blood of one king and mirror a patriarchal hierarchy in the Catholic church. In Tolkien each individual is alone, but because he works within an intricate matrix of belief there is an underlying affirmation that goodness will triumph over evil by grace. Howard's hero is as secular as Morris's but even more isolated. In his isolation he is also a catalyst, a super-man, not by token of any divine right but by dint of his own strengths.

In the passage just quoted, Howard not only expresses Co-nan's recognition that he is "a lone adventurer" but shows that he makes his claim on the hearts of the people eloquently and effectively in a manner other than through inheritance. This is the manner in which he won the throne in the first place—the people have a ready recognition not only of survival of the fittest but of kingship of the fittest. Howard holds forth a variation of Plato's philosopher-king, a vision of oligarchy in which physical strength, courage, instinctive rightness of thinking, and respect for individual freedom are united. Conan is the embodiment of this sort of king.

But at the moment, his subjects think he is dead. By the time Conan encounters Servius (106–7), we realize that, like Xaltotun, Conan has undergone death and resurrection symbolically a number of times. In addition to his apparent death in the battle of the opening pages, he has descended into the underworld and experienced a deathlike paralysis, unconsciousness, and awaken-ing. From the perspective of Servius, then, Conan appears, like the risen Christ to his disciples, to be a symbol of death and res-urrection: a king risen from the dead though a mountain has fallen on him.

It seems more than coincidental that the names of those sur-rounding Conan in the time of occupation bear Roman names. Servius, after all, is a name derived from the Latin *servus,* mean-ing "slave," the same root of the Anglo-Saxon word *serf.*[9] Servius informs Conan that the Countess Albiona is to die under the ax at midnight in the Iron Tower "because she would not become the mistress of Valerius." Albiona is another Latinate word, from the root *albus,* or "white." Albion is the old literary name for Great Britain, perhaps because of its white cliffs, but the "white" implied in Albiona's name is also a symbol that contrasts with the darkness of all of the book's enslaving forces. It is across a great cultural chasm that Servius watches Conan at the end of chapter 8, when Conan determines to attack the tower to free Albiona:

> Servius was again aware, as in the past, and now more strongly than ever, of something alien about the king. That great frame under the

mail mesh was too hard and supple for a civilized man; the elemental fire of the primitive burned in those smoldering eyes. Now the barbaric suggestion about the king became more pronounced, as if in his extremity the outward aspects of civilization were stripped away, to reveal the primordial core. Conan was reverting to his pristine type. He did not act like a civilized man would act under the same conditions, nor did his thoughts run in the same channels. He was unpredictable. (116)

Here Howard's fantasy affirms in an even more primordial way an attitude similar to that Morris expressed in his later lectures, as when he declared in 1894 that "the leading passion of my life has been and is hatred of modern civilization"[10] Howard pointed in the same direction with his famous closing lines at the end of the short story "Beyond the Black River": "Barbarism is the natural state of mankind. Civilization is unnatural. It is a whim of circumstance. And barbarism must always ultimately triumph" (Herron, 150).

Howard's words exemplify his skill for turning phrases, but they also indicate his turn back in time beyond the medieval to the primordial. And paradoxically, it is the primordial man, the uncivilized barbarian, who determines to ride against all odds toward the civilized castle, declaring, "I may be a king without a kingdom, but I'm not a man without honor" (*Dragon*, 116). At bottom, Howard finds honor in barbarism, and its ultimate triumph is in an important sense the triumph of good.

This time Conan is aided in his near-impossible task by priests of Asura, a religion that has been driven underground but whose followers feel gratitude for Conan because he did not condone their religious persecution during his time as king. Howard speaks of Conan as possessing "the broad tolerance of the barbarian" (132). Slowly the list of values grows, and tolerance, the respect for freedom of belief, is high on the list.

Yet although honor, tolerance, and freedom are allied with primordial barbarism, the sources of evil, treachery, and sorcery too have ancient roots. Hadrathus, a priest of Asura, states simply, "Age follows age in the history of the world, and now we enter an age of horror and slavery, as it was long ago" (133). Hadrathus explains that his cult's simple purpose is "to seek below the aspect of illusion" (131). In so seeking, he has seen into the heart of the sorcery Conan must confront. Howard renders the mythic history of the world, much as Tolkien does, as one long struggle of the twin forces of good and evil, dark and light. The metaphor coalesces in the jewel that restored Xaltotun to life, the Heart of Ahriman. At first Conan suspects it is the source of Xaltotun's power, but he learns that

> his power is drawn from the black gulf. But the Heart of Ahriman came from some far universe of flaming light, and against it the powers of darkness cannot stand, when it is in the hands of an adept. It is like a sword that might smite at him, not a sword with which he can smite. It restores life, and can destroy life. He has stolen it, not to use it against his enemies, but to keep them from using it against him. (138)

This discovery is another of Howard's intriguing twists: his villain is not drawing power from the jewel. Howard portrays instead "the black gulf" as a separate and potent source of power. Howard's plot contrasts strikingly with Tolkien's in that the powers of Tolkien's silmarils, or of the controlling ring, initially forces of light and goodness, are desired and used by the forces of evil and darkness. In Howard's story, his villain is stealing the power of light in order to lock it away so that it can't be used to illuminate the darkness from which his power comes. In Tolkien the preserved light and the rings' power are achieved by human craft and are associated with technology, but the jewel's illumination in Howard's tale shows nothing of technology. The inexplicable power comes from "a great jewel, like a ruby, but pulsing with blinding fire with which no ruby ever burned. It glows like living flame" (138). The jewel, interestingly, is a metaphor for the earth and for a pulsing, primordial force, a darker and more passionate light that seems far less vulnerable to destruction than Tolkien's delicate trees of light.

Conan gains strength from this information as he pursues the jewel, the Heart of Ahriman, which holds the key to the heart of his kingdom. He follows it toward the South, toward Argos, and reaches Poitain,[11] a disunited land plagued by civil war. Here he is waylaid by a village warlord, Valbroso, who has captured Zorathus, the merchant Conan has been seeking. The merchant, whom Valbroso has strung up naked on a rack, is near death, as Valbroso has been trying to force from him the secret to unlocking a heavy iron chest carved with skulls and dragons that contains the jewel. Conan speaks with Zorathus, who agrees to give the secret to Valbroso. Valbroso greedily follows the directions, pressing certain skulls and finally pushing the carved head of the dragon, where he pricks his thumb. Zoranthus laughs suddenly and wildly, taunting Valbroso with the dragon's fang, which has been steeped in the venom of the black scorpion. The chest springs open, Valbroso dies, and the jewel spills out onto the floor. But as Conan moves toward it, Beloso strikes Conan's head with the heavy iron chest, staggering the hero long enough to allow him to make off with the jewel. Conan gives chase, but reeling from the blow to his helmeted head, he blacks out when his horse loses its footing and Conan is thrown from the saddle.

This time when Conan awakens he finds he has been dragged into the forest by a monster with doglike jaws and manlike hands: "*Ghouls,* men called them, eaters of human flesh, spawn of darkness, children of unholy matings of a lost and forgotten race with the demons of the underworld" (167). It is a bleak and savage struggle, but Conan eventually extricates both himself and his stallion from the threat of these primitive, half-human forces and continues on into Argos, following a route he supposes Beloso has taken toward the port of Messantia. There, through a contact from his pirate days, Conan locates Beloso and sets out toward the house where he is staying, only to find a furtive figure leaving the house as Conan approaches. Inside he finds Beloso slain and the mark of the cult of Set on his body.[12] Conan is attacked in the dark by other figures but fights his way out to pursue the vanishing dark priest of Stygia, who now has possession of the jewel. However, at the shore he is assaulted by thugs sent by Publio to kill him. They leave him for dead, racing off to report their job complete and to doctor their wounds. But Conan, merely unconscious, is shanghaied by a nasty crew of slave traders and awakens to find himself aboard ship at sea.

Meantime, the four mysterious, unstoppable Khitans, capable of killing by a touch and of reading the future in imaginary symbols drawn on the carpet, have located Publio. They discover that Publio's men have, allegedly, slain Conan. When the Khitans check, however, they find blood on the sand, but Conan's body is gone—another image of resurrection. The Khitans demand a ship from Publio and continue their relentless pursuit.

Conan's awakening aboard the slave-trader ship results in one of the book's most violent and uncivilized episodes. As he realizes fully that he has been captured and doomed to servitude along with the black slaves, Conan thunders, "Death to the masters!" and begins freeing the captives one by one with gigantic blows from his ax, which "rose and fell without pause, and with every stroke a frothing, screaming black giant broke free, mad with hate and the fury of freedom and vengeance" (194). Conan's rage is limitless, and with the help of the black slaves he sets free, he slaughters all the whites aboard the ship. Both Conan and the slaves are described as "giants." Howard writes vividly:

> Then it was massacre. The Argosseans . . . could not stand against the maddened giants, led by the tigerish barbarian. Blows and abuse and hellish suffering were avenged in one red gust of fury that raged like a typhoon from one end of the ship to the other, and when it had blown itself out, but one white man lived . . . and that was the blood-stained giant about whom the chanting blacks thronged to cast themselves prostrate on the blood deck and beat their heads against the boards in an ecstasy of hero-worship. (194–95)

There is a kind of religious ecstasy in the scene, and Conan at this moment seems to represent the triumph of barbarism that Howard predicts. It is a reenactment in shortened version of the path by which the barbarian first won his kingdom. It is the triumph of primordial, intrinsic freedom, temporarily violated by the slave masters, who represent "civilized" society and its slave-dependent economy. The picture Howard offers of the barbarian is not pretty, but it is a portrait of primordial heroism and a radical rejection of those who chain the heroic, independent spirit:

> Conan, his mighty chest heaving and glistening with sweat, the red ax gripped in his blood-smeared hand, glared about him as the first chief of men might have glared in some primordial dawn, and shook back his black mane. In that moment he was not king of Aquilonia; he was again lord of the black corsairs, who had hacked his way to lordship through flame and blood. (195)

Howard has his freed slaves voice their triumphant responses in cadences unmistakably prophetic, in the rhythms of the Old

Testament: "Now will the Stygians howl like dogs in the night, and the black dogs of Kush will howl. . . . there will be wailing of women and the thunder of the spears" (195). The voice of freedom seems to echo the biblical history of the wandering tribes of Israel, who eventually achieved their freedom from slavery in Egypt. There is an overtone of the repeated biblical theme that the low shall be raised up. And beyond the affirmation that the instinctive, independent spirit of the individual should be freed, there is a lyrical celebration of the power of the fantasy narrator, whose imagination is able to invent, slice through, and hew its way out of any corner. Howard here depicts his own version of the liberation that is at the core of the fantasy genre. The ship with its crew of free men, now led by a natural leader, becomes a metaphor for the ship of state as it sweeps "southward like a living thing, her oars pulled now by free and willing hands" (197). The natural, "barbaric" social order that triumphs preserves freedom and achieves an ideal, organic society, such as that of the state of Aquilonia, vital and thriving under Conan before the onslaught of dark forces. These strands of Howard's tale echo Morris's utopian instincts and Tolkien's biblical grounding. But in Howard's Conan saga, lurking at the edge of the idealism, faith, and strength is an overwhelming darkness and despair that can at any moment gain the upper hand. Howard's grounding in biblical rhetoric also lacks the bedrock of faith in language and in grace that permeates the Tolkien mythos.

The extent of the dark powers in *The Hour of the Dragon* is given voice in Orastes's late but urgent confessions in the royal palace in Tarantia as Amalric and the two kings, Tarascus and Valerius, as they contemplate the chaos that overruns their lands. Orastes has recognized, too late, the extent of the evil Xaltotun represents. He explains that he knows the individual has limits and therefore limits of evil influence, since he can sin "only to the extent of . . . personal individuality" (236). What he sees through Xaltotun is the depth of ancient evil magnified over time, for "behind Xaltotun lie a thousand centuries of black magic and diabolism, an ancient tradition of evil. He is beyond our conception" (236–37). Yet Orastes has at last attained a faint conception of the dark forces their small, individual acts of evil have unleashed. He suggests that Xaltotun would unweave even the fabric of time "by the sorcery of a gigantic blood-sacrifice such as the world has never seen. He would enslave the world, and with a deluge of blood *wash away the present and restore the past*" (237). This is the dark opposite of the New Testament metaphors of forgiving the sins of the past through the blood the lamb. Instead, Howard presents the dark reality that the blood may be literal and a "blood-sacrifice" so great as to undo the present. He presents the dangers of romanticizing a past that may very well be more evil than the present. His grasp of the enslaving power of evil and of its accretion of force or magnitude over time may be part of what led to Howard's suicide in 1936.[13] In any case, whatever the author's possible reluctance to face his own demons, in Conan he has imagined a hero equal to the challenge.

Orastes has grasped that Xaltotun seeks the literal restoration of Acheron and the old order he represents. Traditionally, Acheron is the river of woe in Hades, across which the dead are ferried by Charon. Howard's fantasy portrays the enduring reality of evil and the nearly unfathomable strength required for a successful struggle against it, perceptions that are easily lost to "civilized" readers who enjoy the veneer of material comfort in their everyday lives. He insists that we view what is built on the surface of the present in terms of what is beneath it. The evil in his fiction flows from beneath the surfaces, from catacombs and tombs and other underground sources. But in the end, paradoxically, followers of an underground religion come to Conan's aid.

While Xaltotun savors the blood sacrifices of the armies being slaughtered below him, he stands at an ancient altar on a mountaintop, ready to sacrifice a virgin for the final sorcery with which he plans to assure his victory. But suddenly he finds on the summit beside him the dark-hooded priest Hadrathus, whose religious freedom Conan preserved, and the old peasant woman with her wolf. They witness Xaltotun's final defeat as Hadranthus produces the Heart of Ahriman from beneath his black robes, and a beam of "blinding blue light" undoes the spell of necromancy with which the book began. Xaltotun is reduced to a shriveled mummy and carried back to Acheron by spirit horses while Hadrathus and Zelata bear mute witness. In a final symbol of romantic comedy, Howard has Conan reunite with Zenobia, and Conan restates in his own marriage the book's liberation motifs: "She was a slave in Nemedia, but I will make her queen of Aquilonia!" (275).

The final pages tie together too neatly, perhaps, but this is in the nature of Howard's fantasy, and as a wholesome order is restored, a slave transformed into a queen is a powerful image with which to close.[14]

Chapter 7

COMPLETING THE CIRCLE: LANGUAGE, POWER, AND VISION

Over the course of nearly three decades—from her 1964 short stories "The Word of Unbinding" and "The Rule of Names" through her 1990 novel *Tehanu,* the last book of the Earthsea cycle—Ursula K. Le Guin has created a fantasy world where language deeply matters. Earthsea's magic is based on language, and a knowledge of the secret aspects of language is the essence of power. Character, place, and plot all play important parts in the success of Le Guin's fiction, but her explorations of language in the style, tone, and themes that unfold in her works seem the heart of her achievements.

The significant presence of language at the center of Le Guin's artistic vision in the Earthsea books is in some ways comparable to the linguistic inspiration that J. R. R. Tolkien acknowledged underlies *The Lord of the Rings;* he said in his introduction to the second edition that his work was "primarily linguistic in inspiration" (*LOTR,* 1:3). Even the titles of Le Guin's earliest Earthsea stories—"The *Word* of Unbinding" and "The Rule of *Names*" (italics mine)—reiterate the importance of language in her work. Yet although the creators of Middle-earth and Earthsea share a love of language, these two authors who have been so influential in defining the shape of modern fantasy differ significantly in the details and results of their approaches.

Both writers embody in their work an intensification of the basic characteristic of fantasy writers to emphasize the use and invention of language itself. It is an impulse at once modern or postmodern—like that of the visual artist who pays as much attention to the medium as to the content—and ancient, echoing the magic of the word as preserved on the earliest Egyptian fragments of fantastic hieroglyphics, the magical aspects of White's Gramayre, Frye's belief that "the real hero becomes the poet." A close examination of Le Guin's Earthsea cycle, including some observations of the similarities and differences in Le Guin's and Tolkien's linguistic emphases, may help to clarify the structural and thematic implications of the works' interplay of language, power, and vision, particularly as they are resolved in *Tehanu*.

First, it is important to observe that Le Guin consciously builds on the techniques and characteristics of fantasy Tolkien established. *The Lord of the Rings* was popularly perceived as a trilogy (and helped create great popularity for trilogies and cycles of tales), and Le Guin's Earthsea cycle first achieved its popular identity as "the Earthsea trilogy"—*A Wizard of Earthsea, The Tombs of Atuan,* and *The Farthest Shore*—published over four years, between 1968 and 1972. Le Guin carefully mapped the books' terrain and used some of Tolkien's favorite landscape features, such as mountain, cavern, and sea, as their most significant settings. As in Tolkien's fiction, the imaginary world includes a mythological creation story that gives depth and roots to present time, and the origin of Earthsea even specifically mirrors elements of Tolkien's creation myth. According to Le Guin, Earthsea began with the word *Éa,* uttered by Segoy when he caused the earth to rise up from the seas. Though the myths differ in many respects, the word that brings the world into being in Tolkien is practically the same: *Eä.* Tolkien's word is defined as verb and noun: "*Eä!* Let these things Be!" or "the World that Is."[1] Le Guin varies her word by removing the diaeresis on the *a* and placing a diacritical stress on the first letter, *Éa.* Her word also deftly mirrors the beginning and end of the word for her world, Earthsea—*E* from the first letter of "Earth," *a* from the final letter of "sea."[2]

Another literary technique Tolkien used that is strongly established in *The Wizard of Earthsea* is the frequent allusion to ancient oral traditions and poems (all of them the author's creations), the songs and stories that preserve Earthsea's history. Primary among these is *The Creation of Éa*, five lines of which are used as an epigram for the first book, and which is quoted from and alluded to in the subsequent volumes. Other important texts Le Guin refers to include *The Deed of Ged, Deed of Enlad, Matter of the Dragons, Song of the Sparrowhawk, Deed of the Young King*, and the *Deed of Erreth-Akbe*. The finding of a ring is important, and the ring is written with nine runes of power. (In Tolkien there is one Ring that rules nine Rings of Power.) There is the sinking of an island like Atlantis, Soléa, which was lost beneath the sea. (In Tolkien it is Númenor, also called Akallabêth or Atlantë.) There is a dragon, too, in Earthsea—more than one, in fact, but whereas the dragons in Tolkien are evil forces to be destroyed, in Le Guin what begins as a childish perception of dragons as evil creatures that must be destroyed ends with man and dragon speaking the same language and ultimately sharing the same identity.

Having noted some of the similarities between Tolkien and Le Guin, it is appropriate to state some differences as well. Le Guin, although interested in a language base, is not a philologist. She provides only suggestive linguistic detail in her novels, offering the most extensive information about Old Speech, the language of creation, wizards, and dragons, and only scant examples and details of other language systems. In fact, Le Guin has said,

> No use trying to make a lexicon of Hardic or of the True Speech; there's not enough in the books. It's not like Tolkien, who in one sense wrote *The Lord of the Rings* to give his invented languages somebody to speak them. That is lovely, that is the Creator Spirit working absolutely unhindered—making the word flesh. But Tolkien is a linguist, as well as a great creator.[3]

The Earthsea cycle, although its works are closely interconnected, or interlocked, is clearly composed of four distinct novels, in contrast to Tolkien's single *Lord of the Rings*, which is manifestly one book, divided into three volumes only artificially. Critic Richard West has noted what he calls the "interlace structure" of *The Lord of the Rings*,[4] and in Tolkien's novel the interlacing is so complete that it extends beyond that book to include *The Silmarillion* and many of the other supporting texts that remained unpublished during his lifetime.

Le Guin's novels philosophically are rooted in Eastern as well as Western traditions and have an individual psychology of revelation significantly different from the scriptural pattern of revelation underlying Tolkien's works. Characters, too, are much more individual in Le Guin, and the women more important. Her books are more intimate, less vast and cosmic in scope. There is a consistent tenderness in the tone of her poetic prose and in the interactions of her characters. The works evince a lyrical impulse quite different from Tolkien's harsher epic mode. Love is a different emotion in her work and assumes a different scale of importance. The contrasts are found not only on the emotional and stylistic levels; the physical created world of Earthsea is vastly different in conception from Tolkien's Middle-earth. There is far less solid ground in Le Guin, and lands are far less physically interconnected. Hers is a world of islands, many of them tiny. One of the most significant episodes takes place on rafts, where the physical ground that supports human civilization is nothing more than timbers strung together to make individual crafts that congregate for a time each year to form a kind of tribe or village.[5]

Le Guin's creatures have a unity different from the markedly distinct races found in Tolkien.[6] All the islands are filled with people, the only apparently different species being Dragons (who are ultimately shown to share identity with people too). In Tolkien we have Hobbits and Dwarves, Elves and Ents, Giants and Trolls, and more. (Le Guin originally included a troll character in "The Word of Unbinding" but decided it was a "mistake" and so abandoned it in the novels.)

Whereas Tolkien's mythos involves a splintered world of loss, of separate peoples forever fragmented and divorced from a once perfect, harmonious creation—a pattern that conveniently parallels Western traditions that separate flesh and spirit, god and man, male and female—Le Guin's creation is built on a paradox of identity in which the beginning and the end are one, akin to Eastern traditions in which yin and yang, dark and light, death and life, silence and the word, are one.[7]

In the first book, *A Wizard of Earthsea,* Le Guin establishes the rules of power in Earthsea. Each entity has its "true name," and

those who know and call the name control the entity. Brian Attebery points out in *The Fantasy Tradition in American Literature* that

> Le Guin is taking her concept of magic from a different source than
> Tolkien's. She has gone right past courtly romance and peasant lore
> to the universal beliefs of tribal societies. Hers is the magic of ritual
> name-bestowal, and singing to the hunted animal, and In the begin-
> ning was the Word. Her wizards are shamans, witch doctors. Like
> Claude Lévi-Strauss, she revives the ancient, magical view of the uni-
> verse, the so-called savage mind, as an interesting alternative to our
> mechanistic, scientific view of the cosmos. (Attebery 1980, 168)

This first novel concerns itself with Sparrowhawk's boyhood and
education: "At first all his pleasure in the art-magic was, childlike,
the power it gave him over bird and beast."[8] Le Guin associates
this link of word with power as a childish perception (quite different from Tolkien's characters, who are almost always driven,
even as adults, by desire for power and reenact, generation after
generation, power struggles one with another, waged partly by
the power of word against word as the eternal battle of good and
evil continues to rage). Sparrowhawk's education is the learning
of true names. His mother died before he was a year old, but
Sparrowhawk's aunt, his mother's sister, teaches him a little
magic language—word by word and spell by spell—until, by the
time he reaches age 12, he has mastered all this village witch can
teach him.

Sparrowhawk demonstrates his abilities to apply power by
calling up a fog to confuse invading raiders attacking his village.
The story of his deed is widely told and reaches the wizard
Ogion the Silent, who seeks out Sparrowhawk and gives him his
true name: *Ged.* This is one of Le Guin's clever inventions, an
echo of "God" but for a change of vowel, capable of being pronounced as easily as Jed. Le Guin has fervently denied any connection between Ged and God, but what do artists know about
their own work anyway? She wrote in "Dreams Must Explain
Themselves" that

> A man who read the ms.... thought "Ged" was meant to suggest
> "God." That shook me badly. I considered changing the name in case
> there were other such ingenious minds waiting to pounce. But I
> couldn't do so. The fellow's name was Ged and no two ways about it.

> It isn't pronounced Jed, by the way. That sounds like a mountain moonshiner to me. I thought the analogy with "get" would make it clear, but a lot of people have asked. (*Language,* 47)

Le Guin's preference for pronunciation of Ged with a hard *g* only reinforces its echo of "God"; and if we can believe Le Guin when she says that she "found" the name "in my subconscious," if we take unconscious wordplays and Freudian slips seriously (especially in fantasy), and if we recall that Le Guin has also said, "I am an artist . . . and therefore a liar. Distrust everything I say. I am telling the truth,"[9] it is absolutely clear that Ged is in one sense an artistic invention approximating God but for a vowel.

Ged is apprenticed to Ogion, and his real education begins with Ogion's maxim: "To hear, one must be silent" (*Wizard,* 18). He also begins to be taught by Ogion the principle of balance practiced by the wizards, but life with the quiet, simple mage does not move quickly enough or dramatically enough to satisfy Ged, who "wondered what was the good of having power if you were too wise to use it" (18). Ogion then agrees to send him to the school for wizards on the island of Roke.

At first, there in the presence of the Archmage Nemmerle, he thinks of himself as "a word spoken by the sunlight" (35). But Ged will come to see himself as *both* sunlight and shadow, for the other students' power plays and rivalries of pride lead Ged in a dangerous direction. In this bildungsroman on the archetype of the sorcerer's apprentice (see Attebery 1980, 173), Le Guin provides some passages of very direct teaching. When the Master Hand in the Court of Seeming tries to explain the difference between illusion and real change, he uses a rock, which he names *tolk* in True Speech. The plain rock will recur as an important image in the later books, so this early explanation becomes increasingly resonant as the narratives unfold. Ged has used an illusion spell to make an ordinary rock appear to be a diamond. He wants to know how to make this change actual and permanent. The Master explains that the language of illusion can make the stone look like a diamond, a flower, a fly, an eye, or even a flame—each of the Master's words changing the appearance of the stone to fit the word. But his point is that although it appears to be separate, the stone is a part of Roke Island, an integral part of the larger world. Small words of illusion may alter the appearance, but real change requires a different order of language:

To change this rock into a jewel, you must change its true name. And to do that, my son, even to so small a scrap of the world, is to change the world. It can be done. . . . But you must not change one thing, one pebble, one grain of sand, until you know what good and evil will follow on that act. The world is in balance, in Equilibrium. A wizard's power of Changing and of Summoning can shake the balance of the world. It is dangerous, that power. It is most perilous. It must follow knowledge, and serve need. To light a candle is to cast a shadow. . . ." (*Wizard,* 43–44)

But before Ged understands the cautions and the balance, his pride involves him in a contest with another boy, and he summons up from death the spirit of a legendary beautiful woman, at the same time releasing a dark presence that cannot be recalled: "He sought for protection, but there was none: the thing was not flesh, not alive, not spirit, unnamed, having no being but what he himself had given it—a terrible power outside the laws of the sunlit world" (83).

Ged undergoes a trial by shadow and slowly faces the consequence of what he has done, learning to see the truth in paradox and balance:

Ged had neither lost nor won but, naming the shadow of his death with his own name, had made himself whole: a man: who, knowing his whole true self, cannot be used or possessed by any power other than himself, and whose life therefore is lived for life's own sake and never in the service of ruin, or pain, or hatred, or the dark. In the *Creation of Éa,* which is the oldest song, it is said, "Only in silence the word, only in dark the light, only in dying life . . ." (181)

The last passage, from the *Creation of Éa,* is used as an epigraph in each book in the cycle, reiterating this central principle at each novel's start. This recognition is explained by Ged's good friend Vetch at the end of the book, and the final act marks Ged's full entrance into manhood and his complete sense of his own identity and power. A first cycle is completed. A lesson is learned, a quest closed, a chapter finished.

Here the interlocking but discreet and separate model can be seen (as contrasted to Tolkien's continuous unraveling narrative). There is a completion in each of Le Guin's novels, but the end brings a new beginning. Ged has completed one stage of his life and is ready for the next. His knowledge of himself, his recognition of the sunlight and the shadow of his nature, liberates him from childhood and its childish fears and desires and allows him to move on to a new stage of life.

Ged's journey has taken him from the surface of the world to the depths of the self, as the shadow had to be named and embraced in a fable of identity. When Ged finds half of a broken ring near the end of the first book, Le Guin, employing a literary technique similar to one frequently used by Tolkien, observes that "the truth of his guess he did not learn until, years later, the quest of the Ring of Erreth-Akbe led him to the Kargad Lands, and to the Tombs of Atuan" (142–43). The finding of part of a broken ring, the reference to the new quest, and other clues tie the first book to the second; each detail is used to lock the separate parts of one cycle to the next.

The style, theme, and subject matter of *The Tombs of Atuan* are appropriately more mature. Darkness, silence, tenderness predominate, but there is a harshness and a cruelty that make the gentler aspects all the more clear. The second book narrates a female rite-of-passage drama that parallels the male rites in the first book but is constructed on the basis of opposites in many ways. Tenar is a young girl taken from her family into darkness, robbed of her identity to serve "the Nameless Ones." (Here the literary echo is more strongly that of Morris's young heroine Birdalone in *The Water of the Wondrous Isles,* who was kidnapped as a helpless toddler by the Witch-wife and carried off to captivity in Evilshaw.) In contrast to Ged, who feels power grow within him as a boy, the girl is robbed of her name and identity and power. She is forced to serve the nameless, ancient forces of the tomb, powers "who ruled before the world of men came to be, the ones not named, and she who served them had no name."[10]

She is taught about the wizards: "They have no gods. They work magic, and think they are gods themselves. But they are not" (*Tombs,* 50). When she asks about where they get their power, she is given two answers: "Lies" and "words" (50). Here then is a perspective that views "true names" as lies, that equates words and lies. Ged enters the narrative just after the middle of the book. He has come to the tomb in search of the other half of the Ring of Erreth-Akbe, which when made whole can usher in a reign of peace for all of Earthsea. Tenar (who is called Arha, "the Eaten One," when she loses her given name in a ritual of being devoured by the Nameless Ones) traps Ged there and questions him. He answers honestly, "I came to rob them" (79). The very truth of his reply belies the concept that wizards' words are lies.

Arha is drawn toward this faint bit of light in the darkness of her tombs. She cannot bring herself to kill Ged for violating the territory of the Nameless Ones. Gradually she is attracted to him, the only male in an underground maze of female and eunuchs. Then he calls her by her name, Tenar, triggering a sequence of revelations that begins with a dream in which a woman reminiscent of her mother also whispers "Tenar." Le Guin moves the narrative deep into the psyche and psychology, centering significance in a personal, interior landscape, a dream within dream. In a lyrical passage of great beauty and exhilaration Tenar dreams she wakes, and Le Guin writes, "Her despair grew so great that it burst her breast open and like a bird of fire shattered the stone and broke out into the light of day" (96). Then Tenar *really* wakes and looks into the *real* morning sky:

> High up, so high he caught the sunlight and burned like a fleck of gold, a bird was circling, a hawk or desert eagle.
> "I am Tenar," she said, not aloud, and she shook with cold, with terror, and exultation, there under the open, sunwashed sky. "I have my name back. I am Tenar!" (96)

Unlike Tolkien's quest in *The Lord of the Rings*, the quest here is to find and rejoin a broken ring rather than to destroy a whole and dangerous one. (Again, Le Guin turns a Tolkien-inspired fantasy of recovery toward a Morrisian vision of regaining wholeness on a human, communal, psychologically integrated scale that is more earthly than cosmic.) The reuniting of Tenar with her name—which is also a joining of interior and exterior, light and dark, male and female—begins a process of union and illumination. Ged guides her to recognize her shadows as somewhat akin to the shadow he named and recognized at the end of the first book:

> They have no power of making. All their power is to darken and destroy. They cannot leave this place; they *are* this place; and it should be left to them. They should not be denied nor forgotten, but neither should they be worshiped. The Earth is beautiful, and bright, and kindly, but that is not all. The Earth is also terrible, and dark, and

cruel. . . . They exist. But they are not your Masters. . . . You are free, Tenar. You were taught to be a slave, but you have broken free. (106–7)

From the breaking comes a joining, for the two halves of the broken Ring of Erreth-Akbe can be reunited, and Tenar wears the joined band on her arm as she and Ged leave the tombs together.

Ged then explains to her the nature of the magic he "weaves":

> Once, at the beginning of time, when Segoy raised the isles of Earthsea from the ocean deeps, all things bore their own true names. And all doing of magic, all wizardry, hangs still upon the knowledge—the relearning, the remembering—of that true and ancient language of the Making. (107)

The wizard's training, then, consists of finding out the names and of learning "ways to use the words" (107). There is a romantic notion here that can be traced back to Plato: that learning is remembering, and the wizard's job, like that of the literary artist, is to find ideal ways to use the words. Le Guin makes these aesthetic concerns explicit throughout the cycle by using the term "art magic," and in her incisive commentary in "Dreams Must Explain Themselves" she observes,

> The trilogy is, in one aspect, about the artist. The artist as magician. The Trickster. Prospero. . . . . Wizardry is artistry. The trilogy is then, in this sense, about art, the creative experience, the creative process. There is always this circularity in fantasy. The snake devours its tail. Dreams must explain themselves. (*Language*, 48)[11]

By leaving the tomb, Tenar reenacts an archetypal pattern of death and rebirth: "To be reborn one must die, Tenar," Ged tells her (*Tombs*, 114). In fact, the experience in the tombs is a death and a rebirth for both of them. They have emerged from wordless darkness, a power of death and absence, before the words of the Making, and from a silence that could almost swallow up the voice. The experience is couched in metaphors of dark and light, above and below ground, but the pair emerges at last from the tomb/womb to be reborn surrounded by metaphors of language and silence, for at the end Tenar moves away from her darkness "shrieking in a thick voice not her own, as if a dead tongue moved in her mouth" and almost falls back "into the crumbling, lipless mouth of the Tombs" (122). As the tombs are shaken and the great stones above fall inward, "the raw black lips of the crack closed together" (123).[12]

Both Ged and Tenar are metaphorically reborn, but the experience is most dramatic in terms of Tenar's changed perceptions, for this book is primarily a treatment of the female principle or experience. At the end Le Guin writes simply that "[s]he felt newborn" (131). Ged begins to teach her a new language. And the final image is a memorable one of the two united as they return the Ring, now whole, to Havnor at the center of the Making: "Gravely she walked beside him up the white streets of Havnor, holding his hand, like a child coming home" (146).[13]

The first two books of the Earthsea cycle thus recount coming-of-age stories for two children, a male and a female. Both of them are initiated into secret power centers and become aware of forces larger than themselves: Ged is allied primarily with the powers of light and naming; Tenar is joined to the forces of darkness and silence. Each must meet and embrace the opposite to engage the rite of passage: Ged's naming of his shadow, Tenar's remembrance of her name of light amid darkness. The reader might expect this pattern to be completed by the conjunction of these forces in the cycle's third and once-final novel, *The Farthest Shore*. This is not the case, however. *The Farthest Shore* is the story of Ged's quest as Archmage to repair a tear in the fabric and balance of Earthsea caused by a selfish human quest for immortality. The situation is precipitated by a twisted magician who has escaped death. Le Guin describes the subject as death, for a recognition of one's own mortality "is the hour when childhood ends, and the new life begins. Coming of age again, but in a larger context" (*Language*, 50). Tenar plays no part in this story. It is again a tale of male rites of passage, a second mode of maturation for Ged and a coming-of-age for Arren, heir to the throne of Enlad and descendent of Morred and the ancient kings. That this final novel in the trilogy is male dominated is perhaps one of the reasons Le Guin describes the books as "a four-legged chair missing a leg."[14] The publication of *Tehanu* in 1990 provided the balance.

Tehanu, set nearly two decades later than *The Farthest Shore*, picks up Earthsea's narrative and settles many unresolved issues. Its focus is the corruption of male power under the influence of the twisted values that characterize *The Farthest Shore*, chief among them man's passion for the ultimate power of immortality. The results of this twisted male dominance are made flesh in the curse of a living death for an innocent female child. The narrative describes the events of Tenar's life after her escape from the Tombs of Atuan. She remained awhile on Gont with Ged's mentor, the mage Ogion, then chose to marry a farmer and raise two children. A widow when the story opens, Tenar, who is now known as "Goha"—"which is what they call a little white web-spinning spider on Gont" (*Tehanu*, 1)—assumes the care of a young girl who has been abused and severely burned by the males of her family, pushed into a fire and left for dead.

With the help of two other women, Lark and Ivy, Tenar keeps the child alive, though one side of her face is horribly deformed and one eye has been lost. When the girl is seven, Tenar is summoned to attend Ogion's death. She takes the girl with her and on their long walk tells her a story she heard from Ogion of an old woman from the seaport, whom he recognized by her true name, "Dragon!": "In that first moment . . . it was not woman he saw at all in the doorway, but a blaze and glory of fire, and a glitter of gold scales and talons, and the great eyes of a dragon" (*T*, 11). As he looks again she is a haggard old woman, who refuses to answer if she is dragon or woman but offers instead to sing him a story:

> When Segoy raised the islands of the world from the sea in the beginning of time, the dragons were the first born of the land and the wind blowing over the land. So the Song of the Creation tells. But her song told also that then, in the beginning, dragon and human were all one. They were all one people, one race, winged, and speaking the True Language. (12)

This myth echoes the Platonic legend recounted by Aristophanes in the *Symposium* of a time when man and woman were one. The old woman's story tells how dragons and humans changed over time, but there is a remnant of the undivided people, "great winged beings both wild and wise, with human mind and dragon heart" (13). The story hangs in the air, hinting that this book is about dragons in a major way. After Ogion dies, the dragon Kalessin arrives on the cliff near Ogion's cottage bearing Ged, so weak he is scarcely alive.

The issue of power has clearly been reconceived in this book, which speaks from first to last of gender issues. The exploration of power begins with the plight of Tenar, a widow unable to inherit her husband's farm because the social order requires that it pass instead to the eldest son; then the female child, Therru, is depicted as helpless and victimized nearly to destruction by the men in her family; finally, there is Moss, the witch near Ogion's cottage who is a woman of great strength, depth, and promise. Moss has "lived on a few words of the True Speech" (36), for women are not eligible to become mages. She alerts Tenar, who has been tutored by the wise mage Ogion, to a deeply female power: "He does you great honor, teaching you. But look and see, child, if all he's taught you isn't finally to follow your heart" (37).

The relationship between language, power, and vision evolves throughout the Earthsea cycle, and the reader's understanding, perhaps together with the author's, takes clearer shape over time. At first it appears that language, power, and vision are external phenomena. Language is about control and power drawn from ancient sources. Vision, as in the vision of the dead spirit Ged summons before he is ready to control it in *The Wizard of Earthsea*, is external and imbued with power greater than that of the self. However, even by the end of the first book, Ged has named this exterior shadow vision with his own name, and the language, power, and vision become increasingly interior. In *The Tombs of Atuan* the very claustrophobia of the dark interior spaces leads toward introspection and surrealistic vision, but real power rests with the male God/king outside the tombs, and the woman of potentially the greatest power is shown to have been robbed of all *real* power by having been deprived even of her name. When she responds to Ged's presence without killing him there is something instinctive, perhaps a prompting of the heart, that asserts a kind of vision and ultimately restores language, power, unity, and balance.

In *The Farthest Shore*, as Ged's body ages and weakens he is set against a young foil of great power, for Arren will be king of all Earthsea. Vision wobbles between deceptive external, drug-induced visions of Hazia, delusions-of-power visions fed with the false promise of the ultimate power of immortality. But Arren, who throughout the novel is aware of and amazed at the feelings of love that bind him to Ged, is witness to a process of vision at once hallucinatory and interior. The story's progress through an external geography toward the western island that is the farthest away is ultimately linked through language and metaphor to an interior landscape, for the final lands they cross are death and pain and despair, interior realities that control and shape the external world.

In her final book, Le Guin seems to have felt the need to make explicit the false sexist power plays imposed on the women and perpetuated in the slogans repeated from book one: "*Weak as woman's magic, wicked as woman's magic*" (*Wizard*, 5). Now that Ged has violated the male principle of imposed power, linked to the strong women in this novel he becomes a perfect foil for Le Guin's observations on the male-female balance and the final intertwining of language, power, and vision. From the first she focuses on the heart. Therru's face and one eye have been mutilated by the fire imposed by males. The book becomes in one significant aspect an explicit repudiation of exterior male dominance and a text that seeks to document and thereby exorcise to some extent the violations of balance this dominance has wrought.

Early in the book, in another conversation between Tenar and Moss, the differences between male and female power becomes explicit when Moss explains of wizards, "His power's himself, see. . . . And that's all. When his power goes, he's gone. Empty" (*Tehanu*, 56). When Tenar asks about a woman's power, Moss tells her,

> Oh, well, dearie, a woman's a different thing entirely. Who knows where a woman begins and ends? Listen, mistress, I have roots, I have roots deeper than this island. Deeper than the sea, older than the raising of the lands. I go back into the dark. . . . Before the moon I was. No one knows, no one knows, no one can say what I am, what a woman is, a woman of power, a woman's power, deeper than the roots of trees, deeper than the roots of islands, older than the Making, older than the moon. Who dares ask questions of the dark? Who'll ask the dark its name? (57)

Tenar replies, "I will. . . . I lived long in the dark."

Tenar's calm in the face of darkness, her willingness to try to put even the most ancient unilluminated roots under the power of language, suggest that the capability for vision may provide the consumate opportunity for insight and for transformation. The ultimate male power has been thought to be embodied in the dragonlord, "a man dragons will talk to" (68). Tenar finds she is a "woman dragons would talk to" (68), and this is a "new thing" she must understand and find some way to express.

As Ged speaks to her of his own loss of power—"All I had in the end was one cup of water, and I had to pour it out on the sand, in the bed of the dry river, on the rocks in the dark. So it's gone. It's over. Done" (78–79)—Tenar's eyes catch a glimpse of the stars, and she sees one called "Tehanu" in her own language. It is a glimmer of light in darkness, of language in silence, but it awakens an intuition of vision beyond language; it is something she intuits about Ged and Therru both but expresses first in terms of Ged: "Before he had his name, before he had knowledge, before he had power, the hawk was in him, and the man, and the mage, and more—he was what we cannot name. And so are we all" (84). This expression of vision and power beyond language, beyond naming, beyond the most ancient time is grasped by women, and Le Guin reinforces here that something like this instinct of heart prompted the link between Tenar and Ged that liberated them both from the darkness and the tombs. This same instinct has drawn her toward Therru, who will prove to offer an even more significant recovery of the balance by the end of the book. (It also echoes the tender adolescent, almost sexless leap of love Arren feels for Ged in *The Farthest Shore*.)

The book's central point or fulcrum occurs nearly at the midpoint of the text, embodied in a vision and captured in an eloquent image. In another conversation with Moss about the differences between men and women, Tenar says,

> It seems to me we make up most of the differences, and then complain about 'em. I don't see why the Art Magic, why power, should be different for a man witch and a woman witch. Unless the power *itself* is different. Or the art. (109)

Moss then sums up succinctly: "A man gives out, dearie. A woman takes in" (109). Although there is truth and insight in Moss's statement (and it parallels sexual archetypes as well as the narrative patterns Le Guin has woven—Ged gave out his cup of water; Tenar took in Ged and Therru), it is a vision only of opposites, like light and dark; it is a recognition of differences rather than an intuition of oneness, wholeness, or identity.

Tenar seems uniquely capable of seeing that vision, which is rendered in an image provided by an old mentor, Fan the weaver, a man who does a woman's work. He shows her the other side of the fan from which he takes his common name, a painting of dragons. Then he instructs her to hold the fan up to the light:

> She did so, and saw the two sides, the two paintings, made one by the light flowing through the silk, so that the clouds and peaks were the towers of the city, and the men and women were winged, and the dragons looked with human eyes. . . . Tenar turned the fan once more before the light, then remounted it as it had been, the dragons hidden in darkness, the men and women walking in the light of day. (115)

At the center of the book is this vivid perfection of a whole, which at any given moment is invisible. The two sides come together, light and dark, yin and yang, male and female, human and dragon. This is a quiet epiphany, a moment of illumination: real change is no change at all but merely a change in perception.

Tenar begins to teach Therru the old songs of the Making and the Old Speech, the things Ogion tried to show her and asked her in turn to teach the child. In so doing she naturally turns to Ged, for they have joined together in love and enjoy an intimacy and depth of understanding in their union that is another kind of insight and power, a positive dimension that Ged now realizes is a result of his giving up his power. Tenar tells him of her intuition that Therru should learn the language only "from a true speaker of it" (218), which, being a woman, she has never been. Ged says that "no man is that," and they conclude that only dragons speak the True Speech as their native tongue but that even they perhaps do not actually learn it. "My guess would be that the dragon and the speech of the dragon are one. One being," Ged says. "They do not learn. . . . They are" (218).

In the book's final chapter, called "Tehanu," when both Ged and Tenar are emptied of power, humiliated, about to be destroyed by the last thrusts of the perverted, male shadow-power Ged gave his final cup of art magic to quench, the narrative shifts into the child's mind. Therru speaks with dragons in what turns out to be her native tongue, the True Speech, which she does not learn but *is*. Kalessin brings a breath of fire to cleanse the evil and to prepare the way for a complete rebirth. The child speaks in "the words of the Making" and calls Ged by the name Segoy. There is a sense of union and of new beginning as the child and the dragon are seen as one, as the two sides of the fan are one. It is a closing of the cycle or circle that promises unity and renewal: a circle that is the ancient symbol of the whole; real change, but in a sense no change at all—a change merely of perception as Ged, identified at the end with Segoy, creator, God, begins again the cycle of creation of which he is both end and beginning. It is the Eastern circle composed of yin and yang, light and dark, male and female, that makes the whole. It is the Western myth expressed by Aristophanes in Plato's *Symposium* in which the creatures of the world are originally round, "back and sides forming a circle" until division splits their circle into parts.[15] According to Aristophanes, this division results in the force of love, which can reunite that which was divided:

> this meeting and melting into one another, this becoming one instead of two, was the very expression of his ancient need. And the reason is that human nature was originally one and we were whole, and the desire and pursuit of the whole is called love. (Plato, 158)

In the Earthsea cycle Le Guin explores the language and the power of the earth to arrive at the conclusion that the whole is greater than its parts. This final book makes clear the violations, degradations, and divisions wrought primarily through men's various attempts to wield male power over other men, women, and the world. It offers, though, a final vision of the whole in which the dragon and the speech of the dragon are one, human nature and dragon nature are one, past and present (Ged and Segoy) are one, end and beginning are one. It offers a vision of identity that is powerful—not in terms of control but in terms of love. It is a final statement of identity in which a vision of the whole is achieved through a love force that includes all language, power, and vision in the circle of its wide embrace. It is the concrete metaphor that echoes through Tenar's closing words as she and Ged return with their simple, ordinary love to the simple cottage of their art-mage teacher Ogion, a declaration that resounds with art and the fullness of life: " I think we can live there."

Notes and References

Chapter 1

1. Dennis M. Kratz, "Development of the Fantastaic Tradition through 1811," in *Fantasy Literature: A Reader's Guide,* ed. Neil Barron (New York: Garland, 1990), 3; hereafter cited in the text.
2. Harold Bloom, "*Clinamen:* Towards a Theory of Fantasy," in *Bridges to Fantasy,* ed. George E. Slusser, Eric S. Rabkin, and Robert Scholes (Carbondale, Ill.: Southern Illinois University Press, 1982), 5; hereafter cited in the text.
3. Robert Scholes, "Structural Fabulation: An Essay on Fiction of the Future," *University of Notre Dame Ward Phillips Lectures in English Language and Literature,* vol. 7 (Notre Dame: University of Notre Dame, 1975), 29.
4. Orson Scott Card, *How to Write Science Fiction and Fantasy* (Cincinnati, Ohio: Writer's Digest, 1990), 22. Card has award-winning credentials in both science fiction and fantasy writing. The first two volumes of his Ender series won back-to-back Hugo and Nebula Awards in 1985 (*Ender's Game*) and 1986 (*Speaker for the Dead*); this was the first time these prizes for best science fiction book of the year had been won successively by one author. His awards for fantasy include both the World Fantasy Award and the Mythopoeic Fantasy Award.

His novels in the Tales of Alvin Maker series (*Seventh Son, Red Prophet,* and *Prentice Alvin*) are among the most impressive contemporary American fantasy fiction.

5. Eric S. Rabkin, *The Fantastic in Literature* (Princeton: Princeton University Press, 1976). Rabkin presents an influential theoretical discussion using the groundwork of structuralist criticism but also developing a less extreme and limiting alternative to the theories of Todorov. Rabkin's parameters seem more descriptive of a large number of works commonly accepted as being part of the canon of quality fantasy.

6. The exact origins of this papyrus are not known. Known as P. Leningrad 1115, it was discovered in the Imperial Museum of St. Petersburg in Russia and is now located in Moscow. Several translations are available; I have relied on Miriam Lichtheim, *Ancient Egyptian Literature: A Book of Readings,* vol. 1 (Berkeley: University of California Press, 1975).

7. From this tale forward, fantasy embraces the tradition of narratives of heroes' journeys. As the genre evolves, the hero's journey becomes a nearly universal structural component. The genre has in turn transmitted it to other popular contemporary modes, including science fiction, and the formula has also become a heuristic device in contemporary cinema—particularly in animated features. Christopher Vogler's *The Writer's Journey: Mythic Structures for Storytellers and Screenwriters* (Studio City, Calif.: M. Wiese Productions, 1992) makes this point clear. Further critical insights are to be found in such works as Joseph Campbell's *The Hero with a Thousand Faces* (New York: Pantheon, 1949) and Evans Lansing Smith's *The Hero Journey in Literature: Parables of Poesis* (Lanham, Md.: University Press of America, 1996).

8. The Westcar Papyrus, probably transcribed around 1652 to 1554 B.C.E., is now located in Berlin and is known as P. Berlin 3033. For translations of the complete tales I have relied on Lichtheim, *Ancient Egyptian Literature.* For the fragmentary tales and for general charm and flavor, however, I recommend W. M. Flinders Petrie, *Egyptian Tales Translated from the Papyri,* 2 vols. (New York: Stokes, 1896). Petrie organizes the "Tales of the Magicians" by their tellers—for example, "Khafra's Tale," "Baufra's Tale," and "Hordedef's Tale." His

renditions, although perhaps not as academically accurate as Lichtheim's, are highly readable. Moreover, they reflect the understanding of these stories in England in the nineteenth century, when modern fantasy was being invented.

9. The tablets containing *The Epic of Gilgamesh* were discovered and excavated in 1853. Henry Rawlinson immediately began deciphering the tablets at the British Museum. (J. R. R. Tolkien would later be appointed Rawlinson and Bosworth Professor of Anglo Saxon at Oxford University, a position honoring the great philologist.) Upon Rawlinson's death, the work was carried on by his assistant, George Smith, who translated first the tale of the great flood, which he published together with an outline of the epic in about 1873. The publication caused considerable excitement, since the tale, transcribed from a manuscript written 1,500 years before Homer, recounted a significant event recorded in the Old Testament.

10. The earliest versions of the Book of the Dead date from about 1570 to 1304 B.C.E.; the book was refined in the Ptolemaic period, 322–330 B.C.E.

11. The relationship between the primal story of creation in the Old Testament and the stories created each night by Scheherazade in *The Arabian Nights* is explained by J. R. R. Tolkien through the metaphor of "sub-creation," the responsibility of humankind to create in turn because they are made in the image of the Creator. See chapter 3, on Tolkien, for further discussion.

12. Leslie Marmon Silko, *Storyteller* (New York: Seaver Books, 1981); Louise Erdrich, *Tracks* (New York: Henry Holt, 1988); Piers Anthony, *Tatham Mound* (New York: Morrow, 1991); Piers Anthony and Richard Gilliam, eds., *Tales from the Great Turtle: Fantasy in the Native American Tradition* (New York: Tor, 1994).

13. Just after the turn of the century, in 1905, the last great breakthrough in translating ancient texts occurred when François Thureau-Dangin produced the first translation of Sumerian texts, the earliest identified writing to date.

14. Lin Carter, "About *Phantastes* and George MacDonald: Beyond the Gates of Dream," in MacDonald, *Phantastes* (New York: Ballantine, 1970), vii.

15. His given name was Edward John Moreton Drax Blunkett (1878–1957), and he became the 18th Baron Dunsany. From a family established in Ireland in Norman times in County Meath, north of Dublin, Dunsany was heir to the family seat, the twelfth-century Castle Dunsany. Dunsany rhymes with "Sun-rainy."

16. *Letters of James Stephens,* ed. Richard Finneran (London: Macmillan, 1974), 204.

17. Douglas A. Winter, foreword to E. R. Eddison, *The Worm Ouroboros* (New York: Dell, 1991), ix.

18. Paul K. Alkon, *Science Fiction before 1900: Imagination Discovers Technology* (New York: Twayne, 1994), 118; hereafter cited in the text as *Science Fiction.*

19. Donald L. Lawler, "The Biography of the Life of Manuel," in *Survey of Modern Literature,* vol. 1, ed. Frank N. Magill (Englewood Cliffs, N.J.: Salem Press, 1983), 96; hereafter cited in the text.

20. John Clute and Peter Nicholls, eds., *The Encyclopedia of Science Fiction* (New York: St. Martin's Griffin, 1995), 152; hereafter cited in the text.

21. Northrop Frye, *Anatomy of Criticism: Four Essays* (New York: Atheneum, 1967); hereafter cited in the text as Frye 1967.

Chapter 2

1. Northrop Frye, *The Secular Scripture: A Study of the Structure of Romance* (Cambridge, Mass.: Harvard University Press, 1976), 4; hereafter cited in the text as Frye 1976.

2. Fiona MacCarthy, *William Morris: A Life for Our Time* (New York: Knopf, 1995), 15; hereafter cited in the text.

3. William Morris, *Golden Wings and Other Stories,* with an afterword by Richard Mathews (Van Nuys, Calif.: Newcastle Publishing Company, 1976), 89; hereafter cited in the text as *Golden.*

4. Sidney Cockerell, introduction to J. W. Mackail, *The Life of William Morris,* no. 521 in the World's Classics Series (London: Oxford University Press, 1950).

5. E. D. Lemire, ed., *The Unpublished Lectures of William Morris* (Detroit: Wayne State University Press, 1969). The introduction and two appendices, "A Calendar of William Morris's Platform Career" and "A Bibliographical Checklist of Morris's Speeches and Lectures," are particularly useful.

6. Allusions to John Ball are conspicuous in *The Once and Future King* by T. H. White, whose recovery and reimagination of Arthurian England is indebted to Morris's *Dream of John Ball* and to his Arthurian poems.

7. William Morris, "The Gothic Revival," in Lemire, ed., *The Unpublished Lectures.*

8. Tolkien wrote his influential essay "On Fairy-Stories" in 1938 and 1939. See the discussion of his main points in chapter 3.

9. May Morris quotes from Cockerell's letters in her introduction to *The Collected Works of William Morris,* vol. 18 (London: Longmans, Green, 1913), xxxiij.

10. William Morris, *The Well at the World's End,* bk. 1, *The Collected Works of William Morris,* vol. 18 (London: Longmans Green and Co., 1913); hereafter cited in the text as *Well.*

Chapter 3

1. Humphrey Carpenter, *Tolkien: A Biography* (Boston: Houghton Mifflin, 1977), 15; hereafter cited in the text.

2. J. R. R. Tolkien, "On Fairy-Stories," in Tolkien, *Tree and Leaf* (Boston: Houghton Mifflin, 1989), 44; hereafter cited in the text as "FS."

3. T. A. Shippey, *The Road to Middle-earth* (Boston: Houghton Mifflin, 1983), 6, 10; hereafter cited in the text.

4. J. R. R. Tolkien, "*Beowulf:* the Monsters and the Critics," *Proceedings of the British Academy* 22 (1936): 245–95.

5. Rosemary Jackson, *Fantasy: The Literature of Subversion* (London: Methuen, 1981).

6. J. R. R. Tolkien, *The Lord of the Rings* (Boston: Houghton Mifflin, 1987) 1:75; hereafter cited in the text as *LOTR.*

7. See Randel Helms, *Tolkien's World* (Boston: Houghton Mifflin, 1974), for amplification of these and other parallels.

Chapter 4

1. J. R. R. Tolkien to Edith Bratt [October 1914], *Letters of J. R. R. Tolkien,* ed. Humphrey Carpenter with Christopher Tolkien (Boston: Houghton Mifflin, 1981), 7; hereafter cited in the text as Carpenter and Tolkien.

2. Christopher Tolkien, interview with the author, 25 July 1987.

3. Christopher Tolkien to the author, 7 January 1990.

4. Evidence for the decline in Morris's popularity in terms of critical response to his work can be judged from the listings in Gary Aho's comprehensive annotated bibliography *William Morris: A Reference Guide* (Boston: G. K. Hall, 1985). Listings starting in about 1914 drop dramatically; there were only six items in print in 1915, seven each for 1916 and 1917.

5. Victor Brombert describes and explains these three approaches to the hero in his introductory essay "The Idea of the Hero," in *The Hero in Literature,* Victor Brombert, ed. (Greenwich, Conn.: Fawcett Publications, 1969), 11–21.

6. The "fellowship" of the Ring is a collection of odd, mismatched fellows who have little in common and a tendency to go their separate ways.

7. There are interesting parallels between Thiodolf's hauberk and the necklace charm Ralph wears in *Well.* Ralph moves into a more complex relationship with the supernatural. It should be noted, too, that Tolkien's hero eventually takes off his supernatural charm when he rids himself of the ring at last.

8. J. R. R. Tolkien, prologue to *The Fellowship of the Ring* (New York: Ballantine, 1965), 20–21.

9. Frodo's isolation is emphasized by the fact that he was orphaned and adopted. The biographical correspondence to Tolkien's own life is unmistakable. However, the point here is not merely to point out a connection but to indicate that fantasy, with its self-conscious use of Freudian and Jungian

psychology, is a genre that projects personal history as part of its imaginative expression.

10. Verlyn Flieger, "Frodo and Aragorn: The Concept of the Hero," in *Tolkien: New Critical Perspectives,* ed. Neil D. Isaacs and Rose A. Zimbardo (Lexington, Ky.: The University Press of Kentucky, 1981), 59–60; hereafter cited in the text as Flieger, 1981. See also the complete essay, 40–62.

11. An appendix to *Lord of the Rings* contains "The Tale of Aragorn and Arwen," which does provide a clearer basis for their marriage.

Chapter 5

1. Sylvia Townsend Warner, *T. H. White: A Biography* (New York: Viking, 1968), 23, 26; hereafter cited in the text. The author is quoting White from a lecture entitled "The Pleasures of Learning," given on a U.S. lecture tour during the last year of his life.

2. The impulse is strikingly similar to that of Tolkien, who asserted, "The incarnate mind, the tongue, and the tale are in our world coeval" ("FS," 24).

3. White, *The Once and Future King* (New York: Ace Books, 1987), 10; hereafter cited in the text as *Once.*

4. White's final publication of *The Once and Future King* was composed of revised versions of the three parts that had originally been published individually in book form: *The Sword in the Stone* (1938), *The Witch in the Wood* (1939, significantly revised as "The Queen of Air and Darkness" in *Once*), and *The Ill-Made Knight* (1940). A concluding section not previously published, "The Candle in the Wind," was also added.

5. Morris's sole surviving oil painting, called *Queen Guenevere* or *La Belle Iseult* (1857–1858), is now in the Tate Gallery in London. Only the title of his first painting, now lost, survives: *Sir Tristram After His Illness in the Garden of King Mark's Palace Recognized by the Dog He Had Given Iseult*. After Dante Gabriel Rossetti proclaimed "that the *Morte d'Arthur* and the Bible

were the two greatest books in the world" (MacCarthy, 97), Burne-Jones and Morris enthusiastically selected scenes from *Le Morte d'Arthur* as subjects for their commission to paint murals (with Rossetti, Arthur Hughes, and others) in the Oxford Union. Morris's subject was "How Sir Palomydes loved La Belle Iseult with exceeding great love out of measure, and how she loved not him again but rather Sir Tristram" (MacCarthy, 130).

One of the most useful sources for information on Arthurian legend is the "Camelot Project" on the Internet: [http://rodent.lib.rochester.edu/camelot/mainmenu.htm].

For general background, here is a brief excerpt from the free online reference material:

King Arthur is the figure at the heart of the Arthurian legends. He is said to be the son of Uther Pendragon and Ygraine of Cornwall. Arthur is a near mythic figure in Celtic stories such as *Culhwch and Olwen*. In early Latin chronicles he is presented as a military leader, the *dux bellorum*. In later romance he is presented as a king and emperor. One of the questions that has occupied those interested in King Arthur is whether or not he is a historical figure. The debate has raged since the Renaissance when Arthur's historicity was vigorously defended, partly because the Tudor monarchs traced their lineage to Arthur and used that connection as a justification for their reign. Modern scholarship has generally assumed that there was some actual person at the heart of the legends, though not of course a king with a band of knights in shining armor—though O. J. Padel in "The Nature of Arthur" argues that "historical attributes of just the kind that we find attached to Arthur can be associated with a figure who was not historical to start with." If there is a historical basis to the character, it is clear that he would have gained fame as a warrior battling the Germanic invaders of the late fifth and early sixth centuries. Since there is no conclusive evidence for or against Arthur's historicity, the debate will continue. But what can not be denied is the influence of the figure of Arthur on literature, art, music, and society from the Middle Ages to the present. Though there have been numerous historical novels that try to put Arthur into a sixth-century setting, it is the legendary figure of the late Middle Ages who has most captured the imagination. It is such a figure, the designer of an order of the best knights in the world, that figures in the major versions of the legend from Malory to Tennyson to T. H. White. Central to the myth is the downfall of Arthur's kingdom. It is undermined in the chronicle tradition by the treachery of Mordred. In the romance tradition that treachery is made possible because of the love of Lancelot and Guinevere.

White uses elements from both traditions in his novel.

6. White incorporated this episode in his revised section based on *The Sword and the Stone* after his publisher persuaded him that a fifth book, "The Book of Merlyn," would make the volume too long and would not be its most appropriate conclusion. The material was published posthumously as *The Book of Merlyn: The Unpublished Conclusion to "The Once and Future King"* (Austin: University of Texas Press, 1977); hereafter cited in the text as *Merlyn*.

7. As if to underscore the change, White does include a final verse duet sung by Lancelot and Gwenever: "their voices, no longer full in tone like those of people in the strength of youth, were still tenacious. . . . If they were thin, they were pure." The song is sadly beautiful and courageous, and it ends, "All might, all gone" (540).

8. T. A. Shippey, "The Once and Future King," in Frank N. Magill, ed., *Survey of Modern Fantasy Literature* (Englewood Cliffs, N.J.: Salem Press, 1983), 1,153.

9. The emphasis here on the heroic "invention of civilization" in Arthur's court is in marked contrast to Robert E. Howard's barbaric empires, which are discussed in the next chapter.

Chapter 6

1. Don Herron, ed., *The Dark Barbarian: The Writings of Robert E. Howard* (Westport, Conn.: Greenwood Press, 1984), Appendix A, "Robert E. Howard's Library," 191–92; hereafter cited in the text.

2. David Pringle, "Edgar Rice Burroughs," in *The Science Fiction Encyclopedia,* Peter Nicholls, ed. (New York: Doubleday, 1979), 96.

3. Brian Attebery, *The Fantasy Tradition in American Literature* (Bloomington: Indiana University Press, 1980), 118; hereafter cited in the text.

4. This assessment seems generally accurate, though Burroughs's simplicity is also appealing. His writing connects at the subconscious level, so Freudian and Jungian analyses can be intriguing, and there are thematic motifs of some interest, including questions of identity and the relationship between time and evolution. Burroughs's Pellucidar novels, including *Tarzan at the Earth's Core* (1930), explore life inside a hollow earth in which time is suspended and dinosaurs coexist with beastlike men. *The Land That Time Forgot* (1918) similarly explores the temporal dimension in a setting near the South Pole where creatures undergo metamorphoses through evolutionary phases. The variety of Burroughs's invention and his simple, direct plots have also proven to have lasting entertainment value.

5. Robert E. Howard, *Conan the Conqueror,* ed. and intro. L. Sprague de Camp (New York: Lancer, 1967).

6. Though de Camp's more heavily edited paperback edition of *Conan the Barbarian* is widely available, I have chosen to use the text of *The Hour of the Dragon,* ed. Karl Edward Wagner (New York: G. P. Putnam's Sons, 1977), which follows Howard's original version published in *Weird Tales;* hereafter cited in the text as *Dragon.* The two books are essentially the same, but de Camp used a heavier editorial hand to "clean up" Howard's original.

7. Howard quoted in Marc A. Cerasini and Charles E. Hoffman, *Robert E. Howard,* Starmont Reader's Guide 35 (Mercer Island, Wash.: Starmont House, 1987), 16–17; hereafter cited in the text.

8. The scenes are full of interesting similarities and differences. Shelley's manufactured creature was built of pieces chosen for their beauty, but the resulting monster is instantly hideous and repugnant to its creator. Howard's resurrected mummy, on the other hand, has genuine beauty and magnetism. I would recommend to any reader a thoughtful comparison of Howard's scene with Shelley's opening to chapter 5 in *Frankenstein.*

9. Other Latin-based names include Valerius (*vale*=farewell), who rules Aquilonia, and Emilius Scavonius (Scavonius seems related to scavenger).

10. William Morris, "How I Became a Socialist," in *Political Writings of William Morris,* ed. and intro. A. L. Morton (New York: International Publishers, 1979), 243.

11. Here in the choice of name there is an interesting echo of William Morris's setting in "Sir Peter Harpdon's End" Poictou, in which he speaks of the Poitevin church, a province on the Atlantic coast of West France. Later a similar name is used by James Branch Cabell in his history of Dom Manuel of Poictesme.

12. Religious groups, many of which are based on real groups that flourished in antiquity in Egypt or Africa, play significant roles in Howard's Conan stories. Set is one of the nine great original deities in the Egyptian creation myths. Set's brother, Osiris, embodied the principle of good; Set represented the principle of evil.

13. The supreme evil in Howard's work is always linked to the loss of freedom, to slavery. Evil is thus opposed to fantasy's goal of liberation.

14. Howard's fortuitous ending has less conviction than do his moments of great evil and potential destruction. Though I have not said as much about his life as I have of Morris's, White's, and Tolkien's, his personal experiences do find clear expression in his work, and the powers of darkness that he conveys so strongly surely provide metaphorical hints of reasons for his suicide. He killed himself just after learning that he would have to face the death of his beloved mother, the most important female in his life. The happy ending here in Conan's case seems a matter of wishful thinking, and the frequency with which Conan is saved by a woman perhaps supplies a key to what might have helped preserve Howard's life: if only a slave who would be queen had come to his rescue.

Chapter 7

1. Tolkien, *The Silmarillion* (Boston: Houghton Mifflin, 1977), 20; hereafter cited in the text as *Silmarillion.*

2. The word may also be another play on the paradoxes of ends and beginnings, once and future, antiquity and futurity,

which run throughout the fantasy genre and which T. H. White emphasized so strongly.

3. Ursula K. Le Guin, *The Language of the Night: Essays on Fantasy and Science Fiction* (New York: HarperCollins, 1989), 47–48; hereafter cited in the text as *Language*.

4. Richard C. West, "The Interlace Structure of *The Lord of the Rings*," in *A Tolkien Compass*, ed. Jared Lobdell (La Salle, Ill.: Open Court, 1975), 77–94; hereafter cited in the text as West.

5. Brian Attebery observes in *The Fantasy Tradition in American Literature* that "Physically, Earthsea most resembles the island groups between Asia and Australia, where, probably not by coincidence, some of the anthropological research that resulted in our present understanding of magic and myth was conducted. These islands show the same diversity within a common cultural framework as Earthsea, and the scale is similar" (Attebery, 171).

6. Attebery also comments on this unity: "Running counter to the divisive influence of geography is a common heritage. Most of Earthsea speaks a single tongue, derived ultimately from the true, dragonish speech. Tales and legends pass freely from island to island, and the oldest are found from one end of the world to the other" (Attebery, 169).

7. Le Guin has spoken and written frequently about her Eastern influences. In her essay on the Earthsea trilogy she notes her "interest in the *I Ching* and Taoist philosophy evident in most of my books" (*Language*, 49). The principle of yin-yang is used in Taoist and Chinese philosophy to indicate the active and passive principles of the universe. The yang, the male force, is light, active, generative; yin, the female, is dark, passive, receptive. From their interaction all things come into existence. "Segoy" may be one name for yin-yang.

8. Le Guin, *A Wizard of Earthsea* (New York: Bantam, 1975), 6; hereafter cited in the text as *Wizard*.

9. Le Guin, intro. to Le Guin, *The Left Hand of Darkness* (New York: Ace, 1977), iv; hereafter cited in the text as *Darkness*.

10. Le Guin, *The Tombs of Atuan* (New York: Bantam, 1975), 15; hereafter cited in the text as *Tombs*.

11. This circularity, which Le Guin elsewhere alludes to as a spiral—"The story of the book is essentially a voyage, a pattern in the form of a long spiral" (*Language*, 46)—is a poetic metaphor like W. B. Yeats's "gyre." It is finally affirmed artistically by the alteration of the Earthsea trilogy to the Earthsea *cycle* with the 1991 publication of *Tehanu*.

12. The image of the cavern as both mouth and tomb evokes the most primitive archetypes of the Great Mother. The book is filled with rich symbolism of dark power, ancient and not to be construed except perhaps by the male, as evil. The book's Jungian and Freudian dimensions are marvelously rich and should be explored in depth. Le Guin has said, "The subject of *The Tombs of Atuan* is, if I had to put it in one word, sex. There's a lot of symbolism in the book, most of which I did not, of course, analyze consciously while writing; the symbols can all be read as sexual. More exactly, you could call it a feminine coming of age. Birth, rebirth, destruction, freedom are the themes" (*Language*, 50).

13. At this point, the male hero having led the woman out of darkness, having taught her the real language she should speak, and having led her like a little child into the city, my plot summary may make Le Guin sound like she is writing patriarchal history as fantasy. In the experience of reading the whole book, however, this is not the overall impression. Tenar/Arha possesses a different and equally important power and experience, a point Le Guin clarifies in *Tehanu* as Tenar's strengths become more evident and as another nameless female child victim becomes a hero.

14. Le Guin, *Tehanu* (New York: Bantam, 1991), 255 (appendix); hereafter cited in the text.

15. Plato, "Symposium," trans. Benjamin Jowett, in *Great Books of the Western World*, vol. 7 (Chicago: Encyclopedia Britannica, 1952), 157; hereafter cited in the text as Plato.

Bibliographic Essay

Reference Works

Everett F. Bleiler's *The Checklist of Fantastic Literature* (Chicago: Shasta, 1948) was the standard bibliographical reference for fantasy for many years, and he added more than 1,000 new titles when he issued a revised edition (Firebell, 1978). Diana Waggoner provided one of the first comprehensive reference works on fantasy as a distinct genre with *The Hills of Faraway: A Guide to Fantasy* (New York: Atheneum, 1978). She delimited the genre by excluding science fiction, horror, utopias, and picture books but included works written for children. Applying criteria from Tolkien and Frye, she offered a theoretical framework and divided the book into eight categories of fantasy: mythopoeic, heroic, adventurous, ironic, comic, nostalgic, sentimental, and horrific. She offered nearly 1,000 entries, including plot summaries and critical observations, for works arranged within these categories by author. Other useful reference works followed in quick succession. L. W. Currey provided collectors the information necessary to identify first editions of books by 215 authors up to June of 1977 in *Science Fiction and Fantasy Authors: A Bibliography of First Printings of Their Fiction and Selected Nonfiction* (Boston: G. K. Hall, 1979). Roger C. Schlobin compiled a selected bibliography of fantasy works "with strong adult appeal" from 1858 to mid-1979 in *The Literature of Fantasy: A Comprehensive Annotated*

Bibliography of Modern Fantasy Fiction (New York: Garland, 1979). Of the three, Waggoner is probably the most interesting for the critical perspective she brings to her work.

For critical focus on fantasy as a distinct genre, there are five essential general reference works. Neil Barron's *Fantasy Literature: A Reader's Guide* (New York: Garland, 1990) is a superb survey and critical introduction that includes outstanding critical summary essays on the development of fantasy up to 1988 for both adults and young adults. Following each overview essay are comprehensive, well-selected bibliographies, with intelligent annotations, of all the most important works within that time frame. Barron's companion volume *Horror Literature: A Reader's Guide*, edited by Neil Barron (New York: Garland, 1990) offers similar standards of excellence for darker fantasy. For more extensive individual critical discussions, the five-volume *Survey of Modern Fantasy Literature*, edited by Frank N. Magill (Englewood Cliffs, N.J.: Salem Press, 1983), contains full critical essays on most of the seminal works and includes a first-rate collection of essays on theories, themes, motifs, and special topics. Similarly, *Supernatural Fiction Writers: Fantasy and Horror*, edited by Everett F. Bleiler (New York: Scribner, 1985), assembles in chronological order substantial, well-written essays on 148 authors from the second century C.E. (beginning with Lucius Apuleius) to the 1980s. David Pringle's *Modern Fantasy: The Hundred Best Novels* (London: Grafton, 1988; rpt. New York: Bedrick, 1989) affords a unified critical perspective on the author's selection of the 100 best fantasy novels, and Pringle's choices reflect his intelligence and good taste. More recently he has edited *The St. James Guide to Fantasy* (New York: St. James, 1995), in which he and 44 other critics offer short introductory essays and bibliographies for more than 400 fantasy authors up through 1994.

The most recent, comprehensive, and up-to-date reference is *The Encyclopedia of Fantasy*, edited by John Clute and John Grant (New York: St. Martin's, 1997). Its many strengths include an excellent theoretical grounding in the genre, incisive entries (over 4,000, including literature, film, video, music, art, and mixed media), cross references to authors, topics, themes, and motifs, and links to another pioneering reference work that remains invaluable for both fantasy and science fiction, *The Science Fiction Encyclopedia*, originally edited by Peter Nicholls (Garden City, N.Y.: Doubleday, 1979), and enlarged and updated under joint editorial direction with John Clute (New York: St. Martin's Griffin, 1995; also available in a multimedia CD-ROM edition). Nicholls, Clute, and Grant are unsurpassed as editors of the best single-volume encyclopedias in the field, and Nicholls and Clute construe the category of science fiction broadly enough to encompass innumerable fantasy authors, works, and themes. The nearest science fiction rival is *The New Encyclopedia of Science Fiction,* edited by James Gunn (New York: Viking, 1988). One additional major fantasy reference guide is expected this year: *Magill's Guide to Science Fiction and Fantasy Literature,* a multivolume update and expansion of Magill's *Survey of Science Fiction Literature* (1979) and *Survey of Modern Fantasy Literature* (1983), discussed previously.

Historical and Theoretical Studies

Only fairly recently have critics begun serious discussion of fantasy as a distinct genre. With a few notable exceptions, most critics previously considered fantasy to be simply one of many wrinkles of popular fringe fiction that they grouped (together with science fiction, gothic fiction, ghost stories, and horror) under the broad umbrella of "the supernatural." George MacDonald contributed some useful starting points for understanding the traditions and characteristics of fantasy as a genre in his 1893 essay "The Fantastic Imagination" and extended them with numerous examples in *A Dish of Orts: Chiefly Papers on the Imagination, and on Shakespeare* (London: Sampson, Low, Marston, 1893). MacDonald's theories were regarded at the time more as defenses of his own writing than as the basis for further critical development. However, some of the most respected subsequent literary critics and historians have also acknowledged the need for attention to fantasy's distinctive generic qualities. E. M. Forster in *Aspects of the Novel* (New York: Harcourt Brace, 1927) includes interesting chapters on "Fantasy" and "Prophecy," in which he discusses some of the mythological interests and poetic qualities that characterize the fantasy mode. J. R. R. Tolkien's Andrew Lang lecture "On Fairy-Stories," delivered at St. Andrews in 1939, was expanded and published in a volume entitled *Essays Presented to Charles Williams* (Oxford: Oxford University Press, 1947). The revised edition includes an important statement of theory, "On Stories," by C. S. Lewis. The latter essay, grouped with some of Lewis's other writings on fantasy theory and on other authors, was published in *On Stories and Other Essays on Literature* (New York: Harcourt Brace, 1982). Tolkien's essay has also been published together with his story "Leaf by Niggle," in *Tree and Leaf* (London: George Allen and Unwin, 1964; several subsequent editions have also been published).

In the late 1950s M. K. Briggs wrote the first of her volumes on supernatural motifs, *The Anatomy of Puck: An Examination of Fairy Beliefs among Shakespeare's Contemporaries and Successors* (London: Routledge and Kegan Paul, 1959). *Pale Hecate's Team: An Examination of the Beliefs on Witchcraft and Magic among Shakespeare's Contemporaries and His Immediate Successors* (London: Routledge and Kegan Paul, 1962) and *The Fairies in Tradition and Literature* (London: Routledge and Kegan Paul, 1967) followed. These are rich resources for fantasy imagery and helped heighten appreciation for its reach and achievements. Her work was supplemented and extended by Theodore Ziolkowski in his *Disenchanted Images: A Literary Iconology* (Princeton, N.J.: Princeton University Press, 1977).

While Briggs and Ziolkowski explored the imagistic vocabulary of fantasy, other critics in the early sixties attempted to describe fantasy's relationship to mainstream literature to define its unique characteristics. British writer Colin Wilson examined the work of such writers as J. R. R. Tolkien, H. P. Lovecraft, and E. T. A. Hoffmann in *The Strength to Dream: Literature and the Imagination* (London: Gollancz, 1961), and C. S. Lewis, in *An Experiment in Criticism* (Cambridge: Cambridge University Press, 1961), defended fantasy's literary validity in the context of a broader, original, personal response to literature.

By the end of the sixties, Tolkien's popularity with a new generation of readers, together with a rapidly expanding, impressive array of new fantasy authors, had attracted increasing serious critical attention to the genre. The first important theoretical discussions saw print: Robert Scholes's *The Fabulators* (1967), revised as *Fabulation and Metafiction* (Carbondale: University of Illinois Press, 1979), is a thoughtful consideration of the genre's qualities and an exploration of experimental techniques in postmodern fiction by Borges, Barth, Coover, and others. Tzvetan Todorov's *Introduction à la littérature fantastique* (1970), translated by Richard

Howard as *The Fantastic: A Structural Approach to a Literary Genre* (Cleveland, Ohio: Case Western Reserve University Press, 1973), was the first serious scholarly attempt to comprehensively define the genre; and speaking for and to the wide popular, nonacademic audience, Lin Carter's *Imaginary Worlds: The Art of Fantasy* (New York: Ballantine, 1973), is a book full of perceptive insights despite its mixed purposes of appealing to a general reader, promoting the Ballantine adult fantasy series, and expressing the opinions and observations of an experienced professional writer and editor of fantasy.

Both Scholes and Todorov are continuing influences in serious criticism, though they often are criticized themselves, Todorov particularly for his restrictive approach. Todorov departs from Northrop Frye's theory of genres to define fantasy partly in terms of structural characteristics, but his book leads him toward a narrow critical definition with criteria that fall under the general rubric of "reader response." When C. N. Manlove published his *Modern Fantasy: Five Studies* (Cambridge: Cambridge University Press, 1975), he broadened fantasy's definition to include fiction that evokes wonder and that contains elements of the supernatural or impossible. Manlove develops his approach, which is useful and clear, at much greater length and includes subcategories and examples. However, in his book he critiques the fantasy genre as being insufficient to support major literary achievements. I have found his general discussion and definition more useful than his specific interpretation and critical analysis. Carter, on the other hand, still seems to me to be undervalued as a resource. Though he lacks academic precision, his instincts are sound, and many of his observations and suggestions offer grounds for further work, perhaps coupled with extensions of Frye's theories in *Anatomy of Criticism* and *The Secular Scripture,* both of which I have already discussed in the body of this book.

Another important trio of works first appeared in print in 1976. W. R. Irwin's *The Game of the Impossible: A Rhetoric of Fantasy* (Carbondale: University of Illinois Press, 1976), as its title suggests, defines fantasy as fiction that deals with violations of what is normally thought of as being possible. Eric S. Rabkin's *The Fantastic in Literature* (Princeton, N.J.: Princeton University Press, 1976) casts an even wider net, asserting that the fantastic imagination is a significant "mode of human knowing" and offering a spectrum model in which one type of writing gradually moves toward another. Bruno Bettelheim won a National Book Award for his psychoanalytical exploration of fairy tales and their significance in the moral development of children in *The Uses of Enchantment: The Meaning and Importance of Fairy Tales* (New York: Knopf, 1976). Bettelheim's close readings and discussions of fairy tale symbols offer insights applicable to a broad range of fantasy writing, and his treatment is considered landmark, suggestive of how the various enchantments found in fairy tales speak to fundamental human needs. His work has also been criticized for psychoanalytic exaggeration and has been most usefully critiqued and counterbalanced by Jack Zipes in *Breaking the Magic Spell: Radical Theories of Folk and Fairy Tales* (Austin: University of Texas Press, 1979), *Fairy Tales and the Art of Subversion: The Classical Genre for Children and the Process of Civilization* (New York: Wildman Press, 1983), and *Fairy Tale As Myth/Myth As Fairy Tale* (Lexington: University Press of Kentucky, 1994). Zipes offers insights into political themes in the fairy tale tradition, particularly as a response to political oppression. The impulse toward liberation that he describes has been faulted for being as narrowly obsessed with politics as Bettelheim is with psychology, but taken together these studies can significantly advance our thinking about the matrix of values in fantasy literature.

Stephen Prickett's *Victorian Fantasy* (Bloomington: Indiana University Press, 1979) offers historical and critical perspectives on the fantasy genre as it developed from the gothic novel through Victorian period and concludes that fantasy is "the most philosophic form of fiction." Another book published the same year collects philosophical-critical essays by one of the most important contemporary American fantasy authors, Ursula K. Le Guin. In *The Language of the Night: Essays on Fantasy and Science Fiction,* edited by Susan Wood (New York: Putnam, 1979), Le Guin demonstrates that many of the philosophical, political, and psychological issues Victorian authors raised remain concerns of contemporary authors. Le Guin's impressive intellectual breadth and insight deepen our respect for and understanding of the contemporary evolution of the genre. Her essays also point out significant feminist motifs in her work, motifs that have been concerns in fantasy from Morris's earliest stories to the present.

The decade of the 1980s was rich for its fresh critical perceptions of fantasy. It began with what remains the best discussion of fantasy in the United States—Brian Attebery's *The Fantasy Tra-*

dition in American Literature: From Irving to Le Guin (Bloomington: Indiana University Press, 1980). The book, a watershed critical survey, documents the extent to which fantasy has pervaded mainstream American literature and demonstrates how other texts usually relegated to the literary periphery as works for children or fantasy fans are more properly seen in the context of a significant American literary tradition.

Rosemary Jackson's *Fantasy: The Literature of Subversion* (London: Methuen, 1981) steps forward from Todorov's somewhat off-target psychoanalytic approach to consider how the genre's immersion in the impossible threatens and subverts established political, social, and economic conventions. Psychologically she associates the impulse of fantasy with the desire for what is forbidden. Her intelligent discussions are enriched with tools of Marxist and structuralist criticism and with approaches suggested by Jacques Lacan, Julia Kristeva, and other recent influential literary theorists. By discussing examples from Dickens, Dostoyevsky, Stevenson, Pynchon, and others, she ties her approach to mainstream literature but blurs her effectiveness with purer forms of fantasy. Nonetheless, she also breaks considerable new ground. Similarly, Christine Brooke-Rose, in *A Rhetoric of the Unreal: Studies in Narrative and Structure, Especially of the Fantastic* (Cambridge: Cambridge University Press, 1981) finds significant elements of fantasy in works by Henry James, Washington Irving, and others. She also devotes a full chapter to Tolkien, but she seems unable to apply her critical acumen as effectively to purer fantasy. Nonetheless, her examination of rhetorical strategies, intertextuality, and a spectrum of significant literature and critical theory not only helps advance fantasy criticism but helps place it usefully within the broader literary spectrum.

Casey Fredericks's *The Future of Eternity: Mythologies of Science Fiction and Fantasy* (Bloomington: Indiana University Press, 1982) is a more down-to-earth study of "science fiction and myth" and contains an especially useful chapter, "In Defense of Heroic Fantasy." Heroic fantasy is also discussed in C. N. Manlove's *The Impulse of Fantasy Literature* (Kent, Ohio: Kent State University Press, 1983); the work is an extension of approaches Manlove pioneered in *Modern Fantasy*, but here he tags works by Morris, Dunsany, Eddison, and Beagle as "anaemic fantasy" and skews his generally insightful critical discussions with his own fiercely held brand of literary dogmatism, which is more frequently prescriptive than receptive. By contrast, Kathryn Hume's *Fantasy and Mimesis: Responses to Reality in Western Literature* (New York: Methuen, 1984) is a welcome relief in its recognition that dominant mimetic paradigms have shaped mainstream critical responses to fantasy. Hume's book offers some new ways to assess the full spectrum of fantasy in literature, which includes such postmodernist authors as Barth, Calvino, and Pynchon.

Two works that benefit from feminist perspectives are Thelma J. Shinn's *Worlds Within Women: Myth and Mythmaking in Fantastic Literature by Women* (New York: Greenwood, 1986) and Charlotte Spivack's *Merlin's Daughters: Contemporary Women Writers of Fantasy* (New York: Greenwood, 1987). Taken together, these works are articulate reminders of the strong women authors in the genre: Andre Norton, Evangeline Walton, Marion Zimmer Bradley, Doris Lessing, Ursula K. Le Guin, Susan Cooper, Patricia McKillip, Vera Chapman, and many others.

Brian Attebery pulls a healthy number of the most important critical approaches together in his *Strategies of Fantasy* (Bloomington: Indiana University Press, 1992). Attebery's work benefits from his own previous study *The Fantasy Tradition in American Literature* and offers a practical synthesis of much of the contemporary theoretical and interpretive scholarship. He includes outstanding discussions of genre theory and background, conventions of story and character, postmodernism, and "science fantasy." His success in fusing philosophically and critically complex theoretical tools with instinctively (and sometimes inspired) commonsense approaches offers a useful model for future scholarship in the field.

Anthologies

Borges, Jorge Luis, Silvina Ocampo, and Adolfo Bioy Casares, eds. *The Book of Fantasy*. New York: Viking, 1988.

    Borges published and republished his own stories in many variant editions. The same tendency underlies his work as an editor. This collection, which was first published in Argentina in 1940, was revised twice and finally translated and published in English in 1988. Its scope is global, with an emphasis on Latin American authors. By choosing a great range of works, some dating from the seventeenth century, the editors offer an unusually broad survey of the spectrum of styles and sensibilities in fantasy literature.

Boyer, Robert H. and Kenneth J. Zahorski, eds. *The Fantastic Imagination: An Anthology of High Fantasy.* New York: Avon, 1977.

A strong collection that includes short stories and excerpts from novels that represent the rich range and style of such fantasy authors as George MacDonald, Lord Dunsany, James Branch Cabell, J. R. R. Tolkien, C. S. Lewis, Lloyd Alexander, Peter Beagle, and Ursula Le Guin.

———. *The Fantastic Imagination II: An Anthology of High Fantasy.* New York: Avon, 1978.

This second installment expands the original with work by Kenneth Morris, Evangeline Walton, Patricia McKillip, Vera Chapman, and others. There are examples of sword and sorcery but nothing by Robert E. Howard, and on the whole this is not as strong an anthology as the first.

———. *Dark Imagining: A Collection of Gothic Fantasy.* New York: Dell, 1978.

This solid paperback anthology includes works in a spectrum that overlaps fantasy and horror. Contents are divided into gothic high fantasy (MacDonald, Merritt, Howard, Leiber, etc.) and gothic low fantasy (Doyle, Hodgson, Blackwood, White, Bradbury, Beagle, etc.).

———. *The Phoenix Tree: An Anthology of Myth Fantasy.* New York: Avon, 1980.

The emphasis is on the mythic aspects of fantasy in these stories and excerpts from novels by Borges, Dunsany, Lovecraft, Richard Adams, and others.

Carr, Terry, ed. *New Worlds of Fantasy.* New York: Ace, 1967, 1970, 1971.

———. *Year's Finest Fantasy.* New York: Berkley, 1978, 1979.

———. *Fantasy Annual.* New York: Pocket Books, 1981, 1981, 1985.

Carr's annual collections interpret fantasy in a very broad generic sense and include works that run the gamut from science fiction to horror. Most of the fiction is deserving of "best of the year" distinction and thus one useful way of sampling some vintage writing, although the range suggests the difficulty in identifying "pure" fantasy.

Carter, Lin, ed. *Flashing Swords.* New York: Dell, 1973, 1974, 1976, 1977, 1981.

Lin Carter's numerous contributions to modern fantasy include his cultivation of a popular audience for heroic fantasy of the sword and sorcery type. In these five volumes he published original work by himself, as well as by Poul Anderson, Fritz Leiber, Michael Moorcock, Andre Norton, Jack Vance, and many others.

Carter, Lin, and Arthur W. Saha, eds. *The Year's Best Fantasy Stories.* 14 vols. New York: Daw, 1975 (Carter edited vols. 1–6; Saha edited vols. 7–14).

Carter's preference for heroic fantasy in the sword and sorcery mode made his annual selections distinctive and interesting for the light they shed on a developing sense of the genre, though his choices were not always of the highest literary quality. Saha's editorial orientation is more difficult to gauge, but this was a popular annual series.

Datlow, Ellen, and Terri Windling. *The Year's Best Fantasy and Horror.* New York: St. Martin's, 1988–.

This outstanding annual anthology has taken its place beside *The Year's Best Science Fiction* (ed. Gardner Dozois) as a premier survey of contemporary genre fiction. The editors provide consistently excellent introductions, and their inclusion of poetry as well as horror fiction helps make for rich and rewarding reading.

Leiber, Fritz, and Stuart David Schiff, eds. *The World Fantasy Awards. Vol. 2.* New York: Doubleday, 1980.

An excellent collection of top stories from World Fantasy Awards. See entry for Gahan Wilson.

Manguel, Alberto, ed. *Black Water: An Anthology of Fantastic Literature.* London: Lester and Orpen Dennys, 1983. Rpt. *Black Water: The Book of Fantastic Literature.* New York: Clarkson Potter, 1984.

One of the most comprehensive and weighty (literally—some 972 pages!) anthologies of fantasy, *Black Water* collects 72 stories from throughout the world. Its inclusion of such mainstream authors as Graham Greene, D. H. Lawrence, Herman Hesse, and Henry James suggests its editors' orientation toward strong literary content. The work, which is an impressive context for a few strong modern works by Ray Bradbury, Ursula Le Guin, and others, enlarges one's conception of the scope of fantasy.

Saha, Arthur W. See Carter and Saha, *The Year's Best Fantasy Stories.*

Silverberg, Robert, and Martin H. Greenberg, eds. *Fantasy Hall of Fame.* Arbor House, 1983.

This major collection includes 22 stories chosen by a poll conducted at the World Fantasy Convention to identify the world's best fantasy stories. The result is a solid anthology of work from Poe to Le Guin.

Wilson, Gahan, ed. *First World Fantasy Awards.* New York: Doubleday, 1977.

An outstanding compilation of stories that have been nominated for or received the annual World Fantasy Award.

Windling, Terri, ed. *Faery!* New York: Ace, 1985.

This is an unusual group of 20 stories that have ancestry in fairy tales and fairy myth from sources around the world, including Celtic, European, South American, and even Chinese sources.

Windling, Terri, and Mark Arnold, eds. *Elsewhere.* New York: Ace, 1981, 1982, 1984.

A series of anthologies of heroic fantasy stories of strong literary quality and wide generic range by such authors as García Márquez, Angela Carter, Joanna Russ, and Fritz Leiber. The 1981 collection received the World Fantasy Award as best anthology.

Individual Writers and Works

William Morris

The work of William Morris can best be appreciated in the context of his extraordinary range of artistic, literary, and political activity. Two biographies are most useful: an early one by a member of the Morris circle—J. W. Mackail's *The Life of William Morris* (London: Longmans, Green, 1899)—and a recent comprehensive biography, Fiona MacCarthy's *William Morris: A Life for Our Time* (New York: Knopf, 1995). A nearly complete bibliography of critical writings about Morris can be found in Gary L. Aho, *William Morris: A Reference Guide*(Boston: G. K. Hall, 1985), and in David and Sheila Latham, *An Annotated Critical Biography of William Morris* (New York: St. Martin's, 1991), which is updated by a biennial bibliography in *The Journal of the William Morris Society*.

For a succinct treatment of Morris's literary work, Frederick K. Kirchhoff's *William Morris* (Boston: Twayne, 1979), which contains a chapter on his fantasy novels, is hard to beat. Works that focus directly on Morris's fantasy writing include a collection of essays edited by Carole Silver and Joseph R. Dunlap, *Studies in the Late Romances of William Morris* (New York: William Morris Society, 1976). For an individual interpretation of the importance of Morris's fantasy writing and for critical readings of all the stories and novels see my *Worlds Beyond the World: The Fantastic Vision of William Morris* (San Benardino, Calif.: Borgo Press, 1978), in which I argue that "English fantasy literature begins with William Morris." Carole Silver provides a literate exploration of traditional elements of literary romance in Morris's work in *The Romance of William Morris* (Athens: Ohio University Press, 1982).

J. R. R. Tolkien

The standard biography is Humphrey Carpenter's *Tolkien: A Biography* (London: Allen and Unwin, 1977), which is readable and reliable. For a more complete understanding of Tolkien's literary interactions with his colleagues, Carpenter's *The Inklings* (London: Allen and Unwin, 1978) provides innumerable insights into the development of his literary theories and his literary friendships with C. S. Lewis, Charles Williams, and others.

A comprehensive guide to the critical literature is provided by Richard C. West in *Tolkien Criticism: An Annotated Checklist* (Kent, Ohio: Kent State University Press, 1970, rev. 1981). For a critical introduction, Deborah and Ivor Rogers's *J. R. R. Tolkien* (Boston: Twayne, 1980) is excellent. Paul H. Kocher's *Master of Middle-earth: The Fiction of J. R. R. Tolkien* (New York: Houghton Mifflin, 1972) is a thorough, serious, and thought-provoking study that led the way in critical evaluation of Tolkien's work. My discussion of Tolkien's fantasy through *The Silmarillion* is available in *Lightning from a Clear Sky: Tolkien, the Trilogy, and "The Silmarillion"* (San Bernardino, Calif.: Borgo Press, 1978). A second edition of this work, greatly expanded to include all the posthumous volumes edited by Christopher Tolkien, is slated to be published in 1998. Until then, Kathryn F. Crabbe's *J. R. R. Tolkien* (New York: Ungar, 1981; rev. 1988) includes brief discussions of some of the posthumous volumes.

For greater depth, the two most insightful books to date are T. A. Shippey's *The Road to Middle-earth* (New York: Houghton Mifflin, 1983) and Verlyn Flieger's *Splintered Light: Logos and Language in Tolkien's World* (Grand Rapids, Mich.: Eerdmans, 1983). Shippey effectively applies academic insights into philology to Tolkien's work. Flieger uses Own Barfield's critical theories and a sensitivity to both Tolkien's personal and symbolic dimensions to explore layers of philosophical and theological complexity in his literary work.

T. H. White

Surprisingly little has been written about this author who, brought Arthur, Merlin, and Camelot to life so vividly for modern readers. A good starting point is the insightful *T. H. White: A Biography* (London: Cape-Chatto and Windus, 1967; rpt. New York: Viking, 1968) by White's friend and fellow author Sylvia Townsend Warner. Warner is perhaps best known for the adroit short stories, some about Elfland, that she published in the *New*

Yorker and elsewhere, but her poems and novels fill many volumes, and her fantasy writings include the novel *Lolly Willowes, or, The Loving Huntsman* (1926). The range of White's work can now be fully appreciated thanks to Francois Gallix's *T. H. White: An Annotated Bibliography* (New York: Garland, 1986). The best critical introduction is John K. Crane's *T. H. White* (New York: Twayne, 1974).

Robert E. Howard

Perhaps partly because of his origins as a pulp writer, Howard has not attracted a great deal of critical attention. For a biographical and creative overview, the best single volume is probably *The Last Celt: A Bio-Bibliography of Robert Ervin Howard,* ed. Glenn Lord (West Kingston, R.I.: Donald M. Grant, 1976). Also useful is L. Sprague de Camp, Catherine Crook de Camp, and Jane Whittington, *Dark Valley Destiny: The Life of Robert E. Howard* (Griffin, N.Y.: Bluejay, 1983), and Novalyne Price Ellis, *One Who Walks Alone: Robert E. Howard, The Final Years* (West Kingston, R.I.: Donald M. Grant, 1986). A good critical survey is found in a collection of essays edited by Don Herron, *The Dark Barbarian: The Writings of Robert E. Howard, A Critical Anthology* (Westport, Conn.: Greenwood Press, 1984). Darrell Schweitzer offers a readable and perceptive discussion of Howard's work in *Conan's World and Robert E. Howard* (San Bernardino, Calif.: Borgo Press, 1979). Mark A. Cerasini and Charles Hoffman contribute useful additional critical insights in *Robert E. Howard* (Mercer Island, Wash.: Starmont House, 1987).

Ursula K. Le Guin

The sophistication of Le Guin's fiction, poetry, drama, and nonfiction has already attracted a number of excellent critics, but more time needs to pass before we can fully appreciate the dimensions of her life and work. Elizabeth Cummins Cogell offers a good starting point in *Ursula K. Le Guin: A Primary and Secondary Bibliography* (Boston: G. K. Hall, 1983), though Le Guin has published a great deal since the early 1980s. Elizabeth Cummins's more recent critical overview, *Understanding Ursula K. Le Guin* (Columbia: University of South Carolina Press, 1990), offers many useful insights. There are also three other excellent short critical treatments to recommend, each of which include some biographical information: Charlotte Spivak's *Ursula K. Le Guin* (Boston: Twayne, 1984), George Edgar Slusser's *The Farthest Shores of Ursula K. Le Guin* (San Bernardino, Calif.: Borgo Press, 1979), and Barbara J. Bucknall's *Ursula K. Le Guin* (New York: Ungar, 1981). Although there is no definitive biography, materials from these sources can be supplemented by the good biographical essay Joe De Bolt wrote for *Ursula K. Le Guin: Voyager to Inner Lands and to Outer Space* (Port Washington, N.Y.: Kennikat Press, 1979). De Bolt's book leans toward science fiction, but it also features a survey of criticism by James W. Bittner and three essays on the Earthsea trilogy. Bittner undertakes a more detailed critical examination of Le Guin in his *Approaches to the Fiction of Ursula K. Le Guin* (Ann Arbor, Mich.: UMI Research Press, 1984), an intelligent and fruitful book. A variety of critical essays on Le Guin's early work can be found in *Ursula K. Le Guin*, ed. Joseph D. Olander and Martin Harry Greenberg (New York: Taplinger, 1979), and Bernard Selinger's *Le Guin and Identity in Contemporary Fiction* (Ann Arbor, Mich.: UMI Research Press, 1988), which places her work in a wider contemporary context, contains good discussions of her fantasy novels and stories. Brian Attebery seems particularly sensitive to Le Guin's techniques and sensibilities and offers helpful insights in both of his general studies of fantasy, *The Fantasy Tradition in American Literature* and *Strategies of Fantasy* (previously cited).

Recommended Titles

This is a selected list of works chosen for their influence for their illustration of the range and types of fantasy. For a more comprehensive reading list consult the general reference guides to fantasy mentioned in the Bibliographic Essay.

Adams, Richard (1920–). *Watership Down*. London: Rex Collings, 1972.
> This book for younger readers won the 1973 Carnegie Medal and the Guardian Award for Children's Fiction. A well-written tale in the talking-animal tradition, it recounts the tale of three rabbits, whose warren is also a microcosm of the world, as they come of age and attain knowledge.

Alexander, Lloyd (1924–). *The Book of Three*. New York: Holt Rinehart, 1964.

——. *The Black Cauldron*. New York: Holt Rinehart, 1965.

——. *The Castle of Llyr*. New York: Holt Rinehart, 1966.

——. *Taran Wanderer*. New York: Holt Rinehart, 1967.

——. *The High King*. New York: Holt Rinehart, 1968.
> Together these five books by Lloyd Alexander are known as The Chronicles of Prydain, after the land of Prydain, in which they are set. Loosely based on the Welsh *Mabinogion,* the novels recount the progress of Taran, a young assistant pig keeper, as he matures while engaged in heroic quests. These quests, to help preserve the land from the threat of the dark forces of Arawn, enable Taran to emerge in the end as the High King. Although Alexander's books were written with younger readers in mind (*The High King* received the prestigious Newberry Medal), their lyrical style, so-

phisticated construction, and complex, appealing characters invite comparison with Tolkien's *The Hobbit* or White's *Sword in the Stone,* books for readers of all ages. The series's theme is Taran's maturation, and as the books progress, they, like their hero, grow less simple and even more interesting.

Anderson, Poul (1926–). *The Broken Sword.* New York: Abelard Schuman, 1954. Rev. New York: Ballantine, 1971.

Elements of saga literature and the *Poetic Edda* surface in original and effective guise in Poul Anderson's first fantasy novel, published when he was 27. Anderson's subsequent career brought him greater fame as a science fiction writer (he won Hugo and Nebula Awards), but this rich and darkly lyrical fantasy tale of a human changeling—especially the 1971 revised edition—remains powerful and original.

Anthony, Piers pseudonym of Piers Anthony Dillingham Jacob; (1934–). *Hasan.* San Bernardino, Calif.: Borgo Press, 1977.

This charming reworking of a story from *The Arabian Nights* first appeared in *Fantastic Stories* in 1969. The work, which affirms Anthony's familiarity with and influence from Persian sources, establishes his own narrative skill as a storyteller as well as his talent for mixing pleasurable humor and pure imaginative invention into tales with underlying serious, even archetypal significance.

——. *A Spell for Chameleon.* New York: Ballantine, 1977.

(And the Xanth series, 1977-date, 20 titles so far.)

The Xanth series has had a huge influence on younger generations of readers and has not only put Florida on the fantasy map (since the land of Xanth is based on Florida's geography) but has also won Anthony a diverse and loyal fan base second to none.

——. *Split Infinity.* New York: Ballantine, 1980.

(And the Apprentice Adept series, 1980–1990; seven titles.)

This first book in Anthony's Apprentice Adept series introduces an unusual approach to the genre in that the books are consciously written in a style that is half science fiction and half fantasy (thus the "split" of the title). Two parallel worlds, one based on science and one on magic, present alternate realities. In this first book, the young serf Stile, a champion jockey, discovers the fantasy realm of Phaze.

——. *On a Pale Horse.* New York: Ballantine, 1983. (And the Incarnations of Immortality Series, 1983–1990; seven titles.)

This first book in the Incarnations of Immortality series explores fantasy's (and Anthony's) unique ability to embody abstractions. In the novel, an incarnation of Death engages in symbolic interactions written with the goal of helping readers come to terms with the inevitable end of life. The seven novels in the series undertake similar treatments through incarnations of Death, Time, War, Fate, Mother Earth, Evil (the devil), and Good (God).

Barth, John (1930–). *The Floating Opera*. New York: Appleton, Century, Crofts, 1956.

——. *The Sot-Weed Factor*. New York: Doubleday, 1960.

——. *Giles Goat-Boy; or, The Revised New Syllabus*. New York: Doubleday, 1966.

——. *Chimera*. New York: Random House, 1972.

——. *The Last Voyage of Somebody the Sailor*. Boston: Little Brown, 1991.

——. *Once Upon a Time: A Floating Opera*. Boston: Little Brown, 1994.

Barth earned his deserved reputation as one of America's best living novelists for his experimental mainstream literary fiction. Only gradually have critics begun to notice the pervasive presence of fantasy in nearly all his books. As if to underscore the point himself, Barth has constructed recent works that reveal their fantasy roots in their very titles: in *The Last Voyage of Somebody the Sailor*, which draws on *The Arabian Nights*, Scheherazade and Sinbad lurk behind the book's tales-within-tales; *Once Upon a Time* alludes to the fairy tale tradition, which is appropriate for a story about the gift of a magic pen that facilitates time travel and about the reconstruction of reality.

Barthelme, Donald (1931–1989). *Snow White*. New York: Atheneum, 1967.

——. *The Dead Father*. New York: Farrar Straus, 1971.

——. *The King*. New York: Harper and Row, 1990.

Another important mainstream novelist, Barthelme stretches definitions of realism and fantasy alike with elements of surrealism and absurdity. *Snow White* subverts the fairy tale with sexual impurity and dark, satirical comedy. *The Dead Father* employs a quest structure and the tale-within-a-tale technique in a dadaist comedy that explores traditions of male lineage and relationship (the internal story is a mock medieval translation of a work entitled "A Manual for Sons"). *The King* presents Arthurian characters in a World War II context.

Baum, L(yman) Frank (1856–1919). *The Wonderful Wizard of Oz*. Chicago: Geo. M. Hill Co., 1900.

Baum wrote in his introduction that his book "aspires to being a modernized fairy tale," and it fulfilled that aspiration. Though written for children, Baum's creation of a fresh, consistent imaginative world with original American characters is a remarkable achievement that continues to influence the shape and style of fantasy.

Beagle, Peter S. (1939–). *A Fine and Private Place*. New York: Viking, 1960.

The demarcation lines between life and death dissolve in a Bronx cemetery. Beagle explores ghostly and human love with humor and real feeling.

——. *The Last Unicorn*. New York: Viking, 1968.

A solitary unicorn quests for her lost mates. In parallel, allied journeys, a bumbling magician and an outlaw woman move toward
new life roles. The book is an American fantasy classic, an exploration of the road from innocence to insight in which the author
blends humor, love, fear, and intellect into a well-knit stylistic and
thematic whole.

———. *The Folk of the Air*. New York: Del Rey, 1986.

———. *The Innkeeper's Song*. New York: Roc, 1993.

Beagle waited nearly 20 years after *The Last Unicorn* before publishing a new work of fantasy, and although these two more
recent works may not rise to the landmark status of his masterpiece, they are works of substance that enhance his reputation.
The Folk of the Air, which explores the borders of reality and imagination, moves from Berkeley, California, in the radical sixties and
seventies into imagined and actual creations of the past. *The
Innkeeper's Song* is a somewhat darker but lyrical work of magic
and lost love. Both books are well worth reading.

Bellairs, John (Anthony; 1938–1991). *The Face in the Frost*. New York:
Macmillan, 1969.

Two wizened wizards—Prospero and Roger Bacon—combine
forces to oppose the evil wizard Melichus. Bellairs laces the proceedings with his flair for mystery and with learned wit and
humor.

Blackwood, Algernon (1869–1951). *The Human Chord*. London: Macmillan, 1910.

When a young man responds to an advertisement for a secretary
who must have knowledge of Hebrew and a good tenor voice, he
encounters a retired clergyman who experiments with the magical
powers of sound, using it to alter physical form and actually
restructure matter. The quest is for a blending of sound, a "human
chord" of four perfect notes that will be the name of God and will
transform those who can create it into deities themselves. Blackwood presents thematic issues with complex symbolism and
metaphysical depth, which results in an original and challenging
novel.

———. *The Centaur*. London: Macmillan, 1911.

The classical mythic centaur—half man, half beast—forms the
backdrop for a story shaped by the author's identity as a man who
believed in the supernatural, explored Buddhism and occultism,
and found the human mind capable of visionary insights into an
ordinarily invisible world. In this book two men on a sea journey
encounter a mysterious Russian who offers access to a reality
where the familiar and primitive coalesce. Only one of the travelers is capable of comprehending the vision.

Blaylock, James P. (1950–). *The Elfin Ship*. New York: Del Rey, 1982.

———. *Homunculus*. New York: Ace, 1986.

Blaylock's first novel, *The Elfin Ship*, was followed by *The Disappearing Dwarf* (1986) and *The Stone Giant* (1989; Elfin Ship series), books that established him as an accomplished new writer able to embroider a nineteenth-century cast of elves, dwarfs, goblins, and giants with a range of contemporary irony and humor. With the publication of *Homunculus*, he revised Victorian sensibilities even more dramatically by producing what may be the model steampunk fiction, set in an alternative-history London where different technologies color a fantasy reality full of twisted conspiracy for the hero Langdon St. Ives. Blaylock received both the Philip K. Dick Award and the World Fantasy Award in 1986. The steampunk concept, which he is credited with concocting in collaboration with his friends Tim Powers and K. W. Jeter, has attracted other authors to the mode, which affords an intriguing interface between fantasy and science fiction. The St. Ives series continues in *Lord Kelvin's Machine*, 1991.

Borges, Jorge Luis (1899–1986). *Fictions*. New York: Grove Press, 1962.

——. *Labyrinths*. New York: New Directions, 1964.

——. *Dreamtigers*. Austin: University of Texas Press, 1964.

——. *The Aleph and Other Stories, 1933–1969*. New York: E. P. Dutton, 1978.

These collections of deft metaphysical stories contain much of Borges's best-known writing, and many of the titles appear in more than one collection. The tales—some of them in the form of essays, scholarly articles, or reviews—explore the power of language in fantasy worlds whose existence materializes through encyclopedia entries ("Tlön, Uqbar, Orbis Tertius"), acts of scholarship that reveal double meanings and double authorship ("Pierre Menard, Author of Don Quixote"), a man with memories so complete that he can experience nothing new ("Funes the Memorious"), an infinite library full of unfathomable books ("The Library of Babel"), and a single book in which the narrator searches in vain to find the same page twice ("Holy Writ").

Bramah, Ernest (1868–1942). *The Wallet of Kai Lung*. London: Grant Richards, 1900; New York: Page, 1900.

British writer Ernest Bramah Smith invented an imaginary Chinese storyteller, Kai Lung, who relates tale after tale with humor, imagination, and an amazing flowery Chinese style. This is the first of a series of novels and short-story collections that continued to appear up to 1940 (*Kai Lung Beneath the Mulberry Tree*).

Burroughs, William S. (1914–1997). *Cities of the Red Night*. London: Calder, 1981; New York: Holt, Rinehart and Winston, 1981.

Famous for his experimental prose style, in which he employs cut-up techniques to fuse dissociated texts and striking, unexpected images, Burroughs pushes at the edges of fiction in ways that defy categorization. The realities he evokes in *Cities* and in other novels include elements of science fiction, surrealism, dadaism, crime novels, pornography, and history; what emerges is a mode of fantasy intensely personal and poetic: experimental fantasy that takes full advantage of the powers of imagination, symbol, language, and myth.

Cabell, James Branch (1879–1958). *The Cream of the Jest.* New York: McBride, 1917.

——. *Jurgen.* New York: McBride, 1919.

——. *Figures of Earth.* New York: McBride, 1921.

These three titles represent some of the highlights of what became, eventually, an 18-volume edition of *The Biography of Manuel.* Cabell's mythic imagination is gradually stretched in the interlocked stories, which center around a swineherd called Dom Manuel in the imaginary French province of Poictesme. Cabell's ironic, complex style is demanding, but his work is rich and impressive, forming a milestone in American fantasy. See discussion in text.

Calvino, Italo (1923–1985). *Cosmicomics.* New York: Harcourt Brace and World, 1968.

——. *t zero.* New York: Harcourt Brace Jovanovich, 1969.

——. *If on a Winter's Night a Traveller.* New York: Harcourt Brace Jovanovich, 1981.

Calvino is one of the most original, idiosyncratic writers on the world fantasy stage. His experimental and intellectually demanding fiction has had considerable influence, and it appeals through its sheer inventive energy and its mind-boggling mix of intellect and humor. The "Our Ancestors" trilogy (*The Cloven Viscount,* 1951; *The Baron in the Trees,* 1957; and *The Non-Existent Knight,* 1959), which marks Calvino's move into allegorical fantasy, contains comic fables with touches of magic realism and is well worth reading. However, in the three works listed in this entry, Calvino is more confidently experimental, pressing the conventions of the novel and expanding the generic boundaries of fantasy fiction. The offbeat cosmic character called Qfwfq, a nearly boundless, eternal presence that spans forms ranging from primordial matter and dinosaur to intergalactic dust, links *Cosmicomics* and *t-zero,* interconnected fables full of wordplay and mind games. Like Borges, Calvino is drawn to labyrinthine metaphors and tales within tales, an interest that reaches apotheosis in *If on a Winter's Night a Traveller,* a novel about reading a novel entitled *If on a Winter's Night a Traveller,* written by an author named Italo Calvino. The relationship between imagination, word, and world is brilliantly explored in this inventive variation of *The Arabian Nights.*

Card, Orson Scott (1951–). *Seventh Son.* New York: Tor, 1987.

This is the start of a series of novels, the Tales of Alvin Maker, in which Card carries on a new strain of compelling, complex religious fantasy based on the *Book of Mormon* rather than on the Bible.

Carroll, Lewis (pseudonym of Charles Lutwidge Dodgson; 1832–1898). *Alice's Adventures in Wonderland*. London: Macmillan, 1865.

———. *Through the Looking-Glass, and What Alice Found There*. London: Macmillan, 1871.

These classic "children's books" form part of the archetypal background of all contemporary fantasy. They are highly recommended reading for adults, who see them with new eyes.

Carter, Angela (1940–1992). *The Infernal Desire Machines of Dr. Hoffman*. London: Hart Davis, 1972. Also published as *The War of Dreams*. New York: Harcourt Brace, 1974.

Dr. Hoffman is a villain out to destroy all reason and reality. Carter writes about the epic struggle to resist his efforts in a surrealistic and nearly hallucinatory style.

———. *The Passion of New Eve*. London: Gollancz, 1977.

A man traveling to a future war-ravaged United States is swept up in feminist issues when he undergoes a sex-change operation and is transformed into a pagan goddess.

———. *Nights at the Circus*. London: Chatto and Windus, 1984.

A kind of picaresque adventure that features the life and loves of Fevvers, a giant circus woman who has real wings.

Chesterton, G. K. (Gilbert Keith; 1874–1936). *The Man Who Was Thursday: A Nightmare*. London: Arrowsmith, 1908.

Chesterton was a genuine man of letters, a social critic, moralist, poet, and essayist whose Catholicism provided a religious underpinning to his literary work. In this mock thriller, detective Gabriel Syme's quest for the leader of a group of anarchists leads to multiple reversals of apparent reality and to a frantic pursuit of "Sunday," the leader of a group whose members are code-named for the days of the week. John Clute writes in *The Encyclopedia of Science Fiction* that Chesterton's "magic-carpet London . . . marks a significant stepping-stone . . . between the world of Charles Dickens and that of Steampunk" (211).

Collodi, Carlo (pseudonym of Carlo Lorenzini; 1826–1890). *The Story of a Puppet; or, The Adventures of Pinocchio*. London: Unwin, 1892. Trans. from Italian by M. A. Murray of *Le avventure di Pinocchio*, 1882.

This important children's fantasy not only is an effective cautionary tale about telling the truth but touches on the nature of the creative process and of the relationship between creator and creation. For those familiar only with the Disney version of the story, a reading of the original is definitely in order.

Crowley, John (William; 1942–). *Little, Big*. New York: Bantam, 1981.

With near-perfect and profound simplicity, Crowley pioneers a modern mode of fantasy that clearly connects to familiar urban realities but opens links to strange and unexpected worlds. Crowley's thematic insights, complex allusions, and original voice in the love story of Smoky Barnable and Daily Alice Drinkwater mark this work as a contemporary masterpiece.

Dickens, Charles (1812–1870). *A Christmas Carol.* London: Chapman and Hall, 1843.

Ebenezer Scrooge's trip through time and space is one of the earliest time-travel fantasies and is a short masterpiece by one of England's most accomplished "mainstream" novelists.

Donaldson, Stephen R. (1947–). *Lord Foul's Bane.* New York: Holt Rinehart and Winston, 1977.

——. *The Illearth War.* New York: Holt Rinehart and Winston, 1977.

——. *The Power That Preserves.* New York: Holt Rinehart and Winston, 1977.

These first three books of Donaldson's Chronicles of Thomas Covenant are powerful and original contributions to modern fantasy. Using the metaphor of extraordinary illness (the hero is afflicted with leprosy), Donaldson explores the psychology of incurable sickness and gradual death coupled with unbelief. His fantasy emerges ironically almost in spite of itself in a style at once epic and immediate. These first three books achieve such breadth and unity of vision, giving the feeling of one novel broken into three for the convenience and economic interest of the publisher, that they cry out for comparison with Tolkien's work. They are particularly impressive in that they remain so resolutely limited to a fantasy that denies the complete pattern Tolkien described: Donaldson's is a fantasy of loss and limited escape in which there is little prospect of recovery or consolation.

Dunsany, Lord (Edward John Moreton Drax Plunkett; 1878–1957). *The Gods of Pagana.* London: Elkin Matthews, 1905.

——. *Time and the Gods.* London: Heinemann, 1906.

Dunsany's first two volumes of short stories set the standard for sustained creation of a complete alternative reality. The realm of Pagana is new myth, and Dunsany creates it in poetic prose with philosophical depth and lyrical beauty.

——. *The King of Elfland's Daughter.* London: Putnam, 1924.

Dunsany explores the relationship between fantasy and reality: a human prince at the edge of Elfland seeks the Elfland princess for a bride. Once the borders of the lands of magic and reality have been breached (he successfully marries her), the united couple's difficulties in finding happiness in this "mixed marriage" in either reality become apparent.

Eddison, E. R. (1882–1945). *The Worm Ouroboros.* London: Jonathan Cape, 1922.

This novel is often cited as the archetypal heroic fantasy. It takes place in the same world (but uses different characters) as that explored in Eddison's more conceptually experimental Zimiam-vian trilogy—*Mistress of Mistresses* (1935), *A Fish Dinner in Mimison* (1941), and *The Mezentian Gate* (1958), unfinished (except in notes) at the author's death. Although the trilogy is ambitious and impressive, *The Worm Ouroboros* is the single work by Eddison that must be read—it is a complex allegorical masterpiece that circles back on itself in remarkable ways.

Finney, Charles G. (1905–1984). *The Circus of Dr. Lao*. New York: Viking, 1935.

A remarkable short masterpiece in which a Chinese magician brings his circus to small-town America, thus releasing the secret fantasies and desires of the residents. Finney succeeds in conveying both sensual and spiritual complexity.

Haggard, H. Rider (1856–1925). *She*. New York: Harper and Brothers, 1887.

Reincarnation adds an occult dimension to a young man's journey to deepest Africa in search of Ayesha, "She-Who-Must-Be-Obeyed," the powerful and immortal queen who killed him in a previous life. This strong and sensual woman remains a remarkable Victorian creation. (For further discussion of Haggard, see the text.)

Holdstock, Robert (1948–). *Mythago Wood*. London: Gollancz, 1984.

Holdstock has written both fantasy and science fiction and has a fan following for his Berserker series (written under the name Chris Carlsen) as well as for his Raven books (written under the name Richard Kirk). Other of Holdstock's pseudonyms include Ken Blake, Robert Faulcon, and Robert Black. But clearly his greatest achievement to date is his Mythago series, which in addition to *Mythago Wood* include *Lavondyss: Journey to an Unknown Region* (London: Gollancz, 1988), *The Hollowing* (London: HarperCollins, 1993), *Merlin's Wood, or The Vision of Magic* (London: Harper-Collins, 1994), and *Ancient Echoes* (New York: Roc, 1996). He received the World Fantasy Award for *Mythago Wood*, a love story that takes place after World War II in a haunted-forest setting, in which where "mythagos," or materialized spirits of old tales, legends, and songs, play out their archetypal fates in eternal repetition. Both love and adventure abound in a truly memorable beginning to what is certain to remain one of the landmark fantasy series of the late twentieth century.

Howard, Robert E. *The Hour of the Dragon* (*Conan the Conqueror*). Karl Edward Wagner, ed. New York: Putnam, 1977. (For a discussion of Howard's other collections of stories, see the text.)

Hudson, W. H. (1841–1922). *A Crystal Age*. London: Fisher Unwin, 1887.

An early fantasy story in which the hero slips into a future utopian society that exists in idyllic, ecological harmony.

——. *Green Mansions: A Romance of the Tropical Forest*. London: Duckworth, 1904.

Set amid the tropical forests of South America, this novel once again enables Hudson's ecological interests to remain thematically important. However, the book has much in common with Haggard's "lost race" fantasy tradition. The young Venezuelan hero brushes destiny with a magical girl named Rima, who can communicate with all natural creatures. She is rumored by the natives to be a devil and is ultimately destroyed—a loss for the hero and for ecological vision.

Le Guin, Ursula K. (1929–). *A Wizard of Earthsea*. Berkeley, Calif.: Parnassus Press, 1968.

——. *The Tombs of Atuan*. New York: Atheneum, 1971.

——. *The Farthest Shore*. New York: Atheneum, 1972.

——. *Tehanu: The Last Book of Earthsea*. New York: Atheneum, 1990.

See the text for a discussion of these works.

Leiber, Fritz (1910–1992). *Swords in the Mist*. New York: Ace, 1968.

——. *Swords Against Wizardry*. New York: Ace, 1968.

——. *The Swords of Lankhmar*. New York: Ace, 1968.

——. *The Knight and Knave of Swords*. New York: Morrow, 1988.

This partial listing of Leiber's wonderful sword and sorcery tales is intended merely to whet the fantasy appetite. All the books in the Fafhrd and the Gray Mouser series are worth reading. Leiber, adept at science fiction as well as at fantasy, is the writer's writer when it comes to his refinement of the sword and sorcery tradition begun by Robert E. Howard. The good-hearted, brawny barbarian Fafhrd is a kind of Leiber alter ego, and the clever, diminutive companion Mouser is modeled after Leiber's close friend Harry Otto Fischer. The tone of the interlinked stories ranges from dark to comic, but Leiber is always readable and engaging. *Swords of Lankhmar* is a novel expanded from earlier pulp stories; *The Knight and Knave of Swords* includes a novella, *The Mouser Goes Below*, and the final series book published during his lifetime, *Ill Met in Lankhmar*, another novella, was issued with a novella by Charles de Lint (New York: Tor, 1990). Leiber's many honors include six Hugo Awards; three Nebula Awards, and a Grand Master Nebula; two World Fantasy Awards; and the Bram Stoker Lifetime Achievement Award.

Lewis, C. S. (1898–1963). *Out of the Silent Planet*. London: Lane, 1938.

This first book of Lewis's Space trilogy is sometimes classified as science fiction, but it is fundamentally space fantasy. A friend of Tolkien's and a pivotal member of the Inklings, Lewis exerted formative influences on modern fantasy and helped demonstrate its strengths as a medium for embodying philosophical and theological ideas. The whole series, which also includes *Perelandra* (1943) and *That Hideous Strength* (1945), is recommended reading.

——. *The Lion, the Witch and the Wardrobe*. London: Macmillan, 1950.

The first of Lewis's seven tremendously popular books in the Chronicles of Narnia, which have become children's classics and are often enjoyed equally by adults who read them aloud to their children. Peter, Susan, Edmund, and Lucy step through a wardrobe into the magical land of Narnia, where they meet a majestic lion named Aslan and come to know the heroism necessary to survive the dire conflict between good and evil. Again, although I have listed only one title, I recommend the whole series.

Lindsay, David (1876–1945). *A Voyage to Arcturus*. London: Methuen, 1920.

A masterpiece of metaphysical fantasy that sweeps the reader away in a cosmic, near-hallucinatory quest through layers of illusion toward Truth. The imagery, metaphors, and characters are original and compelling, and the names alone are suggestive of Lindsay's inspired inventiveness—Maskull, Krag, Nightspore, Crystalman, Surtur, and Muspel. Lindsay makes allusions to Norse and other mythologies and to Christian and other mystical traditions, but he is no preacher, and his book's refusal to reach and preach an answer remains one of its enduring strengths.

MacDonald, George (1824–1905). *Phantastes: A Faerie Romance for Men and Women*. London: Smith Elder, 1858.

MacDonald's subtitle places this allegorical struggle against temptations of the flesh in the fairy tale tradition. This is a pioneering work of fantasy fiction but is somewhat limited by its determination to convey lessons symbolically.

———. *Lilith*. London: Chatto and Windus, 1895.

A narrator named Vane (a nearly painful pun by the author, who, as a clergyman, was acutely aware of earthly vanity and whose children's story *At the Back of the North Wind* [1871] was focused, like a weather vane, on knowing which way the wind blows) passes into a mirror world (probably the influence of family friend Lewis Carroll) and becomes involved in the conflicts between Adam and Eve and between Adam's legendary evil second wife, Lilith. MacDonald achieves a more complex effect in this book and creates a seminal work of fantasy in the Christian allegorical tradition.

McCaffrey, Anne (1926–). *Dragonflight*. New York: Ballantine, 1968. (Part of the Dragon series.)

This first book in McCaffrey's Dragon series is worth noting, for its own merits as well as for the opportunity to represent the merit of the whole series and of the related books for younger readers (such as *Dragonsong*, 1976, and *Dragonsinger*, 1977). McCaffrey's context is essentially science fiction—a remote and long-lost space colony where humans and magic dragons live in telepathic harmony. The numerous fantasy elements, from magic to the archetypal fantasy beast, the dragon, are apparent even in this short description. The books are popular reading and are interesting for their mix of genre elements.

Moorcock, Michael (1939–). *Stormbringer.* London: Jenkins, 1965.

The first of a series of novels centered on the mercurial Elric of Melniboné, a weak albino of elfin descent who draws strength from his sword Stormbringer, a weapon that drains the souls of opponents to strengthen Elric. This book narrates the end of the Elric story, and Moorcock later wrote volumes of "prequels" to recount earlier adventures. The novel gives a glimpse of Moorcock's literary energy, which has resulted in his astoundingly lengthy bibliography of science fiction, fantasy, and mainstream novels, as well as short stories, plays, and many more impressive works by this writer of immense imaginative talent.

——. *Gloriana; or, The Unfulfill'd Queen.* London: Allison and Busby, 1978.

Set in an alternative history of Elizabethan London, *Gloriana* is in many ways Moorcock's fantasy tour de force. History and allusion —with especially heavy plays on *The Faerie Queene*—add intellectual complexity and wit to a complicated story of a pipe-smoking queen who yearns for sexual fulfillment. The book showcases the range and strengths of Moorcock's many talents.

Morris, William (1834–1896). *A Dream of John Ball.* London: Reeves and Turner, 1888.

——. *News from Nowhere; or, An Epoch of Rest.* Boston: Roberts Brothers, 1890.

——. *The Story of the Glittering Plain.* Hammersmith, England: Kelmscott Press, 1891; Boston: Roberts Brothers, 1891.

One of Morris's most immediately appealing tales, this novel gains interest from its hero's rejection of immortality in the land of the undying so he can return with his beloved to make a meaningful life in the mortal world.

——. *The Wood Beyond the World.* Hammersmith, England: Kelmscott Press, 1894; London: Lawrence and Bullen, 1895.

——. *The Well at the World's End.* Hammersmith, England: Kelmscott Press, 1896; London: Longmans, Green, 1896.

——. *The Water of the Wondrous Isles.* Hammersmith, England: Kelmscott Press, 1897; London: Longmans, Green, 1897.

——. *The Sundering Flood.* Hammersmith, England: Kelmscott Press, 1897; London and New York: Longmans, Green, 1898.

——. *Golden Wings. Svend and His Brethren.* Portland, Maine: Thomas H. Mosher, 1900.

Each of these important early volumes by Morris—and I have not listed all of them—is worth reading for a grounding in the origins of fantasy. I have singled one out for discussion in the text, and that might well be a good starting point.

Myers, John Myers (1906–1988). *Silverlock*. New York: Dutton, 1949.

Shandon Silverlock travels to a magical, mythic commonwealth where his quests cause him to cross paths with literary characters intricate and varied enough to snare any reader. This is a tour de force is a literary parade of allusions and characters, from Homer and Shakespeare to Twain, who sprout a fantasy family tree.

Norton, Andre (Alice Mary; 1912–). *Witch World*. New York: Ace, 1963. (Part of the Witch World series, 1963–{ }, which is comprised of more than 20 novels and collections to date, including numerous short stories.)

A prolific and influential author, Norton is a gifted writer for young people as well as for adults. What started in this first book, a step from science fiction into fantasy in which Englishman Simon Tregarth enters the planet known as Witch World through an ancient stone entrance in Cornwall, blossomed into a series in which Norton explores various magical and psychic powers in a realm where the most influential characters are usually women (who possess the power of magic). Norton's concern with social, moral, and emotional ideals undergirds her obvious skill and pleasure in pure storytelling.

Peake, Mervyn (1911–1968). *Titus Groan*. London: Eyre and Spottiswoode, 1946; New York: Reynal and Hitchcock, 1946.

——. *Gormenghast*. London: Eyre and Spottiswoode, 1950; New York: British Books Center, 1950.

——. *Titus Alone*. London: Wyre and Spottiswoode, 1959; New York: Weybright and Talley, 1967.

Sometimes known as the Titus Cycle or the Gormenghast Trilogy, these three novels from a multitalented artist and author are among the twentieth century's fantasy classics. In these books, which are linked by the character Titus (who is only two years old in the first novel), Peake blends gothic settings and grotesque sensibility with humor and intelligence. The author's early death of a degenerative disease (possibly encephalitis) affected his brain, and he never completed a final text for *Titus Alone,* which was probably not intended to be the end of the series, since portions of a manuscript for a fourth Titus novel also survive.

Powers, Tim. *The Anubis Gates*. New York: Ace, 1983.

——. *Dinner at Deviant's Palace*. New York: Ace, 1985.

——. *Last Call*. New York: Morrow, 1992.

Tim Powers, who knew Philip K. Dick well, has twice received the Philip K. Dick Award, in 1984 and 1986. He was also recipient of the World Fantasy Award in 1993. His accomplishments are particularly notable as fusions of science fiction and fantasy techniques, first exemplified in *The Anubis Gates* in his ground-breaking version of the steampunk mode he developed with his friends James Blaylock and K. W. Jeter. *Anubis Gates* involves time travel to an alternative Victorian London with guest appearances by Coleridge and Lord Byron and a dark underworld where horror and black humor mix. *Dinner at Deviant's Palace* brought Powers his second Dick Award for a more heroic, complex fantasy in postholocaust California. *Last Call,* which clinched Powers's World Fantasy Award, is set in modern California and employs mythic motifs from the legend of the Fisher King to show the consequences of a gambler's bargain for his life. Powers is an original new voice in fantasy who builds on traditions while breaking new ground and avoiding formulaic fiction.

Pratt, Fletcher (pseudonym of George U. Fletcher; 1897–1956). *The Well of the Unicorn.* New York: Sloane, 1948.

——. *The Blue Star.* New York: Ballantine, 1969.

Known for his science fiction and for his collaborations with L. Sprague de Camp (*The Incomplete Enchanter,* New York: Holt, 1941; *The Compleat Enchanter: The Magical Misadventures of Harold Shea,* New York: Doubleday, 1975), Fletcher also created one of the earliest modern American heroic historical fantasies with *Well of the Unicorn.* Magic misfires in the book but genuine heroism is attained when Airar Avarson and the magician Meliboë resist invading Vulkings to save their freedom. *The Blue Star,* in some ways a better novel, wasn't published on its own until after the author's death (it was first printed as a novella in the anthology *Witches Three,* New York: Twayne, 1952). In *The Blue Star,* magic can be transferred from witches through a powerful Blue Star, which enables the possessor to read others' minds. Pratt deals not only with issues of personal maturity, empowerment, and relationship but also with politics and social order.

Rushdie, Salmon (1947–). *Grimus.* London: Gollancz, 1975. There is irony in the fact that Rushdie, born in India and educated there and in England, should have been among the first to employ Native American myths in modern fantasy. *Grimus* is the surrealistic story of an American Indian who has been granted immortality and wanders through surrealistic, interdimensional realities in search of death. Rushdie's writing is philosophical, satirical, innovative, and entertaining.

——. *The Satanic Verses.* London: Viking, 1988.

The author's best-known book because its publication resulted in Iran's Ayatollah Khomeini issue of a *fatwa* (death sentence) against the author for blaspheming Islam. Rushdie combines satirical wit and formidable intelligence in a satirical magic-realist style somewhat in the tradition of James Branch Cabell. The complex plot is impossible to summarize, but Rushdie bitingly satirizes transplant-Indian culture in Britain, politics, religion (through the modality of Islam), and even his own authorship (his alter-ego poet is a disguised eunuch who lives in a brothel).

Scarborough, Elizabeth Ann (1947–). *The Healer's War*. New York: Doubleday, 1989.

> Scarborough has been a prolific author of humorous fantasy and has collaborated with Anne McCaffrey on three novels that incorporate both science fiction and fantasy elements. *The Healer's War,* a serious fantasy based partly on her experiences as an army nurse during the Vietnam War, won the Nebula Award in 1989. A change of direction from her lighter works, this book explores issues of religious understanding, the confrontation of evil, and dimensions of magic that emerge from intense realism in a controversial contemporary war.

Stephens, James (1880?/1882?–1950). *The Crock of Gold*. London: Macmillan, 1912.

> Stephens has written an adult fairy tale novel that draws from Irish legends. The book, which has an uneasy allegorical atmosphere, is highly charged with an intricate philosophical contest of dichotomies: flesh and spirit, intellect and instinct, reason and emotion.

Tolkien, J. R. R. (1892–1973). *The Hobbit; or, There and Back Again* London: Allen and Unwin, 1937.

——. *The Fellowship of the Rings*. London: Allen and Unwin, 1954; Boston: Hougton Mifflin, 1954.

——. *The Two Towers*. London: Allen and Unwin, 1954.

——. *The Return of the King*. London: Allen and Unwin, 1955.

——. *The Silmarillion*. Ed. Christopher Tolkien. London: Allen and Unwin, 1977; Boston: Houghton Mifflin, 1977.

> See the text for a discussion of these works.

Twain, Mark (pseudonym of Samuel Langhorne Clemens; 1835–1910). *A Connecticut Yankee in King Arthur's Court*. New York: Webster, 1889.

> This ironic, comic treatment of Arthurian legend is claimed for both science fiction and fantasy and probably belongs on both lists as a good example of Rabkin's discussion of his "spectrum" metaphor for fantastic literature, in which one mode makes gradations into another. Some of the Arthurian components and impossible events in Twain's novel seem characteristic of fantasy, but since the greater part of the book has to do with the narrator's anachronistic introduction of technology into Arthurian England, science seems to gain the upper hand, though Twain condemns its misapplication.

Updike, John (1932–) *The Centaur*. New York: Knopf, 1963.

> Greek myth becomes more than metaphor or allusion in this critically acclaimed novel set in the real American landscape in Pennsylvania in the late 1940s. The centaur of the title is a schoolmaster, transformed into Chiron. Updike extends other characters into

projections from ancient Greek mythology, and the myths receive new life when moral issues and imagination in the present connect powerfully with roots in antiquity. Updike is an acknowledged master prose stylist whose literary work stretches fantasy techniques into the mainstream.

——. *The Witches of Eastwick.* New York: Knopf, 1984.

Suburban America is transformed with humor and sometimes real danger of dark forces as three women cultivate their supernatural powers. The incongruities provide insights into values and ample ground for Updike's wit.

Walton, Evangeline (1907–). *The Virgin and the Swine.* Chicago: Willet Clark, 1936. Rpt. *The Island of the Mighty.* New York: Ballantine, 1970.

This retelling of a portion of the great Welsh epic *The Mabinogion* is a tangible demonstration of the power of contemporary fantasy to recover and renew ancient fantasy sources. Walton explores essentially the same tales Lloyd Alexander taps, but Walton's style and approach are more elevated, almost biblical. She later followed this poetic work of adult fantasy with three other books drawn from the same Welsh sources and issued in Ballantine's adult fantasy series: *The Children of Llyr* (1971), *The Song of Rhiannon* (1972), and *Prince of Annwn* (1974). Walton remains unsurpassed in rendering these enthralling stories, which probably date from the eleventh century, to enrich the mythic present.

White, T. H. (1906–1964). *The Sword in the Stone.* London: Collins, 1938.

——. *The Witch in the Wood.* New York: Putnam, 1939.

——. *The Ill-Made Knight.* New York: Putnam, 1940.

——. *The Once and Future King.* London: Collins, 1958; New York; Putnam, 1958. (Unifies *The Candle in the Wind* and revised versions of each of the previous titles listed here.)

——. *The Book of Merlyn: The Unpublished Conclusion to "The Once and Future King."* Austin: University of Texas Press, 1977.

For a discussion of these works, see the text.

Williams, Charles (1886–1945). *War in Heaven.* London: Gollancz, 1930.

Williams introduces a unique combination of supernatural fantasy and symbolic murder mystery in his first published novel. The story involves the discovery of a corpse and the attempt to turn the Holy Grail to evil ends. That the ideal Grail is part of the plot of a mundane murder is prototypical of Williams's metaphysical plot elements. This book, as well as Williams's other work, is significant for its thematic reach, conceptual invention, and historic influence, including his personal influence on Tolkien and Lewis as an associate of the Inklings.

——. *The Place of the Lion.* London: Gollancz, 1931.

A magician introduces Platonic ideal forms that range from ideal mythical creatures (such as the lion and phoenix) to human ideals (such as wisdom).

——. *Many Dimensions*. London: Gollancz, 1931.

The magic Stone of Solomon can bring great wealth and power and is capable of infinite replication (each time it is divided it produces two stones of equal power). Williams raises moral questions about how such power should be used, or *if* it should be used, in the world.

Wolfe, Gene (1931–). *The Shadow of the Torturer*. New York: Simon and Schuster, 1980.

An impressive beginning to Wolfe's tetralogy, The Book of the New Sun, which mixes elements of fantasy and science fiction in a dying earth in a remote future. The hero Severian, an original variation on the sword and sorcery heroic model, has experiences with space travel, robots, and other science fiction conventions. Severian is afflicted with the inability to forget anything, a fascinating motif in this rich series that by its very nature reinforces fantasy's reach from antiquity to the far future and forgets nothing along the way.

——. *Soldier of the Mist*. New York: Tor, 1986.

Set in Greece in the fifth century B.C.E., this novel begins a series of more classical historical fantasy novels that are structured almost as the antithesis of the New Sun books. Appropriately, the hero of this book, a Greek solder named Latro, can remember only the past 24 hours due to a severe head wound. Loss of memory plays against reality, and breakdowns in perception of cause and effect play against the supernatural in a richly written text.

Zelazny, Roger (1937–1995). *Creatures of Light and Darkness*. New York: Doubleday, 1969.

Zelazny reminds us of some of the earliest mythic roots of fantasy as he transplants Egyptian mythos into space in this interesting novel whose experimental style lies in the gray area in which science fiction and fantasy blend. In some ways it is a successor to his Hugo Award-winning science fiction novel *Lord of Light* (1967), which utilizes Hindu mythology and also shares some hybrid generic qualities, but *Creatures* moves more clearly into the fantasy realm. With its epic heroism, cosmic themes, and writing style that incorporates poetry and poetic prose, the novel remains challenging and impressive.

——. *Nine Princes in Amber*. New York: Doubleday, 1970.

This book, the first in the author's remarkable Amber series (10 volumes to date), exploits the relationship between reality and memory, object and shadow. The hero, Corwin, lost Prince of Amber, awakes in a hospital bed on earth and, as his memory returns, makes his way back to Amber and to his identity there. Again Zelazny's fluid and memorable writing style and thematic intelligence are strengths.

INDEX

paradox: of Conan as hero, 122; of
fortunate fall, 93; in Howard,
133; in Le Guin, 138, 141, 150;
of magic, 117; in Tolkien, 73; in
White, 117. *See also* oxymoron
parallelism, of plot in Tolkien, 76
past: dangers of romanticizing, 133;
restored by blood sacrifice, 133;
as source of evil, 133; in *The
Once and Future King,* 98. *See also*
history
patriarchal traditions, 46–47; in
Tolkien, 78. *See also* gender
issues
Payne, John, trans. of *Arabian Nights,* 15
Peace, 33
peace, in Earthsea, 142
Peer Gynt, 20
Pellinore, King, 80, 98–99, 101,
109–10
Pendragon, King Uther, 107–8
People of the Mist, The, 119
Perelandra, 32
Persia, 2, 15
Peterborough Chronicle, 105
Peter Pan, 17
Peter Pan figure, in Grass, 33
Phantastes, 16, 21, 23
Phantasus. See Tieck
Pharos the Egyptian, 20
philology, 14, 21, 26, 137; definition
of, 59; and Inklings, 31; and
Tolkien, 54. *See also* language;
linguistics
philosopher-king, 127. *See also* king
philosophy: in Howard, 120; lack of
in E. R. Burroughs, 120
"Phoenix on the Sword, The," 29
Picts, 121
Pinocchio, 17
Pippin. *See* Took, Peregrin "Pippin"
pity, in Tolkien, 75
Place of Dead Roads, The, 32
plague, in Howard, 125
Plato, 12; completing the circle in Le
Guin, 151; and Howard, 127;
legend that man and woman
were originally one, 146

Platonism, 13
Plattner Story and Others, The, 19
plot: contrasts between Tolkien and
Howard, 129; in Le Guin, 135
Poe, Edgar Allan, 19; "Fall of the House
of Usher, The" 19, 39; "Tale of the
Ragged Mountains," 25
poet, as hero, 45, 136. *See also* authorship; creator; hero
Poetic Edda, 14
Poictesme, 27
point of view: complex, in White,
113–14; and geography in
Tolkien, 71; shift to child's, in
Tehanu, 15. *See also* narrative
poison, black scorpion venom, 130
politics, White and, 117. *See also*
socialism
Pope, Alexander, 14
Port of Saints, 32
*Portrait of the Artist as a Young Man,
A,* 34, 46
possessiveness, in Tolkien, 63
postmodern fantasy, 34
power: of art-magic in Earthsea, 139;
of darkness and silence in
Howard, 132, 143, 145; in Earthsea, 138; empty to be full of, in Le
Guin, 150; feminine, in *Tehanu,*
147; from flaming light, 129; and
language in Earthsea cycle, 147;
and language in Le Guin, 135; in
Le Guin and Tolkien, 139; of light
and naming, 145; male corruption of, in Le Guin, 145; play, 14;
primitive, in Howard, 119; reconceived, in *Tehanu,* 147; renuncia-
tion of supernatural, in Morris,
90; in Tolkien, 67, 78, 81; in
White, 101, 116; and wisdom, 140
Pratt, Fletcher, 30
Pre-Raphaelites, 4, 124–25; influence
on Morris, 38
present, washed away by blood sacrifice, 133
pride: of Saruman and Sauron, 76;
towers as emblems of, in
Tolkien, 72

The Author

Richard Mathews is the author of *Worlds Beyond the World: The Fantastic Vision of William Morris; Lightning from a Clear Sky: Tolkien, the Trilogy, and The Silmarillion; The Clockwork Universe of Anthony Burgess;* and other critical studies of fantasy and science fiction writers. He coedited *Subtropical Speculations: An Anthology of Florida Science Fiction* with Rick Wilber, including stories by Piers Anthony, Andre Norton, Joe Haldeman, Walter M. Miller Jr., and others. His poetry and criticism have been widely published in periodicals, anthologies, and chapbooks, and his most recent collection of poems is *Numbery* (1995). He is a professor of English at the University of Tampa, where he is editor of the literary journal *Tampa Review* and director of the University of Tampa Press.

The Editor

R onald Gottesman is professor of English at the University of Southern California.